£3

TL―

23/14

The Daily Telegraph

BOOK OF
NAVAL
OBITUARIES

The Daily Telegraph

BOOK OF
NAVAL
OBITUARIES

Edited by

DAVID TWISTON DAVIES

GRUB STREET · LONDON

Published by
Grub Street
4 Rainham Close
London SW11 6SS

British Library Cataloguing in Publication Data
The Daily Telegraph book of naval obituaries
  1.Sailors – Great Britain – Obituaries 2. Naval biography
  I.Davies,David Twiston 1945-
  I. Daily Telegraph II. Daily Telegraph
  III. Book of naval obituaries
  359'.00922'.41

ISBN 1 904010 91 1

Typeset by Pearl Graphics, Hemel Hempstead

Printed and bound in Great Britain by
Biddles Ltd, Guildford and King's Lynn

DRAMATIS PERSONNAE
(in order of appearance)

Admiral Sir Geoffrey Miles
Commander Tom Boyd
Captain Dudley Mason, GC
Captain "Joe" Brunton
Rear-Admiral "Wash" Washbourn
Captain J M Hodges
Admiral Sir William Davis
Commander David Maitland-Makgill-Crichton
Commodore "Peter" Drew
Rear-Admiral "Boggy" Fisher
Admiral of the Fleet Sergei Gorshkov
Lieutenant "Jim" Warren
Captain "Sam" Marriott
Commander Norman Morley
Captain "Hooch" Williamson
Commander Bradwell Turner
Rear-Admiral Sir Ed Irving
Sir Hamish MacLaren
General Sir Peter Hellings
Commander "Jimmy" Wilde
Commander the Reverend Evelyn Chavasse
Commander Hugh Haggard
Captain Ron Freaker
Admiral of the Fleet Lord Fieldhouse
Captain Nigel Clogstoun-Willmott
Vice-Admiral Sir Peter Gretton

Captain Eric Nave
Captain Henry Denham
Rear-Admiral George Ross
Rear-Admiral "Ben" Bolt
Commander Charles Cuthbertson
Captain Gordon Walker
Commander John Hall
Admiral Sir John Hamilton
Captain Barry Anderson
Lieutenant-Commander John Miller, GC
Rear-Admiral Godfrey Place, VC
Commander Graham de Chair
Captain Graham Lumsden
Captain Stanley Leonard
Captain "Fish" Dalglish
Rear-Admiral Johnny Lee-Barber
Admiral "Thirty-one Knot" Burke
Lieutenant Dom Martin Salmon
Brigadier Roy Smith-Hill
Commander Douglas Craven
Commander "Richie" McCowen
Commander Tony Law
Admiral Sir Anthony Griffin
Commander "Rags" Butler
Chief Petty Officer "Lofty" Rogers
Lieutenant Anthony Daniell
Captain Joe Baker-Cresswell
Commodore Geoffrey Marr
Captain Gerry Southwood

Captain Nick Barker
Signalman Gus Britton
Captain Bill McVicar
Chief Petty Officer Frank Miles
Lieutenant Ginger Le Breton
Captain Geoffrey Stanning
Captain Dicky Courage
Lieutenant-Commander Ninian Scott-Elliott
Vice-Admiral Sir Patrick Bayly
Vice-Admiral Sir Roy Talbot
Flotillenadmiral Otto Kretschmer
Colonel Paddy Stevens
Vice-Admiral Sir "Joc" Hayes
Rear-Admiral Roy Foster-Brown
Admiral of the Fleet Lord Lewin
Commander "Jimmy" Gardner
Captain Humphry Boys-Smith
Captain John Cockburn
Lieutenant-Commander John Casson
Rear-Admiral Dennis Cambell
Commander Loftus Peyton-Jones
Captain Paul Bootherstone
Commander Guy Clarabut
Captain Sir David Tibbits
Commander Peter Richardson
Lieutenant-Commander Ken Pattisson
Rear-Admiral Tony Storrs
Vice-Admiral "Rocket" Rod Taylor
Captain Peter Samborne

PREFACE

By Admiral Sir Alan West GCB DSC
First Sea Lord and Chief of Naval Staff

The United Kingdom is, by dint of geography, a maritime nation whose fortunes are, and always have been, inextricably linked with the sea. The sea has fed us, provided us with the means to develop trade, allowed us to build an empire which spanned the globe, defended us and provided us with a field of battle on which to defeat our enemies.

As an island people we have always been fascinated by both the sea and seafarers. From those who have pioneered the exploration of the world's farthest corners, to others whose acts of heroism made such telling contributions in battle, or saved their colleagues from near certain death, each shared a close affinity with and respect for the sea, reflecting the character of the island nation from which they were drawn.

This book tells the stories of one particular group of seafarers – individuals who have had the honour during part of their lives to serve their country in the Royal Navy, the Fleet Air Arm and the Royal Marines. However, such a book would be incomplete if it did not include accounts of others who served so illustriously in the Merchant Navy, or of those who, at certain times, were our enemy at sea.

Some of the men whose lives are retold in these pages were professional naval officers, schooled from an early age in the ways of the sea. Others were drawn from a variety of diverse backgrounds. Yet all were brought together in war to stand as the nation's shield. They came together, professional and volunteer alike, to fight against the enemy and, equally, to surmount the often dreadful perils of the sea. They were not the type of men who set out to be heroes, who sought glory or who regaled others with vainglorious tales of their exploits. In the main they were calm, quiet and unassuming men, who were put to the ultimate test, were not found wanting and, in later life, adopted new challenges in every field of endeavour.

As our nation prepares to commemorate in 2005 the most famous sea battle in history, we recall Admiral Lord Nelson, the commander of the British Fleet at the Battle of Trafalgar, as much if not more than we remember the engagement itself. Two hundred years after Nelson's death on board *Victory*, his strength of leadership, unswerving loyalty, steadfast bravery and unflinching courage in the face of mortal danger are all qualities that have afforded him a place in the hearts of those who appreciate the history of our islands. Such qualities are found in full measure in the tales of those whose exploits are recorded in these pages.

Even the briefest review of the lives in this collection of obituaries reveals something of the robustness of character necessary to live and work at sea. Such characteristics brought out in individuals a heroic nature that was modest, dignified and yet determined and steadfast. These survive still in our country, and can be seen in the men and women who serve in the Royal Navy of today, who remember with honour and pride the selfless acts of those who have gone before. It is in having the opportunity to read of the experiences of people such as these that the principle of service is remembered and the inspiration of their example is handed to the next generation.

INTRODUCTION

Sailors differ from soldiers in never being out of danger. A soldier can feel reasonably secure in camp out of the front line; but even when there is no enemy, a sailor's place is at sea – that ever changing, sometimes benign, often angry element of the natural world.

In the course of editing *The Daily Telegraph Book of Naval Obituaries*, immediately after a companion volume of military lives, I came to appreciate how seamanship is as important as fighting skills in the sea service, and why the line "For those in peril on the sea" is still sung by sailors as a personal appeal to Almighty God. Although the Navy prefers to perform its duties soberly, this does not mean that sailors lack dash. Commander Bradwell Turner became a naval legend in one leap when he boarded the German tanker *Altmark*, and found 300 British soldiers hidden below. The debonair, multilingual Commander David Maitland-Makgill-Crichton thought nothing of setting sail in the teeth of a gale while wearing his pyjamas. Commander Charles Cuthbertson, whose corvette sank in seconds, was the model for the main character in Nicholas Monsarrat's novel *The Cruel Sea*; and when Captain Stan Darling depth-charged a U-boat, whose German crew clung to the conning tower until they could step onto his frigate's quarterdeck without wetting their feet, it was the stuff of film fantasy.

The 106 obituaries in this volume, which appeared in *The Daily Telegraph* and *The Sunday Telegraph* between 1987 and 2004, have never before been published in book form. They have been selected to demonstrate the variety of activities involved in protecting our shores and interests around the world. There is the great convoy captain Vice-Admiral Sir Peter Gretton, who protected merchant ships from the U-boat packs over thousands of miles of the North Atlantic. Admiral Sir Desmond Dreyer was gunnery officer in *Ajax* at the Battle of the River Plate. The painter Commander Tony Law was an aggressive motor torpedo boat captain in the Channel, and Chief Petty Officer "Lofty" Rogers had charge of a 4-inch gun when the auxiliary patrol ship *Li Wo* took on the might of the Japanese Imperial Navy.

Submariners were no less gallant below the waves. Rear-Admiral Godfrey Place won the VC when his midget submarine attacked the battleship *Tirpitz*. There is also Commander "Hughie" Haggard, the languid giant whose crew considered eccentric his love of practising backwards manoeuvres underwater – until the technique saved them from certain disaster. Among the naval pilots are Lieutenant-Commander "Hooch" Williamson, who led the first strike on the Italian fleet at Taranto; and Commander Jimmy Gardner, who flew with Douglas Bader in the Battle of Britain. Rear-Admiral "Ben" Bolt was a fleet observer officer whose reporting impressed even the Italian admiral at Cape Matapan, and Captain Stanley Leonard was the subject of the Navy's first helicopter search-and-rescue operation. No less impressive are the Royal Marines: Colonel Paddy Stevens, who won the MC when he landed on Sword Beach on D-Day; Major-General Derek Pounds, the leader of daring raids behind enemy lines in Korea, and Major Hugh

Bruce, the finest lockpicker incarcerated in Colditz Castle.

Others led more unusual lives. Captain Sam Marriott was captain of the captured submarine known as "His Majesty's U-boat". Captain Geoffrey Stanning was the only "pusser"to be awarded a DSO, after he had taken command of a ship for the first time when all its other officers were killed or wounded at Narvik. For some, highly creditable careers have been overshadowed by non-naval activities. Captain Dicky Courage was the Navy's finest jockey. Commander Ninian Scott-Elliott settled in the Solomon Islands to play the bagpipes at night and drink champagne on the anniversary of the Battle of Trafalgar.

There are also included here those whose work involved less glamorous but equally essential jobs out of the line of fire. Captain Eric Nave broke the Japanese naval ciphers. Rear-Admiral Sir Ed Irving was a reforming Hydrographer of the Royal Navy, and Norman Hancock the architect responsible for the *Swiftsure* nuclear submarine which was so carefully balanced that it had one blank space, known as "Hancock's hole". Admiral Sir Anthony Griffin helped to defuse a mass resignation of admirals by pointing out that this would have meant him becoming First Sea Lord – which all agreed would be "an unacceptable blow to the Royal Navy."

Although the majority of subjects in this book served in the 1939-45 War, a significant number also took part in the First World War, such as Captain "Joe" Brunton, who began before the mast, and Sir Hamish McLaren, a fighter pilot on the Western Front who after the Second World War was responsible for the development the Navy's electrical engineering training branch. Vice-Admiral Sir Peter Berger was *Amethyst*'s navigator in the Yangtse Incident of 1949; Admiral Sir John Hamilton commanded the cruiser *Newfoundland* in the Suez crisis; and Captain Barry Anderson skilfully avoided letting the first Cod War get out of hand. The future head of the Royal Australian Navy, Vice-Admiral "Rocket" Rod Taylor, was mentioned in despatches in Vietnam.

The Navy's most important conflict since 1945 was undoubtedly the Falklands War, which occurred just as the most savage cutbacks were awaited. Fortunately, two veterans of the Second World War were still in the Service. Admiral of the Fleet Lord Fieldhouse was C-in-C Fleet, and Admiral of the Fleet Lord Lewin was the Chief of the Defence Staff who shored up Margaret Thatcher's resolution by assuring her that the Navy could mount a successful expedition 8,000 miles away. The main reason the senior service was able to prove its indispensability in the modern age was the Admiralty. This may no longer be the largest industrial organisation in the world, as it was in the 18th century, but its awareness of duty and continuing history, willingness to adapt and, above all, to put its requirements ahead of that of any individual members, whoever they are, ensures that it remains one of the most formidable British institutions.

Such resolution does not mean that its actions have always seemed fair. Many thought Commodore Peter Drew was treated scandalously when he was court-martialled for scuttling his ship *Manchester*. Captain Nick Baker, of the ice patrol vessel *Endurance*, who made himself highly unpopular at senior levels with his entirely justified warnings about Argentine intentions just before the Falklands war, never achieved flag rank. Yet the Admiralty is not without a sense of humour, and is even prepared to think again about a decision. It very much appreciated Captain Evelyn Chavasse's account of a convoy action written in the form of an article for *Punch*, and it circulated as a model report Commander John Hall's account of the sinking of a U-boat which employed lines from the Greek comic poet Aristophanes. Vice-Admiral Sir Roy Talbot recovered from being denounced as unfitted for command and sent to sea as a watch-keeper, instead of being given command of a destroyer. Perhaps one explanation of such changes of attitude is indicated in the case of Brigadier Roy Smith-Hill, who was notified that their Lordships of the Admiralty were displeased with his failure to prevent the Royal Marines' mutiny in Russia in 1919, but was also told that it at least meant that he had brought himself to their notice. Undoubtedly the most remarkable recovery from official displeasure was that of torpedoman Ginger Le Breton, a leader of the Invergordon Mutiny in 1931 who still went on to be commissioned.

Some, such as Signalman Gus Britton and the Cockleshell hero Marine Bill Sparks, showed little desire for promotion. But many others did. The most dramatic was Rear-Admiral Sir Richard Trowbridge, who joined as a boy seaman and went on to command the Royal Yacht *Britannia*.

The Navy has always been aware of what it owes to those who joined up for major conflicts, either as professional sea officers (Royal Naval Reserve) or as those who have sailed yachts or had no acquaintance at all with the sea (Royal Naval Volunteer Reserve). Members of the Royal Australian Navy, the Royal Canadian Navy and the Royal New Zealand Navy – united by loyalty to the Crown – are another vital element in these pages. There are also merchant seamen such as Captain Dudley Mason, GC, who had to abandon his tanker *Ohio* twice because of enemy attacks on the Pedestal convoy of 1942, and Captain Bill McVicar who steered a lifeboat 1,500 miles to Brazil. And since this book aims to illustrate naval life as fully as possible, a few significant officers of foreign navies are included: "Thirty-one Knot" Burke, hero of the Pacific War; the great U-boat captain Otto Kretschmer; and the Russian naval C-in-C Sergei Gorshkov, who had a sign on his desk declaring "Better is the Enemy of Good Enough."

An obituaries column is always the product of many hands which make small and large contributions in ways often obscure even to them. But this book is firstly the work of the late John Winton (Lieutenant-Commander John Pratt), who was already a bestselling novelist and highly capable historian in 1987 when the paper's obituaries department was seeking specialist writers. With the exception of the late Edward Bishop, an old *Telegraph* hand who had served in the Navy during the war and was already established as our first air obituarist, those approached proved diffident and unsure about what was required. John Winton was different. He accepted the offer of the work at once and when his first piece arrived, on Commander Tom Boyd, we immediately recognised how we had exactly what we needed – a fine storyteller who knew the Navy, its members, its lore and its faults.

After Winton's death in 2001, several other writers lent a hand, including Lieutenant-Commander Jeremy Stocker, Charles Owen and George Ireland, while Geoffrey Hattersley-Smith continued to produce his polar obituaries, of which Captain Sir Alexander Glen is a fine example. Among other expert contributors who have made occasional offerings special mention should also be made of Julian Spilsbury, Air Commodore Graham Pitchfork and the Very Reverend Trevor Beeson. Eventually Captain Peter Hore took over the wheel from Winton. He has continued on John's course, demonstrating a sharp eye for detail and judiciously selecting subjects at a time when the numbers of candidates for the column are multiplying at an ever-increasing rate. It is worth pointing out to those who confidently say, "Well, there cannot be too many left now", that Captain Henry St John Fancourt, who died in 2004, aged 103, turned out not to be the last survivor of the Battle of Jutland. An uncertain number of veterans of the First World War of all services are still with us.

In the 18 years since I became the first deputy to Hugh Massingberd, many writer-editors have worked on the column as it has grown in size and authority to be recognised as being without rival in the English-speaking world. Lewis Jones was first to succeed to the editor's chair. He was followed by Kate Summerscale, Christopher Howse and now Andrew McKie. Among those who have ably aided them are Robert Gray, Claudia FitzHerbert, Aurea Carpenter, Will Cohu, James Owen, Katharine Ramsay, Georgia Powell, Philip Eade and the present deputy editor, Jay Iliff. No more than the Navy could we function without an able support team. These have included

Martine Onoh, Diana Heffer and the present secretary Teresa Moore; mention must also be made of Dorothy Brown, my secretary when I was Letters Editor, a position which for many years was closely involved with the obituaries department. This book could not have come to fruition without the *Telegraph*'s publications manager Morven Knowles, and it has enjoyed the encouragement and support of both Martin Newland, the Editor of *The Daily Telegraph* and his predecessor Charles Moore.

Lastly, tribute must be paid to the man who conceived the idea of the modern obituaries column as a miniature essay form which is authoritative, elegant, witty and sprinkled with recondite information.Hugh Massingberd waited for years before being given the chance to introduce it, with a panache that astonished cynical old Fleet Street. He is still a contributor. It is therefore appropriate that the first obit here, Admiral Sir Geoffrey Miles, who as a schoolboy in 1904 saw the Russian fleet steaming in the Channel after mistakenly attacking some Hull trawlers for Japanese warships, should be the product of his pen.

David Twiston Davies
Chief Obituary Writer

The Daily Telegraph
Canary Wharf, London E14

ADMIRAL
SIR GEOFFREY MILES

Admiral Sir Geoffrey Miles (who died on December 31 1986, aged 96) saw active service during both world wars but witnessed an historic nautical event before he entered the Royal Navy as a cadet in 1905. As a 14-year-old schoolboy at Bedford School,he was walking on Beachy Head when he saw the might of the Russian Imperial Fleet (under Admiral Rozhdestvensky), which was at war with Japan, steaming down the Channel.

The next day young Miles discovered that this armada had just engaged a group of Hull trawlers on the Dogger Bank, and inflicted heavy damage on them in the extraordinary belief that they were Japanese torpedo boats. The result was a diplomatic incident, a hefty payment of compensation as well as a significant revelation of the weakness of the Tsarist navy and the potential of Japanese naval power.

Geoffrey John Austin Miles was born on May 2 1890, and had intended to be a soldier until a Channel crossing at the age of eight won him over to the sea. He was sent to HMS Britannia in 1906, went to sea as a midshipman the next year and, specialising in navigation, was assistant navigator in the Home Fleet flagship *Neptune*. He then was appointed navigator in the despatch vessel *Alacrity* on the China station.

After the outbreak of war he joined the armed merchant cruiser *Empress of Russia* in the Indian Ocean and spent the conflict in submarines and destroyers with the Grand Fleet. He was in *Botha*, the light cruiser *Fearless* and the cruiser *Calliope* before being appointed to the first RN staff course after the war.

Miles served in the cruiser *Coventry* in the Atlantic and Mediterranean flotillas, then was commander of the first and third battle squadrons in the Mediterranean during the mid-1920s before becoming navigator for the battle cruiser squadron of *Hood*. After a spell in the Plans Division of the Admiralty he was promoted captain and commanded *Pangbourne* and the first minesweeping flotilla before joining the Staff College. In 1935-7 he commanded the destroyer *Codrington*, from which he once boarded the cruiser *Miguel de Cervantes* during the Spanish Civil War to protest against interference with British shipping and receive an apology.

He was at the senior officers' tactical school at Portsmouth before becoming flag captain of the battleship *Nelson* in 1939. He was with her when she was mined by one of the first magnetic mines to be laid.

Two years later, in June 1941, he was sent at short notice to Russia as head of the naval section of Lord Beaverbrook's British Mission to Moscow. He was reported attending a Russian play *Here to Those on Passage*, about Russian and British merchant ships, which was produced in Archangel. But, in a letter to *The Sunday Telegraph* more than 20 years later, Miles recalled being struck by "the accuracy of Soviet knowledge of our innermost affairs." Among the intelligence he picked up was the exact number of German U-boats sunk and also the capture of U-110 within two months of its occurrence. The Soviet naval staff also told him of the serious security leak within the British Embassy at Ankara caused by

"Cicero", a German spy who was valet to the British Ambassador.

He immediately passed on this information to London but never heard what action, if any, had been taken. "In retrospect," he continued, "it seems lucky that the Russians and ourselves were fighting a common enemy at the time."

In 1943 Miles went out to India to serve as Deputy Naval Commander, South-East Asia Command, under Lord Louis Mountbatten. From 1944 to 1945 he was Flag Officer Commanding Western Mediterranean and was then posted to Berlin as the senior British representative on the Tripartite Naval Commission.

In 1946, shortly after a mutiny of Indian ratings, he returned to India as Commander-in-Chief of the Royal Indian Navy, a post he retained until the end of the Raj the following year.

Tall dark and slim, with a clearly defined nose and chin, Geoffrey Miles was appointed CB in 1942, KCB in 1945 and KCSI in 1947. His wife, the former Alison Mary Cadell, died in 1981. They had two sons.

COMMANDER
TOM BOYD

Commander Tom Boyd (who died on March 20 1987, aged 72) was a hero of the daring raid on St Nazaire in March 1942, which was an early success of Lord Louis Mountbatten's Combined Operations. The object of Operation Chariot was to destroy the

Normandie liner's dock, the only dry dock on the Atlantic seaboard capable of taking the giant German battleship *Tirpitz*.

Boyd, a 27-year-old lieutenant in the Royal Naval Volunteer Reserve, commanded the motor launch ML60 in a flotilla of small vessels, including torpedo-boats and gunboats, escorting the former United States destroyer *Campbeltown* up the Loire. In the manner of an Elizabethan fireship, *Campbeltown* was packed with several tons of explosives. On the way up the river towards the dock, Boyd remarked to his coxswain: "This is a queer do." "It'll soon be a bloody sight queerer, sir", came the reply.

The attacking force was detected, and came under fierce fire from the shore, but *Campbeltown* successfully crashed the dock gates. Boyd moved close inshore and, under intense fire while brightly illuminated by searchlights, managed to knock out one enemy battery from a range of only 200 yards. Later, still under withering fire, he took ML60 alongside to rescue the survivors of another launch before retiring downriver on one damaged engine.

Although many of the Chariot force were killed or captured, delayed action fuses detonated the charges inside *Campbeltown* hours after the raid, doing enormous damage to the dock and denying *Tirpitz* its possible shelter. Five Victoria Crosses were awarded for the raid, and Boyd was one of four to receive the DSO. The citation spoke of his "great gallantry and skill in bombarding enemy positions on shore at point-blank range."

When, after three days and nights at sea, Boyd eventually sighted the Lizard on the way home, he remarked that he knew the landmark well, having once, as a navigating officer, run another motor launch ashore there, thus earning the sobriquet "T. Lizard Boyd."

Thomas Wilson Boyd, the son of a Hull trawler owner, was educated at St Bees and played rugby for Yorkshire. At the age of 12 he came home from school for the Christmas holidays to be told by his father that he was to sail to Spitsbergen as a "hand" because some of the crews were grumbling.

Boyd later graphically recalled this nautical baptism. The spray froze on the decks; ropes cut sores in his hands; he cried in his bunk at night. Another boy in the crew stole his belt, so young Tom held the thief's head over the side till he was half filled up with saltwater. But the ship's master caught hold of him, saying:"You may be Tom Boyd, junior, but I'm going to give thee a proper hiding."

Such yarns delighted American audiences when Boyd and some others toured the United States to stimulate the sale of War Bonds in the summer of 1942. They were given a memorable "ticker-tape" welcome in New York, where Boyd declared over the public address system: "I can't believe there are so many people in the world or that so many could have turned out to see some very ordinary Englishmen."

Besides his exploits at St Nazaire, Boyd also took part in the evacuation of Dunkirk and served in the Far East. After the war, he became chairman and managing director of the Boyd Line. He was president of the Hull Fishing Vessel Owners' Association from 1958 to 1962 and of the British Trawlers Federation from 1964 to 1966 and 1969 to 1971.

In 1965 he was elected an honorary Brother of Trinity House. He was appointed OBE in 1965 and

CBE in 1967, and was a Deputy Lieutenant for Humberside. Tom Boyd married, in 1937, Barbara Gresham, who survived him together with their son and two daughters.

CAPTAIN
DUDLEY MASON, GC

Captain Dudley Mason (who died on April 26 1987, aged 85) was awarded the George Cross for the epic bravery of the tanker *Ohio* in the relief of Malta during August 1942. As the last and most important of five remaining merchant ships in the Pedestal convoy, *Ohio* limped into harbour lashed between two destroyers so low in the water that her decks were awash. After discharging her cargo of 13,000 tons, she promptly sank.

Mason was chosen for his task after being the youngest master in the service of Eagle Oil, and was given an unprecedently large crew for *Ohio*, one of 14 merchant ships that set off from the Clyde. Previous attempts had failed to break the Axis stranglehold over the island, and the operation was considered so important that three aircraft carriers as well as many other ships from the Mediterranean Fleet were assigned to its protection.

The convoy first met the enemy on August 11 after passing Gibraltar in thick fog, when about 36 German bombers attacked at dusk but scored no hits; several were shot down. The attacks continued next morning. First a merchantman was forced to leave the convoy. Then the elderly carrier *Eagle* was sunk by a

U-boat, followed by a merchant ship and a cruiser; the carrier *Indomitable* was damaged.

The next night seven more merchant ships and two cruisers were sunk, and *Ohio* was hit for the first time. A torpedo badly damaged her steering, broke her communication system and tore a gaping hole in her side. The crew went quickly down to the pump room while Mason steered by hand, without a compass, until she rejoined the convoy the following day.

Ohio now became the centre of enemy attention. Hour by hour her anti-aircraft gunners were in action against constant air attack. At 10 am she was lifted clean out of the water by a stick of bombs; then another bomb exploded in the boiler room, bringing her to a stop, so that she had to be taken in tow.

She was twice abandoned and reboarded. During one evacuation, Mason was so badly burned that an able seaman in a motor launch did not realise who he was, and ordered him to "get cracking" on reloading some Oerlikon guns. Mason quickly and quietly got on with the task for more than an hour before returning to his ship.

The remnants of the convoy finally came within range of the short-range Spitfires on Malta, which held off some of the attacks while minesweepers and motor launches came out to meet them. *Ohio* was hit again in a dusk raid, and *Dorset* was sunk. The destroyer *Penn* and the minesweepers *Rye* and *Ledbury* towed her in turn and fought off more air attacks until the morning of August 15 when *Ohio* finally entered Grand Harbour; her back was broken, and a Stuka had crashed on her deck. The captain of a cruiser signalled "I'm proud to have known you", and cheering crowds with bands were on the quayside to greet her.

The fuel which *Ohio* carried enabled air strikes to be restarted, with the result that Axis shipping losses increased and Rommel's offensive to drive the Allies out of Egypt had to be postponed.

"It was a nice surprise when we got there," recalled Mason afterwards. He and his chief engineer looked so disreputable when they were flown home that they were refused rooms at a London hotel and had to go to a sleazy boarding house. But Mason was later deeply impressed when King George VI asked him to a special audience after his investiture, where the GC had been awarded not just for his own indomitable courage and determination but also for that of every member of *Ohio*'s crew.

Dudley Williams Mason was born on October 7 1901 at Surbiton, Surrey, and went to school at Long Ditton before going to sea as an apprentice at 17. He obtained his master's ticket at 30, and saw service on the Atlantic convoys.

Mason commanded the only British ship in the American invasion of Casablanca and was in the southern United States at the end of the war when the Ministry of Transport asked him to spend a year supervising water supplies at Naples. He returned to Eagle Oil, becoming its marine superintendent briefly before retiring in 1957.

A quiet man of medium height with a dry sense of humour, Dudley Mason was a keen gardener and reader of historical works. He was married twice and left a son.

CAPTAIN
"JOE" BRUNTON

Captain "Joe" Brunton (who died on June 26 1987, aged 90) had an unusually varied sea-going career, ranging from sail to submarines, and from a half-size replica of Drake's *Golden Hind* to Hitler's steam yacht *Grille*.

Thomas Bennett Brunton was born in Derbyshire in 1896, and ran off to sea in 1912. At the age of 16, he was serving before the mast in the barque *Dumfriesshire*, when she rounded Cape Horn; in June 1915 he was still an apprentice when she arrived at Falmouth, loaded with grain after a 157-day voyage from Australia. Diverted immediately to Liverpool by the Admiralty, the vessel was torpedoed and sunk off the Smalls on June 28 by a U-boat.

Brunton later joined the Royal Naval Reserve as a midshipman, serving in the destroyers *Matchless* and *Melpone*, then in Admiral Tyrwhitt's Harwich Force. He transfered to the Royal Navy in 1916, joining the battleship *Centurion* as an acting sub-lieutenant.

After the 1914–18 War Brunton went up to Cambridge under an Admiralty scheme, only gaining a third at Downing College despite First Class passes in his sub-lieutenant's courses. He joined the submarine service in April 1920, where, during a 13-year career he commanded H49, L14, *Otus* – which he took to China – and *Swordfish*. In this period he also had a general service appointment in charge of an A gun turret in the battlecruiser *Hood*. He was promoted lieutenant-commander in 1926, but although spoken of as a "very keen and zealous officer, very painstaking and very hardworking", was passed over for promotion to commander.

However, as secretary of the Royal Naval Sailing Association for some years, Brunton was a successful racing skipper of the yacht *Taimonsham*, which five brother officers had built in Hong Kong and sailed to Dartmouth in 1934. On commemorative occasions he enjoyed the fun of commanding half-size versions of Nelson's *Victory* and Drake's *Golden Hind*.

Although he retired before the 1939-45 War Brunton returned to command the Q ship *Botlea*, one of a number of such decoys which failed to repeat the earlier succcess of ships of the First World War against U-boats. After briefly commanding the destroyer *Vega* on East Coast convoys in 1940, he took command of *Princess Beatrix*, a former ferry between Harwich and the Hook of Holland, in which he won his first Distinguished Service Cross. *Princess Beatrix* was converted as a Landing Ship Infantry (Medium). He carried commandos in her on the Lofoten Islands raid of March 1941, and in August 1942 landed men of the South Saskatchewan Regiment for the Dieppe raid.

That November, Brunton commanded *Princess Beatrix* during the Torch landings in North Africa, following up as part of a shuttle service, ferrying troops from Algiers to the North African harbour of Bone. Admiral Sir Andrew Cunningham, the Allied Naval Expeditionary Force Commander, remembered *Princess Beatrix* and her sister ships with great pride and satisfaction. "Always under air attack, and sometimes under U-boat attack as well, their regular voyages were never uneventful," he said.

In July 1942, *Princess Beatrix* was in the thick of it again during Operation Husky, the landings in Sicily.

Although Brunton was invalided home sick in August, his war was not over. He won a Bar to his DSC as Principal Ferry Control Officer in Force J for the Normandy landings of June 1944. He was in charge of 600 landing craft and, at one stage, 5,000 tons of stores and 1,500 vehicles a day were landing across his beach in the central British sector. Later he commanded *Titania*, depot ship for craft midget submarines and HMS Mountstewart, the Special Services Establishment at Teignmouth for training the crews of "sleeping beauty" canoes, explosive motor boats and other craft used for clandestine warfare.

In 1945 Brunton retired again with the war service rank of captain. The following year he skippered Hitler's steam yacht *Grille* for its Libyan owner but, after a year, found that "unbearable".Brunton worked for MI6 from 1949 to 1954 and then,after a short and unsatisfactory period as a ship's chandler at Gosport, he was trials captain for Thornycroft's,Samuel White's and Camper and Nicholson's.Eventually, he retired to live in Guernsey and then in Spain.

Joe Brunton left a son by his first wife, whom he married in 1922 and who died in 1978. His second wife died in 1982.

REAR-ADMIRAL
"WASH" WASHBOURN

Rear-Admiral "Wash" Washbourn (who died on August 8 1988, aged 78) was the gunnery officer of the New Zealand cruiser *Achilles* during the Battle of the River Plate. Washbourn was on watch early on

December 13 1939, when the *Admiral Graf Spee* was first sighted. He and Captain W E Parry, who had been talking about practicing gunnery exercises later on in the day, both turned to each other and said, "My God, it's a pocket battleship."

In his own words, Washbourn "legged it" to his action station, where he "just had time to wonder whether there was anything in this gunnery business after all,and where I should be in half-an-hour's time, before all my lamps lit up and I was able to say 'Shoot' for the first time in anger."

Achilles suffered one early hit, which badly wounded her captain and caused several other casualties. Of six men near Washbourn three were killed and the others were all wounded. Washbourn took three shrapnel pieces in his "ample frame". But the shock deadened the pain and also the full realisation that those around him had been killed. As they started to fire again, he saw that one man resting in a natural position against his observation instrument was dead. He could not be moved, so the ordinary seaman ordered to replace the dead man had to sit on his remains. Incongruously, Washbourn was amused to see a young boy talking angrily into the telephone to the gun turrets:"I tell you I'm *not dead*. It's me, Dorset, who's speaking to you now. I'm NOT DEAD."

Though outranged and outgunned, the three British cruisers drove *Graf Spee* to take refuge in Montevideo, with *Achilles* following to the limit of the territorial waters. Washbourn recalled how they listened with some bemusement to the BBC describing mythical British fleets off the River Plate. The newsreader's promise of some interesting developments brought a hollow laugh. When Commodore Henry Harwood made his first nightly signal, "My policy is destruction", someone said, "Whose?"

After four days the German captain scuttled his badly damaged ship and took his own life.

Washbourn was awarded the DSO for continuing, while stunned and wounded in the head by a splinter, to control the main armament with the utmost coolness: "He set a magnificent example to the rest of the director tower crew, who all stood to their posts and made light of the incident."

Richard Everley Washbourn was born at Sumner, New Zealand, on February 14 1910, and educated at Nelson College. He entered the Royal Navy in 1917 as the first candidate to pass the New Zealand public school entry exam. He went to Dart-mouth and the training ship *Erebus*. His first ship as midshipman was the cruiser *London*, and he later served in the battleship *Warspite* and the light cruiser *Diomede*.

Following *Achilles* and a period in the gunnery school, HMS Excellent, Whale Island, he served in the battleship *Anson*. In 1942 Washbourn was returning to England from Auckland as a passenger in the Shaw-Savill ship *Waiwera* when she was torpedoed and sunk in the Atlantic. He spent five days in a lifeboat before being picked up and taken to New York, and was recommended to the Admiralty for excellent conduct in helping fellow shipwreck victims in two drifting lifeboats to survive.

After the war he was executive officer and second-in-command of the New Zealand cruiser *Bellona*, where his firmness of purpose did much to mitigate the effects of a serious mutiny over a new pay code in 1947.

He was Commander Superintendent of HMNZ Dockyard, Devonport, in 1950 when he was appointed OBE. He then went to the Admiralty as Deputy Director of Naval Ordnance until 1953. He commanded the minelayer *Manxman* before becoming Chief Staff Officer to Flag Officer (Flotillas) in the Mediterranean.

From 1956 to 1958 he was Director of Naval Ordnance and then commanded the new cruiser *Tiger.* He was appointed CB in 1961 and was Director-General of Weapons from 1960 to 1962. He then returned to his homeland, joining the RNZN and becoming Chief of Naval Staff until he finally retired in 1965.

"Wash" Washbourn was noted for his sense of humour and his letters about his naval life and times were greatly appreciated by their recipients. He described his favourite recreation as beachcombing. He was survived by his wife, June, a son and a daughter.

CAPTAIN
J M HODGES

Captain J M Hodges (who died on August 12 1987, aged 77) won the DSO for his part in the capture of the Vichy French island of Madagascar in May 1942. With the support of naval aircraft from the carriers *Indomitable* and *Illustrious*, the main landing was made to seize the northern town and harbour of Diego Suarez and the nearby island of Antsirane. But after 36 hours, the land forces were held up by a strongly defended Vichy line at the approaches to Antsirane.

A party of 50 Royal Marines from the battleship *Ramillies*, flagship of Rear-Admiral Edward Syfret, the expedition commander, embarked at short notice in the destroyer *Anthony*, commanded by Lieutenant-Commander Hodges who took them on a high speed 120-mile trip through very rough seas round the northern tip of Antsirane.

Hodges brought his ship into a strange harbour in total darkness and, in the face of enemy fire, landed the marines safely onto a jetty. After this unexpected appearance in the rear, Vichy French resistance began to collapse and the town was secured.

Admiral Syfret said: "The *Anthony* carried out her duty with a stout heart and splendid efficiency", adding that her work and that of the landing party were "worthy of the best tradition of the Royal Navy and the Royal Marines."

The son of Admiral Sir William Hodges, John Michael Hodges was born on May 9 1910, and joined the Navy as a Dartmouth cadet in 1923. He was a destroyer commander who escorted Arctic convoys and, during the landings in Normandy, took part in diversionary operations designed to convince the enemy that the landings were to take place elsewhere.

In 1943, he commanded the destroyer *Orwell* which, with *Matchless*, escorted the battle cruiser *Renown*, bringing Winston Churchill, his wife and daughter Mary back across the Atlantic after the Quebec conference. Hodges had as passenger Petty Officer A P Herbert, RNVR, who used his poetic talents to signal to *Renown*:

Return Ulysses soon to show
The secret of your splendid bow.
Return and make your riddles plain
To anxious Ithaca again.
And you Penelope the true
Who have begun to wander, too
We're glad to greet you on the foam
And hope to see you safely home.

To which *Renown* soon replied:

Ulysses and Penelope too
Return their compliments to you
They too are glad to wend their way
Homewards to Ithaca after a stay
With friends from where the land is bright
And spangled stars gleam all the night.
And when he's mastered basic Greek
Ulysses to the world will speak
About the plots and plans and bases
Conferred upon in foreign places.
We thank you from our hearts today
For guarding us upon our way
To chide these simple lines be chary
They are the first attempt of Mary.

Promoted commander after the war, Hodges was executive officer of the cruiser *London* when, in April 1949, she tried to go up the Yangtse River to assist the frigate *Amethyst*. *London* was fired on by communist shore batteries. The captain, the Chinese pilot and a navigating officer were wounded, and it fell to Hodges to turn the ship round in the river and take her safely down to sea.

Hodges's last appointment was as Captain (D) in Londonderry in 1956. He retired that year to Sussex where he bought and ran a successful broiler chicken farm.

He left a widow, Betty, one son and one daughter.

ADMIRAL
SIR WILLIAM DAVIS

Admiral Sir William Davis (who died on October 29 1987, aged 86) had a long, eventful and distinguished naval career in which he experienced most of the vicissitudes of naval life, from mutiny to Mountbatten.

There was nothing bombastic or dramatic about Davis. He was no fireater. But as Vice-Chief of the Naval Staff in the mid-1950s he provided the quiet, competent, unflappable staff platform on which the much more flamboyant personality of Earl Mount-batten,the First Sea Lord,could perform.It was Davis who smoothed over the controversy and mitigated the possible personal consequences for Mountbatten of the "Crabbe Affair";Commander "Buster" Crabbe, the frogman, disappeared while allegedly inspecting the propellers and underwater fittings of the Russian cruiser which had brought the Russian leaders Bulganin and Khrushchev to Portsmouth in 1956.

Davis supported and advised his chief ably and loyally during a seemingly interminable series of other crises. These included the Suez operation (which Mountbatten deplored);the Navy's difficulties over manpower; the abolition of many superfluous naval shore establishments; the rebuilding of the seagoing fleet; and, perhaps most important, the

Navy's response to the swingeing cuts proposed by Duncan Sandys's 1957 White Paper.

The son of a member of the Indian Political Service, William Wellclose Davis was born on October 11 1901,and joined the Navy in 1914,going to Osborne and Dartmouth. His first ship was the battleship *Neptune*, which he joined as a midshipman in 1917.

Specialising in torpedoes and anti-submarine warfare, Davis quickly showed his talents as a staff officer. He was Fleet Torpedo Officer to Admiral Sir Frederic Dreyer on the China station and later Fleet Torpedo Officer and Staff Officer Plans to the C-in-C Home Fleet. He became executive officer of the battlecruiser *Hood* in January 1939, and served in her for the first 18 months of the 1939-45 War. Promoted captain in 1940, Davis went to the Admiralty as Assistant, and later Deputy, Director of Plans and Cabinet Offices.

He was seconded for a time as staff officer to Admiral Keyes in charge of Combined Operations, when he had to exert his powers to smooth troubled waters over Operation Workshop. This proposed landing on the Mediterranean island of Pantelleria was enthusiastically supported by Keyes and espoused by Churchill,and just as fiercely resisted by the Chiefs of Staff and by Admiral Cunningham, the Naval C-in-C Mediterranean. It never took place, but Davis himself emerged with credit, Keyes calling him "the Admirable Staff Officer".

In 1943 Davis was appointed to command the cruiser *Mauritius*. The ship had been left by his predecessor in a very sensitive state of discipline, which was compounded in January 1944 when she arrived in Plymouth Sound with her ship's company expecting to be paid off. Despite Davis's representations to the Admiralty, proper leave was not granted, and the ship had to sail almost at once to return to the Mediterranean. The company thought, not unreasonably, that they were being penalised for previous acts of indiscipline. There was further unrest aboard, including outright refusals of duty.

Such an atmosphere would have discouraged most captains but Davis, with his great gift for making people work together, succeeded in turning the commission into a triumph. *Mauritius* was the only major British warship to take part in the four invasions of Sicily, Salerno, Anzio and Normandy, bombarding enemy shore positions on more than 250 occasions. For the Normandy landings Davis had a Russian general and a Russian air marshal on board – "to see that we really were carrying out a second front and were not delaying any longer," he recalled.

Later *Mauritius* destroyed two enemy convoys in the Bay of Biscay, and finished the year conducting offensive sweeps off the Norwegian coast. Davis himself won a DSO for his part in the Sicily landings, and a Bar for Normandy.

After the war he was Director of Underwater Weapons at the Admiralty, Chief of Staff to C-in-C Home Fleet, and Naval Secretary to the Admiralty, where he served three First Lords. As a rear-admiral he was Flag Officer, Second in Command, Mediterranean Fleet from 1952 to 1954 when Mountbatten was C-in-C. It was made abundantly clear to him that his job was to run the fleet and to be, in effect, the fleet commander while Mountbatten himself dealt with the numerous political and strategic problems in the area.

Davis also "held the fort" for Mountbatten when he went to the Admiralty in 1954 as Vice-Chief of the Naval Staff; his last appointment was in 1958 as C-in-C, Home Fleet, and Nato C-in-C Eastern Atlantic. By then he was the only senior naval officer still serving who had taken part in the 1914-18 War. He was also the first C-in-C to haul down his flag afloat and hoist it again ashore over Nato headquarters at Northwood, Middlesex (the so-called "Führer Bunker").

William Davis was appointed CB in 1952, KCB 1956 and GCB in 1959. From 1959 to 1960 he was First and Principal ADC to the Queen and a Deputy Lieutenant of Gloucestershire, a county he served in numerous capacities during his retirement. Davis took a close interest in naval history and was a frequent and valuable correspondent of such historians as Captain Stephen Roskill.

He married in 1934, Lady Elizabeth Phipps, youngest daughter of the 3rd Marquess of Normanby, who died in 1985. They had two sons and two daughters.

COMMANDER
DAVID MAITLAND-MAKGILL-CRICHTON

Commander David Maitland-Makgill-Crichton (who died on November 16 1987, aged 77) was a dashing wartime destroyer officer, a bon vivant known to his contemporaries as "Champagne Charlie" and a linguist able to translate 40 languages into English; he could speak fluently in a dozen, including every European language except Welsh, Gaelic and Erse.

Crichton's party-loving, hard-drinking image was deceptive. Underneath the debonair appearance and beautifully relaxed manner, there was an able officer prepared to take his ship to sea during a raging gale in the middle of the night while wearing his pyjamas.

In 1940 he won a DSC as first lieutenant of *Express*, one of the last two destroyers to leave the Dunkirk Harbour Mole early on June 3, having made four trips to the Mole and two to the beaches and rescued more than 3,500 men. Crichton was mentioned in despatches two months later when he brought *Express* back to harbour after the 20th Destroyer Flotilla had run into an enemy minefield 40 miles off the Texel on the Dutch coast.

He won another DSO and was mentioned in despatches again for his gallantry during the Malta convoys. He was commanding the destroyer *Ithuriel* on the afternoon of August 12, when she detected the Italian U-boat *Cobalto* and attacked with a full pattern of depth charges. When the submarine was forced to the surface Crichton, who always urged on his destroyers as though they were a pack of hounds, turned to ram.

Ithuriel's stern hit *Cobalto* abaft the conning tower with what Crichton described as "a delightful crunch", and sank her. Admiral Edward Syfret, commanding the operation, took a somewhat cooler view: he thought the submarine was "all in", and the expensive method chosen by the commanding officer of *Ithuriel* was "unnecessary". However, Crichton was duly decorated.

He was mentioned in despatches for a third time in

1943 for services in North Africa while on the staff of Flag Officer Levant. His last destroyer command was in the Mediterranean from 1945 to 1946, carrying out a duty he and his sailors found very distasteful: patrolling the coasts off Palestine to intercept Jewish refugee ships.

A kinsman of the Earl of Lauderdale, David Hugh Maitland-Makgill-Crichton was born in November 1910 and followed his father, a lieutenant-commander, into the Navy, becoming a Dartmouth cadet in 1924. His first ship was the Royal Yacht *Victoria & Albert*.

Even as a boy he had a gift for languages which he possibly inherited from a 16th-century member of his family, James (the "Admirable") Crichton, who also spoke 12 languages. After the 1939–45 War he was executive officer of the cruiser *Gambia* in the Far East and then naval attaché in Copenhagen; he acted as equerry to the King of Denmark for the Queen's Coronation in 1953.

Two years later, he attended a Russian language course at London University, and went to Paris to study the language the following year. He was already fluent enough to act as interpreter for the visit of the Soviet leaders Bulganin and Khrushchev, and then went on to head the naval section at the joint services languages school at Crail.

In 1961 Crichton was an expert witness at the "Portland Spy" trial of Peter and Helen Kroger, who had been transmitting British naval secrets to the Russians by radio from their suburban bungalow at Ruislip; they were the subject of Hugh Whitemore's play *A Pack of Lies*. Crichton testified that anomalies in certain messages proved they were based on

Russian and not English meanings: for instance, the seemingly innocent domestic word "radiator" meant in Russian "transmitter".

Crichton worked at the Ministry of Defence and for Naval Intelligence until he resigned in 1964; but he continued to acquire new languages at the rate of at least one a year. He was a Fellow of the Institute of Linguists, chairman of the Translators Guild and a member of one of the most esoteric naval clubs, the Frinton Society (which is open to former Russian interpreters of the Navy).

He was a bachelor, but became engaged to be married to Mary Parsons earlier in 1987 before his death.

———

COMMODORE "PETER" DREW

Commodore "Peter" Drew (who died on December 20 1987, aged 92) was the shamefully treated captain of the ill-fated cruiser *Manchester* during the Second World War.

While escorting the Substance convoy to Malta in July 1941, *Manchester* was hit by a torpedo dropped from an Italian aircraft. By good seamanship and damage control, Drew and his ship's company brought their ship safely back to Gibraltar. A year later, they were not so lucky. Escorting the Pedestal convoy to Malta, *Manchester* was hit and very badly damaged by two torpedoes fired at close range by Italian E-boats off the Kelibia Roads, Tunisia.

All power was lost, the steering gear was crippled

and the ship took on a 12-degree list to starboard, but Drew was optimistic that she could survive torpedoing a second time. He told the damage control parties: "She'll do 2 to 2½ knots; she can answer the helm sometimes." It was not to be. They were unable to get the ship underway again, and eventually Drew ordered scuttling charges to be placed, and his crew to take to the Carley floats. *Manchester* was scuttled and sank in the early hours of August 13.

Some men were picked up by other warships, but the majority got ashore where they were at once interned and disgracefully treated by the Vichy French, who showed the utmost contempt for every civilised convention regarding the treatment of prisoners of war and internees. One sailor, encouraged to escape with the connivance of bribed French guards, was shot in the back and killed while climbing the wire by those same guards. It was only the coolness and wise leadership of Drew which averted a full-scale prison camp riot, in which more lives would have been lost.

After the successful Torch landings in North Africa in November 1942, the French were forced to release their prisoners. Drew had then to face a court martial, according to the custom of the Royal Navy, for losing his ship. The court found that *Manchester* had been scuttled prematurely and might have been saved.

It was a bitter verdict for Drew after all his efforts for the ship. However, nothing was ever going to touch the great respect and affection in which Drew was always held by the HMS Manchester Association formed after the war. The many members who had shared Drew's experiences in the ship and the prison camp knew how much of their survival they owed to his good humour and leadership.

Harold Drew was born at Oswestry, Shropshire, on March 15 1895 and was educated at the local grammar school and the training ship *Conway*. He joined the Royal Naval Reserve in 1915 and transferred the following year to the Royal Navy where he soon made his mark.

In 1917, when he was only 21, Drew was awarded the DSC for operations in coastal motor boats off the French coast. He specialised in gunnery, and was commended for his technical work on the design of the Navy's high-angle gunfire control systems. In 1927 he was gunnery officer of the cruiser *Suffolk* on first commissioning, with a new design of 8-inch gun turrets and mountings.

One of his first jobs as Deputy Director of Personnel Services at the Admiralty early in the war was to commandeer for naval establishments all Billy Butlin's holiday camps.

Drew never had another seagoing command after *Manchester*. He was maintenance captain at Scapa Flow and then, in 1943, went to a staff appointment in Bombay. He next became director of recruiting and chairman of the committee which organised the victory celebrations, and was appointed CBE.

In 1948 he was appointed ADC to King George VI and went out to India again. For three years, as Deputy C-in-C with the rank of commodore, he played a major role in shaping the organisation and structure of the Indian Navy, which had newly emerged after the turmoil of partition in 1947. He retired in 1952.

Peter Drew was survived by his wife, the former Isabel Nicholson, whom he married in 1921, and their daughter.

REAR-ADMIRAL "BOGGY" FISHER

Rear-Admiral "Boggy" Fisher (who died on April 19 1988,aged 84) commanded the destroyer *Musketeer* in the chase and destruction of the German battlecruiser *Scharnhorst*, off the North Cape of Norway, on Boxing Day 1943.

During long hours of manoeuvring in the dark, bitter cold, *Scharnhorst* twice attempted to attack convoy JW55B on its way to Russia. Twice she was surprised and driven off by the cruisers *Belfast, Norfolk* and *Sheffield*. After the second action *Belfast*, with *Musketeer* and three other destroyers, followed *Scharnhorst* closely, reporting her course and eventually delivering her up to the big guns of the battleship *Duke of York*.

After gunfire had failed to sink *Scharnhorst*, *Musketeer* and other destroyers closed and administered the coup de grace with 11 torpedo hits. Fisher was awarded the DSC.

This was only one incident in a hectic wartime career. In 1940 he commanded the destroyer *Wakeful* at Dunkirk, and had evacuated several hundred soldiers when she was broken in two by a torpedo and sank with great loss of life. Fisher was picked up by the fishing boat *Comfort* which was itself sunk later that day when British ships fired on each other near the Kwinte Whistle Buoy, off the Dutch coast. But once again Fisher was picked up; he was awarded the DSO.

That autumn he went to the Mediterranean where, more than a year later he earned an OBE after taking part in the battle of Cape Matapan, as Staff Officer (Operations) to the Vice-Admiral Light Forces, Vice-Admiral Sir Henry Pridham-Wippell, in the evacuations from Greece and Crete in the spring of 1941.

Fisher was on the bridge of the cruiser *Orion* one morning when British forces were looking for the Italian fleet; *Orion*'s gun crews were sitting out on the tops of their turrets, when another officer on the bridge paused from eating a sandwich and suddenly said to Fisher: "What's that battleship over there? I thought ours were miles away." Fisher's reply was drowned by the whistle of the first salvo of 15-inch shells from the battleship *Vittorio Veneto* pitching close alongside *Orion*. With the other British cruisers *Orion* escaped and that night, in a short but brutal action at close range, three Italian heavy cruisers were sunk.

Fisher then served with the Inshore Squadron which opened up North African ports for Allied use as the Eighth Army advanced. He commanded *Musketeer* with several Russian convoys and later in the Aegean. On one occasion with a day to spare at the "godforsaken" Russian port of Polyarnoe, Fisher organised a regatta between the British ships. Few "hostilities only" sailors had ever pulled an oar in their lives, but the regatta was a huge success, with a home-made totalizator, ex-accountant RNVR officers acting as bookmakers amid "cheering" parties in fancy dress going from ship to ship.

Ralph Lindsay Fisher was born on June 18 1903, and joined the Navy in 1917 as a cadet, going to Osborne and Dartmouth. He wanted to specialise in gunnery but was not selected, so became a non-specialist "salt-horse".

He had a varied career in destroyers and big ships at home and in China. In 1933, when there was a chance sail-training would be reintroduced in the Navy, he sailed round the Horn in the four-masted barque *L'Avenir*, and three years later he and his wife, the former Ursula Carter, spent one leave paddling a small canoe 900 miles down the Danube.

After the war Fisher commanded the destroyer *Solebay* and the aircraft carrier *Indefatigable*, before being appointed Flag Officer Ground Training (Home Air Command), which he described as a "rotten job". He eventually succeeded in having the post abolished "so nobody else ever had to do it".

Fisher, who was appointed CB, retired in 1957 and published his entertaining memoirs, *Salt-Horse* (1985). He was survived by his wife and five daughters.

ADMIRAL OF THE FLEET
SERGEI GORSHKOV

Admiral of the Fleet Sergei Gorshkov (who died on May 13 1988, aged 78) was the creator of the Soviet Navy in the second half of the 20th century.

When he was appointed Commander-in-Chief in 1956 the Soviet Navy was no more than a coastal defence force, an obsolete commissar-ridden "Dad's

Navy", subservient to the Red Army, with low morale and a tradition of non-success going back to the defeat by the Japanese off Tsushima more than 50 years earlier. By the time he was succeeded by Admiral of the Fleet Vladimir Chernavin in 1985, it was judged by contemporaries as a modern well-equipped multi-weapon, multi-function "blue water" power, capable of influencing events and representing the Soviet Union's interests worldwide.

Gorshkov had enormous energy; and he was a hard taskmaster. But like all great naval commanders, he could delegate responsibility. On his desk he had a notice declaring "Better is the Enemy of Good Enough". In the closed bureaucratic society of Soviet Russia, Gorshkov's brilliant manipulation of bureaucracy and media on the navy's behalf was the envy of Western admirals. His writings on naval strategy and tactics were closely studied by Western naval staff.

He could be ruthless. When the crew of the frigate *Storozhevoy* mutinied and took their ship to sea from the Baltic port of Riga in 1975, Gorshkov ordered that she be pursued and sunk, if necessary. Several mutineers were killed, and one ringleader was later executed.

Sergei Georgievich Gorshkov was born at Kamenets Podolsk in the Ukraine in 1910 and joined the navy in 1927, going to the Frunze Higher Naval School. He was a destroyer man from his earliest days, serving first as navigating officer, and then as captain in the Pacific and the Black Sea Fleets.

When Germany invaded Russia in 1941, Gorshkov was in the Black Sea, where he was to remain for most of the war. He commanded the Azov Flotilla in support of the Red Army in the first ferocious battle in the Caucasus in 1941 and 1942. In the latter year he became a member of the Communist Party and, soon after, was appointed deputy commander of the Novorossiysk area. For a time he was acting commander of the 47th Army ashore. When the town of Sebastopol was cut off and besieged by the Wehrmacht, Gorshkov organised one-way "suicide" runs across the Black Sea by destroyers to take food and ammunition to the beleaguered garrison.

By the end of 1943 he was once more commanding the Azov Flotilla, organising seaborne support and assault shipping for the Red Army's landings in the Crimea. The following year he commanded the flotilla in support of operations to recapture the Danube and the cities of Belgrade and Budapest.

After the war he was Chief of Staff, then Commander-in-Chief of the Black Sea Fleet, and in 1955 he was chosen by Khrushchev – who believed, erroneously, that he was a submariner – to get rid of the old battleships and cruisers and take the navy into the nuclear age of new technology with submarines and missiles.

Under Gorshkov the Soviet Navy had more ships and money than his predecessors ever dreamed of. The submarine fleet, launched at the rate of one hull every few months over a period of nearly 30 years, was deemed the equal of the US Navy, with the giant 30,000-ton Typhoon class, the largest submarines in the world.

The navy had its first aircraft carriers, the Kiev class, designed to operate vertical take-off and landing aircraft. Larger full-deck carriers were now being built. The Kirov class battlecruisers became the largest surface warships other than aircraft carriers built for any navy since the 1939–45 War.

There were also huge cruiser and destroyer building programmes, and a new large Kriyak III class of warship for the KGB Maritime Border Troops. At times of crisis, such as the start of the Yom Kippur War in 1973, the Soviet Navy in the Mediterranean equalled the United States Sixth Fleet in strength.

It was unprecedented for its serving head to appear publicly in print, but in 1972–73 Gorshkov wrote a series of 11 articles for *Morskoy Sbornik* (Naval Digest) which were published in the West under the title of "Red Star Rising at Sea". They were later revised and reprinted in a book, *The Sea Power of the State* (1976), and studied as closely in the West as any text of Lenin's.

The book's argument that a strong navy was essential to any great nation, and was a flexible and far-reaching instrument of policy both in peace and war, may have led to Gorshkov's supersession. In the political aftermath following the death in 1982 of Brezhnev (whom Gorshkov had known as a political officer in the Black Sea during the war) there were changes in the commanders of the other military services, and Gorshkov's position of supreme power and prestige may have been weakened.

When at the age of 75 Gorshkov finally stepped down in December 1985, he had served as C-in-C for 29 years, 11 months and two days – the longest of any Soviet commander of any service. In the same period the Royal Navy had 13 First Sea Lords.

Gorshkov's chestful of medals and awards was one of the most splendid in all naval history. Andropov made him a Hero of the Soviet Union for the second

time in 1982, and Chernenko awarded him his Sixth
Order of Lenin in 1985.

LIEUTENANT
"JIM" WARREN

Lieutenant "Jim" Warren (who died on May 24 1988,
aged 76) was one of the first Allied "human torpedo
charioteers", practising methods of clandestine
attacks on enemy harbours and ships in the 1939-45
War which had been pioneered by the Italian Navy.

In 1942 Warren volunteered for the newly formed
Special Submarine Flotilla (later the 12th Flotilla)
which eventually employed two-man human torpedoes, chariots and midget submarines to attack enemy
targets, including the German battleship *Tirpitz*, and
whose members were to win four VCs. Based in
Malta, Warren himself carried out the beach surveys
before the landings in Sicily in 1943.

Together with his wartime comrade, James Benson,
he published a lively history of the flotilla's exploits,
Above Us the Waves (1953), which was later made into
a successful film.

Charles Esme Thornton Warren was born on
January 12 1912 and educated at Bedford School. In
1931 he became the first ex-public schoolboy to join
the Navy as an ordinary stoker. He had hoped to
achieve a commission through the Mate (E) Scheme
and should have done so, having obtained the
necessary early advancement to leading stoker and
high marks in the practical and theoretical examination. But the engineer commander in charge of the

Leading Stokers School at Chatham in 1934 refused to recommend Warren because he did not agree with promotions to commissions from the lower deck.

Instead Warren was offered a free choice of whatever ship he wanted, and he chose to volunteer for submarines. He served in *Rover* on the China station for two years, surviving a serious engine room explosion, and then in *Otis* and *Osiris*. When war came he volunteered for special service.

In 1940 he took part in an operation intended to block the River Danube at the Iron Gate, a narrow gorge near Turnu-Severin in Romania, and thus prevent German access to the oil from Ploesti oil-fields. The plan was discovered and aborted, but several valuable barges and tugs were later brought out.

Warren then became one of the naval liaison staff attached to 50th Middle East Commando based at Heraklion in Crete, raiding enemy outposts in the islands of the Dodecanese. At Suda Bay in Crete he came across his old submarine *Rover*, by then badly damaged by enemy bombing and incapable of diving; but in April 1941, at the height of the evacuation from Greece, Warren was one of the skeleton crew who manned *Rover* while the destroyer *Griffin* towed her to Alexandria.

Warren was finally commissioned in the RNVR in 1944 but had a serious accident that summer when a chariot he was driving went out of control and took him down to a depth of 100 feet. He suffered damage to his lungs and ears which ended his career as a charioteer, and later in life led to almost total deafness.

He was appointed MBE in 1945 and retired from

the Navy the following year. Warren was a tireless publicist for the men of the submarine service. As honorary secretary of the 12th Submarine Flotilla Association, he was not afraid to reprimand Admiral of the Fleet Viscount Cunningham of Hyndhope, his old C-in-C in the Mediterranean, in a letter to *The Daily Telegraph*, for having done less than justice to the flotilla's achievements in his memoirs, and particularly for the failure to mention its human torpedo personnel.

Warren's joint publications with James Benson included *The Admiralty Regrets* (1958), about the submarine *Thetis* lost in Liverpool Bay in 1939, and *Will Not We Fear* (1961), an account of the surrender of the submarine *Seal* in the Skagerrak in 1940. He regularly appeared on radio and television as an expert on submarine affairs.

His marriage in 1942 made Warren probably the only stoker petty officer ever to be married at St George's, Hanover Square. He was survived by his wife, a son and a daughter.

CAPTAIN
"SAM" MARRIOTT

Captain "Sam" Marriott (whose death, aged 73, was reported on May 5 1989) was the captain of what was known as "His Majesty's U-Boat".

In August 1941 an RAF Hudson bomber attacked U-570 and forced its captain to surrender. Marriott was first lieutenant of the crew who brought it to Britain from Iceland. The following year, after Allied

Intelligence had extracted priceless information, Marriott was appointed in command and commissioned it as *Graph* – the codename given to the recovery operation – to serve on three war patrols.

During the first, on October 21 1942, he fired a salvo of four torpedoes at a surfaced German U-boat. The torpedoes exploded after the correct running-time, and *Graph's* crew heard authentic "breaking-up noises". The U-boat was deemed sunk, and Marriott was awarded a DSO. The irony of a U-boat sinking a U-boat caused great jubilation in the navies of the Allies; post-war research, however, shows that U-333 had escaped.

On *Graph's* third patrol, off the Norwegian coast as part of the escort for the Arctic convoy JW51B in December 1942, Marriott saw the German heavy cruiser *Admiral Hipper* through his periscope but was unable to get close enough for a shot.

In 1944 Marriott commissioned the submarine *Stoic* at Cammell Laird in Birkenhead and took it out to the Indian Ocean. After sinking Japanese coastal-shipping off Burma, Malaya and Sumatra, he was awarded the DSC.

As the only U-boat captain in the Royal Navy, he was much in demand when the German U-boats surrendered after VE Day. In May 1945 he brought the captured U-776 up the Thames to Westminster Pier. London dockers and Thames watermen knew what a great victory at sea that U-boat represented. Every crane dipped its jib as it passed up-river, and every tug hooted its siren. Berthed alongside Shadwell Dock, U-776 became the East Enders' submarine. Marriott and his sailors played host to more than 3,000 visitors every day, while up to

25,000 people stared at the submarine from the dockside.

He later took temporary command of surrendered U-boats in Northern Ireland and also commanded the Londonderry Group, which took U-1007 to Latvia to be turned over to the Russians under the Potsdam Agreement.

Peter Barnsley Marriott was born on March 21 1915 and educated at the Nautical College, Pangbourne, before joining the Navy as a cadet in 1931. Like Nelson he was small in stature but determined – and like Nelson he was often seasick. He joined submarines in 1937 and served in *Starfish* and in L26 at the outbreak of war. Later he was first lieutenant of *Urge* and liaison officer to Allied submarines in Dundee.

After the war Marriott served in the carriers *Centaur* and *Victorious*; commanded the submarine *Tabard* in the Mediterranean;and was Chief of Staff to the C-in-C South America and South Atlantic.

Promoted captain in 1955, he was a member of the naval task force for Operation Grapple, the British thermo-nuclear bomb test at Christmas Island in the Pacific. In 1958 he went to Bath as assistant to the Director of Naval Construction and naval adviser on the design of nuclear submarines. His last appointment was Queen's Harbourmaster at Rosyth. He retired in 1964.

In retirement Sam Marriott was, for 10 years, warden of the Norfolk Naturalist Trust nature reserve at East Wretham. He left a widow, Jill, and two sons, who both served in the l7th/21st Lancers.

COMMANDER
NORMAN MORLEY

Commander Norman Morley (who died on September 21 1989, aged 90) was the most decorated Reserve officer of all time, earning himself an entry in the *Guinness Book of Records* as the only man ever to win four Distinguished Service Crosses.

As a lieutenant in Coastal Motor Boat 88, Morley took part in the raid on the harbour of Kronstadt in the Baltic on the night of August 17 1919. The commanding officer of CMB 88 was killed during the attack, and the second-in-command Lieutenant Gordon Steele, took over. CMB 88 penetrated the harbour and, with Morley firing the torpedoes, sank the Russian battleships *Andrei Pervozvanni* and *Petropavlovsk*. Steele was awarded the VC and Morley his first DSC.

Twenty years later Morley rejoined the RNVR, and served in minesweepers for the whole of the 1939-45 War. At Dunkirk in 1940 he was first lieutenant of the minesweeper *Hebe* when she took off hundreds of soldiers, including the Army commander, General Gort,VC.

Morley was mentioned in despatches when commanding the minesweeper *Eastbourne* after clearing an enemy minefield off the Nore in the winter of 1941-42. As commander of the mine-sweeper *Mutine* in the Mediterranean,he took part in the landings in Sicily and at Salerno, where he won a Bar to his DSC, in 1943, and also at Anzio. He won his second and third Bars in command of the minesweeper *Rhyl* during the landings in the south of France in August 1944 and for clearing the harbours of Patras and Itea in Greece early in 1945.

His last command was the minesweeper *Acute*, clearing the harbour and approaches of Genoa after VE Day in May 1945. He knew that, though the enemy might have surrendered,minesweeping had to go on. When asked if he would attend a memorial service on VE Day, Morley replied:"We can't hold up the war just because peace has been declared."

Norman Eyre Morley was born in London in 1898 and educated at Battersea Grammar School. He went to sea in 1914 as an apprentice with the Harrison Rennie Line. In 1916 he joined the RNR and served in the battleship *Iron Duke* as midshipman in Lieutenant Steele's division. Morley took part, aboard a coastal motor boat, in the daring attempt to block the entrance to the German submarine base at Zeebrugge on St George's Day, 1918, when he was wounded.

On leaving the Navy in 1920 he studied architecture at London University and joined Courage, the brewers, eventually becoming their chief architect and property technical director.

When he retired in 1964 he bought a farm at Selborne, Hampshire, where, in the tradition of Gilbert White, he devoted himself to the study of natural history. Morley was a founder member and commodore of Frensham Pond Sailing Club and continued to sail dinghies single-handedly until well into his eighties. He was survived by his wife, Audrey, a son and a daughter.

CAPTAIN
"HOOCH"WILLIAMSON

Captain "Hooch"Williamson (who died on February 24 1990, aged 83) led the daring night attack on the Italian battle fleet at Taranto on November 11 1940.

As a Fleet Air Arm squadron commander, Williamson led the first striking force of Fairey Swordfish torpedo bombers. In the course of that night a total of 21 Swordfish launched from the aircraft carrier *Illustrious* sank or put out of action three Italian battleships, damaged a heavy cruiser, and bombed harbour installations and oil storage tanks.

Williamson himself scored a torpedo hit on the battleship *Conte di Cavour*, sinking her in shallow water; she was later raised but took no further part in the war. His own Swordfish was shot down, or possibly flew so low that it caught a wing tip in the water; and he and his observer were captured to spend the rest of the war as PoWs.

Taranto was a stunning strategic victory, which overnight decisively shifted the balance of capital ship power in the Mediterranean. For the loss of two Swordfish, the aircrews inflicted more damage upon the enemy than the Grand Fleet had achieved at Jutland.Yet this victory, which changed the course of the war, was widely misunderstood. The Admiralty, densely packed with gunnery officers, ignored or discounted it.The BBC reported the action with the headline "The RAF do it again!" – a grotesquely lazy piece of broadcasting which the RAF delighted in at the time and refused ever afterwards to correct.

Williamson received only a DSO, when every man in the Mediterranean fleet believed he deserved the

Victoria Cross; the sailors on *Illustrious* angrily tore down from the noticeboard the first meagre list of Taranto awards. Admiral Sir Andrew Cunningham – who as C-in-C Mediterranean, had fumbled the awards – was full of praise for Taranto in his memoirs; at a post-war dinner in celebration of the operation he confessed that he had not realised at the time what a stroke it was.

A quiet and modest man, Williamson was always ready to lend his logbook and diaries to the many historians of Taranto, but remained reticent about his own part in the great raid. In more than four years as a PoW he never once discussed it with his observer, Lieutenant Norman ("Blood") Scarlett.

Kenneth Williamson was born in 1906 and educated at Osborne and Dartmouth. In 1929 he qualified as a pilot, and it was in the carriers *Courageous* and *Eagle* that he acquired his nickname, for reasons now lost in obscurity. Following a spell in the Directorate of Flying Training he joined *Illustrious* in July 1940 as CO of 815 Naval Air Squadron.

After the war Williamson served in the Admiralty and at such air stations as Lee-on-Solent; Ford, Sussex; and Eglinton, Northern Ireland. In 1948 he joined his old ship *Illustrious* again as Commander (Air). He was also on the staff of Flag Officer Air (Home) and president of the second Admiralty interview board. His last appointment before retiring in 1961 was as Chief of Staff to the Flag Officer Commanding Reserve Fleet.

Williamson was survived by his wife, Joan, a daughter, and three sons who all followed their father into the Service.

COMMANDER
BRADWELL TURNER

Commander Bradwell Turner (who died on March 21 1990, aged 82) led the destroyer *Cossack*'s boarding party in the "Altmark Affair", one of the legendary incidents of the Second World War.

In February 1940 the German tanker *Altmark* had on board some 300 British merchant seamen, captured when their ships were sunk by the raiding German battleship *Admiral Graf Spee*. *Altmark*'s captain was trying to use the shelter of neutral Norwegian waters to make his escape back to Germany.

One attempt by the British to intercept the tanker on February 16 had been thwarted by Norwegian ships, and *Altmark* took refuge in a narrow fjord. That afternoon Captain Philip Vian of *Cossack* demanded of the Norwegians that the British prisoners be handed over to him. The Norwegians replied that they had examined *Altmark* and found no British prisoners. Vian withdrew to seek instructions.

Winston Churchill, who was then First Lord of the Admiralty, ordered Vian to pursue *Altmark*, and, if necessary, to resist any interference by the Norwegians. That night *Cossack* entered the fjord, where *Altmark* tried to ram her and then herself ran aground.

As the two ships came together, Turner − with the leap that made him famous − landed on *Altmark*'s upper deck, followed by the rest of the boarding party. After a brief struggle, in which six Germans were killed, and six wounded, while others fled across the frozen ice to the shore, *Altmark* was captured and her holds were opened.

Turner shouted down:"Any British there?"and was answered by a tremendous yell of: "Yes, we're all BRITISH!" Turner's response became a legend. "Come up then," he said,"the Navy's here!" It was,as Turner recalled many times in later years, a great moment. He was awarded the DSO.

Bradwell Talbot Turner was born on April 7 1907 and educated at Christ's Hospital. He joined the Navy as a cadet in 1921, going to Osborne and Dartmouth.

Turner specialised as a signals officer, and was flag lieutenant to Admiral D'Oyly-Lion,commanding the First Cruiser Squadron in the Mediterranean from 1935 to 1937, before joining the new destroyer *Cossack* as her first lieutenant. Later he went to the Admiralty where he was involved in planning communications and Anglo-American co-operation for the Normandy landings, for which he was made an Officer of the American Legion of Merit.

In 1945 Turner was executive officer of the cruiser *Cumberland* on the South African station, when he contracted polio. He was an invalid for two years, and was left with one permanently lame leg. But he commanded the destroyer *Whirlwind* from 1947 to 1948 and held appointments at HMS Sea Eagle, the shore station in Northern Ireland, in the Admiralty, and with Nato in Washington.

His last appointment from 1954 to 1957 was naval attaché in Oslo. Realising that he had no hope of further promotion, because of his disability, he read law by correspondence course, and was called to the Bar by the Middle Temple in 1956.

He never practised at the Bar, but worked for Marconi until 1972. He became a JP in Chelmsford in 1962 and chairman of the bench 12 years later.

Turner was a tall, dignified man, a perfectionist who loved things to be "just so". The Navy had been his life, and it remained his main interest. He kept in touch with old naval friends, and, in 1980, he attended a "Forty Years On" reunion of old *Cossack* shipmates from the *Altmark* days.

Bradwell Turner was appointed OBE in 1951 and CVO in 1955. In 1937 he married Molly, daughter of Professor W Nixon; they had three daughters.

REAR-ADMIRAL
SIR ED IRVING

Rear-Admiral Sir Ed Irving (who died on October 1 1990, aged 80) was Hydrographer of the Navy from 1960 to 1966, and a highly influential head of his branch. Among other reforms, he persuaded the Admiralty to drop its tradition of converting warship hulls for surveying – a practice which went back to Captain Cook – and to build instead the specially designed Hecla class of ocean survey vessels.

No mere boffin, Irving had a gallant record in the Second World War. In 1941 he was mentioned in despatches for his service as navigating officer of *Scott*, which had the hazardous task of laying beacons to mark out the correct positions for minefields laid off Iceland.

The next year he was first lieutenant of the aged coal-burning survey ship *Endeavour* in the Mediterranean and the Red Sea. During the "Great Flap" of that summer, when Rommel's Afrika Korps stood at El Alamein, *Endeavour* carried out a rapid series of surveys east and south of Port Sudan to find out which harbours might supply the Army if it were forced to leave the Nile Delta.

Irving was also responsible for the coastal surveys before the landings in Sicily and Italy. When the Eighth Army crossed the Straits of Messina in September 1943 he had surveyed the three main landing points and fixed them exactly by arranging for six searchlights to be positioned on the Sicilian side, which gave the assault shipping a perfect navigational transit. He was mentioned in despatches.

A bustling, intense man, he refused to be defeated by circumstances. When he was asked to survey the harbours of North-West Europe after the Normandy landings, the River Scheldt was blocked by sunken ships and mines. Undeterred, he placed his survey boats on commandeered transport barges, and took them through the Belgian canal system to Bruges and up to the Scheldt, where he began his survey at Terneuzen. Irving was appointed OBE in 1944.

Edmund George Irving was born on April 5 1910, and joined the Navy as a cadet at Dartmouth in 1924. His first posting as a midshipman was in the battleship *Royal Oak*. Irving specialised early in hydrography, serving in the survey vessel *Kellett* in 1931 and thereafter in survey vessels around the world until the outbreak of war.

After the war Irving's career alternated between command at sea and service in the Admiralty's Hydrographic Department. He commanded *Sharp-shooter*, *Dalrymple* and *Vidal*, and in 1948 carried out sea trials of the Decca navigational system.

In retirement from the Navy he worked for some

years for Racal. He was a fellow and sometime president of the Royal Geographic Society, and won its Patron's Medal; a trustee of the National Maritime Museum from 1972 to 1981; and acting conservator of the River Mersey from 1975 to 1985.

Irving was ADC to the Queen in 1960. He was appointed CB in 1962 and KBE in 1966. He was twice married:first to Margaret Edwards, who died in 1974; and secondly to Esther Ellison, who survived him, together with a son and a daughter of his first marriage.

SIR HAMISH MacLAREN

Sir Hamish MacLaren (who died on October 15 1990,aged 92) was Director of Electrical Engineering for the Royal Navy from 1945 to 1960 and the central figure in the establishment of its electrical engineering training branch. He also pioneered the scheme whereby naval electrical officers were sent to university to gain engineering degrees, to give them a professional footing equivalent to their civilian counterparts.

After the Second World War MacLaren led the Navy's evaluations of the effects of action damage, shot and fire on the design and performance of electrical equipment in ships; and he was later responsible for a wide range of technical advances, including the change from the old 220 volt DC to 440 volt AC supply in warships – first completed in the destroyer *Diamond* in 1950 – and the development of electrical analogue-computing for naval gunnery.

A son of the manse, Hamish Duncan MacLaren was born on April 7 1898, at Forglen, Banffshire, and educated at Fordyce Academy. He joined the Navy in 1915 and served as an ordinary signalman in a destroyer at Scapa Flow.

After volunteering for flying, he survived a bad crash while training to qualify as a pilot, and was commissioned as a sub-lieutenant in the Royal Naval Air Service, from which he transferred to the RAF when it was formed in April 1918. MacLaren was a bold and skilful pilot,and proved an exceptional flight commander, flying two-seater Airco DH9s and 9As.

His first DFC was gazetted in early November after he had taken part in 36 bombing raids, mostly on docks and shipping in Flanders. It noted that he had always displayed courage, determination and ability despite encountering heavy anti-aircraft fire and invariably larger numbers of enemy planes.When he received a Bar only a month later the citation noted that he had once flown four sorties in one day when he bombed enemy railway junctions in support of the Allied advance on land. On his return from one flight he had been ambushed by a formation of enemy fighters. Although his observer air-gunner Sergeant Barlow was wounded in both legs, he managed to shoot down two of the enemy, and in consequence, was also awarded the Croix de Guerre *avec palme*.

With so strong a fighting record MacLaren might have stayed in the RAF, but after the war he went to Edinburgh University, where in 1921 he took a First in engineering. The same year he was awarded a bursary by the Commission for the Exhibition of 1851, and two years later went to America as a British Thomson Houston Fellow to work with the

General Electric Company.

On his return he remained on the staff at British Thomson in Rugby until joining the Admiralty service as an assistant electrical engineer in 1926. MacLaren then served in the Director of Dockyard's department at Chatham, Devonport and Ceylon; in 1937 he was appointed Superintending Electrical Engineer, HM Naval Base, Singapore.

In 1940 he went to the Admiralty at Bath as Assistant Director of the Electrical Engineering Department. He spent much of the Second World War visiting dockyards around the country, but always tried to be at home on Sunday afternoons for tennis, which he played to county standard. He remained a frustrated aviator throughout the war and followed the doings of the RAF and the Fleet Air Arm avidly: he and his children became experts at aircraft identification.

On retiring in 1960, MacLaren became president of the Institution of Electrical Engineers. He was an excellent public speaker, often said to resemble Field Marshal Montgomery in his crisp delivery. He was appointed CB in 1946 and KBE in 1951.

A most modest man, despite his many decorations, Sir Hamish always said that his greatest achievement was to have converted the Navy from DC to AC. He continued to play tennis and golf, but latterly suffered from deafness, which he said was caused by aero-engine noise and Sergeant Barlow's guns in the open cockpit behind him.

He married, in 1927, Lorna Bluett; they had a son and a daughter.

GENERAL
SIR PETER HELLINGS

General Sir Peter Hellings, the former Commandant General of the Royal Marines (who died on November 2 1990, aged 74) was a shining exponent of the Marines' motto *per mare per terram* (by sea and by land) and probably the only man to have won both the DSC and the MC.

He won his DSC in 1940 as a member of a special marine party hurriedly formed at Chatham and rushed across the Channel to carry out rearguard actions at Boulogne after the fall of France. He then became a company commander in 40 Commando during the Dieppe raid in August 1942. The unit was ordered to land on "White Beach", which was believed to have been captured. In fact it was still in enemy hands, and the commandos' landing craft were met by a storm of fire as they came in. There were many casualties. The CO and second-in-command were both killed, and Hellings's landing craft was hit and broke down. He and his company were lucky to escape under cover of smoke, before being picked up by the gunboat *Locust*.

Promoted second-in-command of 40 Commando, Hellings took part in the Sicily landing in July 1943, and won his MC for gallantry in Operation Devon – the landing at the port of Termoli on the Adriatic coast in October 1943. Having captured the town, the commandos had to defend it for four days after a determined counter-attack by a German Panzer division. Hellings organised the ambush of enemy vehicles approaching the town and for some hours engaged in action with a German tank, firing at close range across the town cemetery.

Afterwards, when Termoli was secured, General Montgomery gratefully ordered the commandos back to Bari where, Hellings said, "there were plenty of girls and drink."

During his tenure as Commandant General from 1968-1971, Hellings proved himself as able a warrior in Whitehall as he had been in the field. It was one of those times when the future of the Royal Marines was uncertain. Hellings enjoyed trust on all sides, though, and the Corps was in safe hands.

Peter William Craddock Hellings was born on September 6 1916, and went to the Nautical College at Pangbourne before joining the Royal Marines in 1935. He specialised in gunnery and served in the cruiser *London* in the Mediterranean from 1937-1938.

In December 1943, after the capture of Termoli, Hellings returned home to join the staff of the Commando group and was mentioned in despatches for his service in operation in North-West Europe. From 1945 to 1946 he commanded 41 and 42 Commando, and he was in Hong Kong for its re-occupation as a British colony in 1945.

After the war, Hellings became a kind of stormy petrel, serving wherever there was trouble. In 1949 he was in Hong Kong again for the Chinese communist offensive against Chiang Kai-shek's troops. He served as brigade major of 3 Commando during the Emergency in Malaya, and commanded 40 Commando in operations against Eoka in Cyprus, where he was mentioned in despatches a second time.

Two years later, he commanded the Royal Marine infantry training school and then became deputy director, Joint Warfare staff. In 1964 he was Chief of

Staff to the Commandant General and, from 1967–8, he commanded the Portsmouth Group of Royal Marines.

Hellings gave the impression of being easygoing and relaxed in manner; but he always had a full grasp of the situation, and never failed to rise to the occasion when something went wrong. As a commando, he practised assiduously with bows and arrows, hoping one day to use them in earnest, and in Hong Kong he kept a pet snake in his bedroom.

He retired in 1971 and became Deputy Lieutenant of Devon two years later. He was Colonel Commandant Royal Marines from 1977 to 1979 and Representative Colonel Commandant from 1979 to 1980. He was appointed CB in 1966 and KCB in 1970.

Peter Hellings was survived by his wife Zoya and a daughter.

COMMANDER
"JIMMY"WILDE

Commander "Jimmy" Wilde (whose death, aged 79, was reported on December 12 1990) was a pioneer in the development of one of the most spectacular weapons in naval warfare – the Landing Craft Tank (Rocket).

These were ordinary LCTs fitted with a second deck over the tank deck, on which were fixed more than 1,000 projectors, each mounting a 5-inch rocket. The rockets were electrically fired in salvoes of 24 at a set range of 3,500 yards, so as to saturate a beachhead with one rocket every 10 yards. As they were launched the craft's upper deck was cleared except for the captain, who stood in an asbestos shelter on the bridge, conning the ship through a strengthened quartz window while the first lieutenant operated the firing panel in the wheelhouse. A rocket craft in action gave a spectacular display of pyrotechnics as volleys of rockets ignited and took off towards the target with deafening roars, sheets of flame and towering columns of black smoke.

The rocket exhaust heated the steel deck so that it had to be constantly sprayed with cooling water. Clouds of steam rising from the hot deck added to the spectacle. The first six rocket craft, including Wilde's, left for the Mediterranean in May 1943 to make their debut at the Sicily landings in July. There, in support of the Highland Division, they put up a sensational performance, opening fire when the leading assault craft were 500 yards from the beach.

The "Jocks" – huddled in their landing craft, feeling tired and seasick while soaked by spray – were heartened to hear the thunderous roars from behind them and the sound of a rushing wind as the rockets passed overhead to detonate with tremendous effect on the beach.

The rocket craft went on to repeat the performance at Salerno in September. Wilde was mentioned in despatches then and later for two actions against German convoys on the west coast of Italy in March and April 1944. Wilde's rocket craft also took part in landings on Elba in June 1944, which were fiercely opposed, and again in the south of France in August. Having progressed from the command of a single rocket craft to a flotilla and then to a squadron, Wilde was promoted commander and awarded the DSC.

James Olaf Stuart Wilde was born on December 15 1910, the son of a naval captain and a godson of Admiral of the Fleet Earl Jellicoe. He went to Dartmouth in 1924 and joined the submarine service in 1933. Two years later he retired from the Navy as a lieutenant and went to work for the Foreign Office in India; but he rejoined at the Cochin naval base in 1939. The following year he served in the cruiser *Kent*, escorting troop convoys in the Indian Ocean and was "snotties' nurse" in charge of the ship's midshipmen, who included Prince Philip.

In 1941 he spent what he called "a very seasick year" as first lieutenant of *Broadway*, one of the 50 aged American destroyers exchanged for bases in the West Indies and Newfoundland. He was mentioned in despatches for the first time after *Broadway* and the destroyer *Bulldog* attacked U-110 on May 9 1941.

U-110 sank while under tow, but not before *Bulldog*'s boarding party had recovered its Enigma cipher machine with that day's settings still on it and numerous codes. This priceless intelligence greatly assisted an Allied break into German machine cyphers (the enemy never knew of the capture).

Wilde left the Navy again in 1946, still on the retired list, then worked for the Allied Control Commission in Hamburg and for the Foreign Office in Libya, Ghana and in Bonn. His wife, Liliana, whom he had met in Italy during the war, died in 1979. They had twins, a son and a daughter.

COMMANDER
THE REVEREND EVELYN CHAVASSE

Commander the Reverend Evelyn Chavasse (who died at Kyrenia, Cyprus, on August 9 1991, aged 84) won a DSO and DSC for gallantry in the Second World War before becoming an Anglican priest.

In 1942 he was appointed to command the destroyer *Broadway*, one of the 50 former US Navy First World War "fourstackers" exchanged for bases on Newfoundland and in the West Indies. Like all her sisters, *Broadway* was rather temperamental: she was prone to suffer power failures, and gave Chavasse some trying times.

He was senior officer of C2 Canadian Escort Group, based at Londonderry, and escorted some 20 Atlantic convoys, proving himself a first-class escort commander. He received a formal letter of appreciation from the Admiralty for the way he handled the defence of convoy ON139 in October 1942, and was awarded the DSC the next year.

In May 1943 C2 Escort Group fought a prolonged battle around the homeward-bound convoy HX237, in which three ships were sunk but three U-boats were destroyed. Ably assisted by a Fairey Swordfish from the escort carrier *Biter* and by the frigate *Lagan*, *Broadway* sank U-89 with her "hedgehog", which threw a pattern of small contact-fused bombs ahead of an attacking ship. This was one of a series of crucial convoy battles which turned the tide of the Battle of the Atlantic in the spring of 1943, and gave the Allies the strategic victory over the U-boats. Chavasse was awarded the DSO.

He then took command of the frigate *Bentinck* as

senior officer of the 4th Escort Group, and escorted more convoys across the Atlantic and in the Mediterranean. Chavasse normally relied on his own and his ship's company's skill and experience, but on at least one occasion he was obliged to seek divine assistance. In March 1944 he was senior officer escorting a convoy of the battleship *Ramillies* and 20 passenger liners, bringing more than 65,000 troops back from Italy to take part in the invasion of Normandy.

The convoy was passing through the Straits of Gibraltar when U-boats were reported ahead, and there was a minefield to port. Chavasse had to decide whether to risk the U-boats or the minefield. "With a sort of blasphemous impropriety," he said, "I filled and lit my pipe, and prayed as I had never prayed before. Ten minutes later I knocked out my pipe and turned to the signalman. 'Make to the commodore, please turn convoy 45 degrees to port'." The convoy steamed across the minefield for an hour, but not one ship was lost.

For a short but enjoyable period in the summer of 1944, Chavasse commanded the luxurious yacht *Philante*, owned before the war by the aircraft designer Tom Sopwith. Next, he was based at Larne, which had a headquarters ship for training escort captains, and then went to Derby House, Liverpool, as Staff Officer (Operations) to the C-in-C Western Approaches, Admiral Sir Max Horton.

That final year of the war in the poorly ventilated underground of Derby House, where Chavasse worked long hours without fresh air or proper rest, took its toll. Afterwards, when he went out to the East Indies on the staff of the C-in-C, Chavasse discovered in the most alarming and dramatic manner that he had tuberculosis: he suddenly began coughing blood all over his white uniform in the middle of an official luncheon in the flagship.

After an operation, he was transferred to the Admiralty as Assistant Director of Naval Intelligence, but he soon suffered a relapse and following a second operation was invalided out of the Navy in 1949.

Twenty-five years later, Chavasse was living on Cyprus as a retired clergyman when the Turks invaded the island. He and his wife, Edith, refused to be evacuated, saying that they had nowhere to go. Instead, affecting his most sublimely confident air, wearing dog-collar and dickey front and waving huge Union Jacks, Chavasse shepherded parties of civilians – men, women and children, British and Greek-Cypriot – through lines of Turkish soldiers.

He had just persuaded one Greek family of six to come out of hiding when a Turkish officer, who spoke neither English nor Greek, drove up in a Jeep and tried to make some sense of what was happening. Chavasse kept saying, "I'm British, old boy, and I am going to take these people to the UNO forces", until the officer eventually gave up, took a baby in his arms and helped to load the car.

Evelyn Henry Chavasse was born into a gallant family on October 10 1906. The fourth son of Major Henry Chavasse, High Sheriff of Co Waterford, he had an uncle, Noel Chavasse, who won the VC and a Bar while serving with the Royal Army Medical Corps during the First World War; Noel's twin, Christopher, who later became Bishop of Rochester, won the Military Cross. In the Second World War Evelyn's older brother Colonel Kendall Chavasse won a DSO and Bar while his youngest brother, Captain Paul Chavasse, won the DSC and Bar; all three brothers were decorated at Buckingham Palace on the same day. In addition, a son of the bishop, also called Noel, who was one of Montgomery's liaison officers, won the MC.

Young Evelyn joined the Navy as a cadet in 1920, going to Osborne and Dartmouth. Much of his pre-war service was spent in the Far East − as first lieutenant of the river gunboat *Scarab* on the China station and then, from 1938 to 1941, on the staff of the C-in-C East Indies, at Colombo.

Soon after leaving the Navy, Chavasse decided to take Holy Orders, and went to Cuddesdon Theological College for training. From 1954 to 1958 he was a curate at the Hampshire coastal parish of Lymington, and then moved to Kidlington, near Oxford.

He returned to Winchester diocese as vicar of Knight's Enham with Swannell, near Andover, at that time a small rural parish. In 1964 he was appointed rector of St Peter's, Jersey. There he quickly became a highly respected figure. He was especially pleased to have the airport in his parish: whenever VIPs arrived he would turn out with the welcoming party.

He retired in 1973, but then went to live in northern Cyprus, where he assumed responsibility for the pastoral care of the small Anglican community. He was appointed OBE in 1975.

An excellent writer, Chavasse once wrote up his official Report of Proceedings of a convoy action in the form of an article for *Punch*, which was much appreciated by the Naval Staff. He also wrote two engaging (though unpublished) books of memoirs,

Up and Down the Yangtse, which told of his time in China, and *Business in Great Waters*, about his war experiences.

Chavasse's first wife, Evelyn, died in 1950, and his second in 1991. He had two sons.

———————

COMMANDER
HUGH HAGGARD

Commander Hugh Haggard (who died on November 17 1991, aged 83) was captain of *Truant*, the third highest scoring British submarine of the Second World War, which was often in the news under such headlines as "Adventure Sub *Truant* Does it Again!"

Haggard took command in April 1940, and began with patrols off the Norwegian coast. One evening in July, when he was on the bridge, he suddenly detected the characteristic shale oil smell from a British torpedo's exhaust. "That's one of ours!" he exclaimed in surprise. It was indeed one of a salvo of six fired at *Truant*, which had been mistaken for a German U-boat by the submarine *Clyde*. The Admiral Submarines, Max Horton, gave both captains the rough side of his tongue: one for being caught on the surface, the other for missing from such short range.

In September, when *Truant* was underway to the Mediterranean, Haggard had been given "strict instructions not to mess about with anything". Nonetheless he could not resist investigating a strange merchant ship sailing alone off the Spanish coast. She proved to be the Norwegian *Tropic Sea*, carrying

8,500 tons of wheat, which had been seized by a German raider off New Zealand months earlier; she was being sailed to France by a German prize crew, who scuttled her when they saw *Truant*.

Haggard took on board the Norwegian captain, his wife and 23 members of the crew of the British SS *Haxby*, who had been made prisoners after their ship was sunk. A Sunderland flying boat later picked up some of the Norwegians from their lifeboat, while the rest, together with the Germans, reached Spain.

The Norwegian captain's wife thoroughly enjoyed her trip to Gibraltar. Haggard gave up his cabin to her, and the wardroom steward brought her breakfast in bed. In a signal to Horton, Haggard claimed the first ever submarine voyage by a woman. He was mentioned in despatches.

Late in 1940 *Truant* arrived in Alexandria, where flotilla morale was low. Seven submarines had been lost, along with their fully trained and experienced crews,with very little to show for it.But Haggard was a lucky captain: he sank an 8,500-ton ship on his first patrol, and he usually found at least one good target every time. Although his successes always appeared to be effortless, he gave much thought to his profession and had some original ideas.

He once pursued a target so close to the Italian shore that *Truant* ran aground in shallow water, while a searching destroyer crossed and recrossed overhead, the keel only inches from *Truant*'s periscope standards. Haggard had practised many times running *Truant* astern while dived.His sailors had thought him daft, but on that occasion, when *Truant* escaped stern first out to sea, the manoeuvre almost certainly saved all their lives.

Standing at six foot five, Haggard could barely fit into his own control room and had to stoop to look through the periscope. His sailors were at first deceived by his patrician good looks and languid manner – he used to give his orders as though requesting the butler to bring him a glass of sherry – but they soon found they had a bold and aggressive commander.

He took *Truant* into a small North African harbour to attack a tanker. It was riding higher than he thought, and the torpedo ran underneath. There was barely room to turn, and Haggard had to do some furious manoeuvring. As *Truant's* conning tower came abreast the target's deckhouse, a man came out, leant over the guard rail and "had a good deal to say". With a cry of "Il Duce", *Truant* passed out of earshot and out of the harbour.

Early in 1942 *Truant* chased targets along the coast of Bali as eagerly as it had done in the Mediterranean. Although Haggard never regarded himself as a very good attacker, he had a happy knack of sinking enemy ships. When *Truant* came home at the end of the year, it had travelled more than 80,000 miles and Haggard's final score, spread around the world from Norway to the Indian Ocean, was 17 enemy ships weighing a total of 70,000 tons.

Haggard was mentioned in despatches a second time, awarded the DSC in 1941 and the DSO in 1942.

Hugh Alfred Vernon Haggard was born on June 21 1908, the son of Admiral Sir Vernon Haggard, who was Admiral Submarines from 1925 to 1927, and the great-nephew of the novelist Sir Henry Rider Haggard. He joined the Navy as a cadet at

Dartmouth in 1921.

Later he confessed that he was "terrified" by the prospect of a naval career but, coming from such a family, "could see no way out". He served as a lieutenant in the Royal Yacht *Victoria & Albert* and in the cruiser *Cardiff*, before joining the submarine service in May 1933. For the next five years he served in *Seahorse*, *Severn*, *Osiris*, *Rover* and *Narwhal*, working at home, in the Mediterranean and on the China station. His first command, in 1939, was the training boat H44 based at Portland.

From 1943 to 1945 he was Commander (Submarines) in depot ships on Holy Loch, at Blyth and in Malta. His last sea-going appointment was as executive officer of the cadet training cruiser *Devonshire* from 1947 to 1948.

"Hughie" Haggard had many friends at all levels in the Navy. One of his best, a submarine CO newly arrived in Alexandria, was briefed for a mission which Haggard thought too dangerous for a com-paratively inexperienced CO. The submarine failed to return. Haggard was horrified when he found out later that his friend had demurred about the patrol, only to be told by the captain of the flotilla:"If you won't do it, Haggard will." Ever afterwards Haggard felt responsible for his friend's death.

He was invalided out of the Navy with tuberculosis in 1954, and joined the Bristol Aeroplane Company in 1957.

Haggard married first,Margaret Dykes,with whom he had a son.After the marriage was dissolved in 1954 he married Lydia Watson, who died in 1984.

CAPTAIN
RON FREAKER

Captain Ron Freaker (who died on December 19 1991, aged 88) was one of the most successful and highly decorated Royal Naval Reserve officers to command convoy escorts in the Battle of the Atlantic.

Although a small man – he had to stand on a biscuit tin to look out over his bridge rail – Freaker was a seaman to his fingertips and a tireless combat captain. In 1941 he was in command of the Flower class corvette *Nasturtium*, escorting the east-bound convoy HX133, when early in the morning of June 27 she received the clear Asdic echo of a U-boat.

In the previous three days *Nasturtium* had already used all her depth charges driving off U-boat attacks, and two sister ships, *Gladiolus* and *Celandine*, were duly summoned to join the attack. *Celandine* received no echo, so *Nasturtium* guided her by steaming over the target,indicating the time to fire by dipping a flag and the location by turning under full helm to leave an aiming mark in her wake. *Celandine* made four attacks while her CO kept signalling "Hope you are not wasting my depth charges." Freaker hastened to reassure him, "You're doing fine. Give him the works."

After four hours, during which *Celadine* never received even a hint of an Asdic trace, U-556 came to the surface,where its crew abandoned ship;all but the engineer officer and three men were picked up. Freaker was awarded the DSO.

In April 1943 Freaker commanded the River class frigate *Jed* in the 1st Escort Group, defending the outward-bound convoy ONS5. The following month the group was on its way to support the eastbound convoy SC130 when it surprised two U-boats on the surface. U-209 dived and fired torpedoes at the frigates, but was then sunk by Jed and the former US Coast Guard cutter *Sennen*. In that month 43 U-boats were lost in all – a casualty rate which shocked the German command and forced the temporary withdrawal of all U-boats from the North Atlantic.

Freaker and his officers (all Reservists) and *Jed*'s sailors (eighty per cent of them "hostilities only") had contributed to a smashing strategic victory for the Allies. The U-boats were dangerous to the end, but were never again the mortal menace they had been that spring.

On June 14 *Jed* and the sloop *Pelican* were escorting convoy ONS10 when a U-boat radio transmission was detected 20 miles ahead. The U-boat went deep, but the ships attacked with depth charges set to detonate between 750 and 900 feet deep. After one pattern from *Jed*, extensive wreckage and human remains came to the surface: that was the end of U-334. Freaker was awarded a Bar to his DSO.

In August *Jed* took part in an offensive in the Bay of Biscay. It involved hunting down U-boats and fighting off Heinkel 177s armed with glider bombs. Freaker was awarded the DSC. In 1945, he was still at sea, in command of *Loch Eck*, one of four frigates of 10th Escort Group supporting convoys around the north coast of Scotland. With the help of Ultra Special Intelligence, which gave accurate and timely information about U-boat sailings from Norway, the group carried out a remarkable patrol off the Shetlands, sinking three U-boats with "squid" and "hedgehog" weapons.

Freaker was awarded a Bar to his DSC.

Ronald Clifford Freaker was born in 1903 and went to sea at 16 as an apprentice with the Blue Star Line, serving on several ships including *Andora Star*, the most luxurious cruise ship of her day. From 1934 to 1938 he served as chief officer and then master of the Royal Research Ship *William Scoresby*. Each year *Scoresby* made a 20,000-mile voyage around the Antarctic, in which up to 900 whales were "tagged" with special darts to record their migration. Whalers who caught a marked whale were paid a small fee.

Freaker was awarded the Bronze Polar Medal, which he received from King George VI at the same investiture as his DSO. He was also awarded the Reserve Decoration, and was a Younger Brother of Trinity House.

In 1945 he joined the Suez Canal Pilotage Service and was a senior pilot when he left in 1956. At home he became a Board of Trade examiner of Masters and Mates in Southampton; in retirement he coached candidates for their Yacht Master's Certificate.

Ron Freaker was survived by his wife, Beatrice, and two daughters.

ADMIRAL OF THE FLEET
LORD FIELDHOUSE

Admiral of the Fleet Lord Fieldhouse (who died on February 17 1992, aged 64) was Commander-in-Chief Fleet at the time of the Falklands conflict and, as the task force commander, was responsible for the planning and direction of Operation Corporate to recover the islands.

He answered directly to the Chief of the Defence Staff, Admiral Lewin, in the task of conducting military deployment and operations to bring about the withdrawal of Argentinian forces and the re-establishment of British administration as quickly as possible. In common with the then First Sea Lord, Admiral Sir Henry Leach, Fieldhouse never doubted that this was possible; but the Navy's confidence contrasted strongly with the attitude of the Ministry of Defence civil servants.

Late in March 1982, when the first rumblings of the old diplomatic storm could be heard, Fieldhouse was in the Mediterranean where Royal Navy ships were exercising. Little was known about the Argentinian opposition. Indeed, the planning for Corporate may be said to have begun with Fieldhouse and the Flag Officer 1st Flotilla, Rear-Admiral "Sandy" Woodward kneeling at the desk of the Admiral's day-cabin in the destroyer *Glamorgan*, studying the ships of the Argentinian Navy in *Jane's Fighting Ships*.

Woodward, who was appointed task group commander at sea, was ordered to sail for Ascension Island with six destroyers and frigates and support from the Royal Fleet Auxiliary. The following month Fieldhouse flew to Ascension Island to confer with Woodward, then returned to direct the war from C-in-C Fleet's HQ in the concrete bunker at Northwood, Middlesex.

Those who served with Fieldhouse at the time were greatly impressed by his imperturbability and good humour, even at times of the greatest stress. He had to fight a war under a most unusual degree of political pressure and exposure. He had to minimise casualties and avoid losing public support for the venture. He had also to bear in mind the Navy's traditionally abysmal handling of press relations, which could effortlessly make a victory look like a defeat.

At Woodward's request Fieldhouse changed the Rules of Engagement to allow the submarine *Conqueror* to sink the Argentinian cruiser *General Belgrano*, which was menacing the southern flank of Woodward's force. But he was merciful in victory, specifically ordering *Conqueror* not to attack ships picking up *Belgrano's* survivors, although *Conqueror* had herself been depth-charged by those same ships.

Lacking the strength for an opposed landing, Fieldhouse accepted Woodward's decision to take a calculated risk in landing the troops at San Carlos. He knew he was thereby flouting one of the bitterest lessons of the Second World War, that one must have at least local air superiority before attempting an amphibious operation. It was a gamble that succeeded triumphantly but could have resulted in terrible losses.

Fieldhouse's leadership was at its best in moments of high drama: the Exocet attack on *Sheffield*, the shock waves from which long reverberated around the Navy; and the losses of destroyers and frigates to bombing, which showed that the Navy's ships were still not capable of defending themselves against deter-mined air attack despite all the money spent.

Past economies and wrong decisions meant that the task force lacked long-range airborne early warning and heavy enough anti-aircraft fire. But in many ways Fieldhouse presided over a curiously old-fashioned war, with many of the tactics the Navy has used for centuries: decoy and deception; blockade and bombardment; covert operations and convoy.

In the end, the Falklands were recovered by what Fieldhouse called a triumph of military capability backed by resolute political will. "All difficulties of short notice, extreme range and appalling weather were overcome by the quality of our people," he said. "They were magnificent.I could not have been better served."

Of Yorkshire stock, John David Elliott Fieldhouse was born on February 12 1928, the son of Sir Harold Fieldhouse, secretary of the National Assistance Board. He joined the Navy in 1941, going to the Royal Naval College at Dartmouth and later Eaton Hall, Cheshire. In 1948 he joined the submarine service. As first lieutenant of *Totem*, he was nick-named "Snorkers" owing to his fondness for sausages – like the Australian first lieutenant in Nicholas Monsarrat's novel *The Cruel Sea*. He passed the commanding officers' qualifying course (the "perisher") in 1955; his first submarine command was *Acheron*.

Fieldhouse subsequently was captain of the submarines *Tiptoe* and *Walrus*; and in 1964, the Royal Navy's first nuclear submarine, *Dreadnought*. He served almost exclusively in the submarine service until 1966, when he took the Joint Services Staff College course at Latimer and then joined the aircraft carrier *Hermes* in 1967 as second-in-command.

Hermes, then the first "all-missile" ship in the fleet, had a busy and successful commission east and west of Suez which included the preparations for the withdrawal from Aden. Her Sea Vixen and Buccaneer aircraft provided a show of strength in the air; and her Wessex helicopters carried out sorties against "dissidents" in Aden and communist agitators in Hong Kong. Fieldhouse took over command of the ship for some weeks when the captain fell ill.

After his own promotion to captain, Fieldhouse's career began to follow the perfect "critical path" to the highest ranks. From *Hermes* he went in 1968 to Faslane in Scotland as captain of the newly-formed 10th Submarine Squadron of Polaris submarines. He next commanded the frigate *Diomede* as captain of the 3rd Frigate squadron, and in 1972 he led Nato's Naval Standing Force Atlantic in the rank of commodore. The following year he went to the Ministry of Defence, first as deputy and then as director of Naval Warfare.

Promoted rear-admiral, he became Flag Officer 2nd Flotilla and then Flag Officer Submarines and Nato Commander Submarines Eastern Atlantic – in effect the first "post-war" officer to hold this post, and the first to have had a nuclear command. He showed his political skills early on by adroitly handling a move from the traditional home at Fort Blockhouse, Gosport, to Northwood. Promoted vice-admiral in 1979, he became Controller of the Navy, responsible for the Navy's ships, stores and equipment.

In the time-honoured way of sea-going officers, Fieldhouse always said he disliked Ministry of Defence jobs. "I joined the Navy to go to sea," he would say, "not to drive a desk at the MoD." In fact, he was an excellent Whitehall warrior, but the most he would admit was that, having had good times at sea, he now had to pay something back. In 1981 he was made C-in-C Fleet, Nato C-in-C Eastern

Atlantic Area and Allied C-in-C Channel. This was a time when an aggrieved and resentful Navy was trying to recover something from what was left after the swingeing cuts imposed by the then Secretary of State for Defence, John Nott.

It was a measure of how well Fieldhouse restored both the Navy's *matériel* and its morale that it was able to undertake Operation Corporate so successfully less than a year later. In December 1982 Fieldhouse became First Sea Lord and Chief of the Naval Staff – only the second submarine officer ever to do so. He fought the Navy's corner with great skill and guile, eventually restoring much of its position and proving more than a match for the slyest civil servant.

He defended the choice of Trident to replace Polaris as Britain's independent deterrent, arguing that it was still by far the most cost-effective option. He accused the European nations, including Britain, of what he called "sea blindness", and urged a much greater political appreciation of the virtues of worldwide sea-power, especially for Britain, which was still an island.

In spite of his face and figure (he enjoyed good food and wine) and the benign, avuncular, almost Dickensian aspect of himself which he liked to show to the world in conversation and jokes, naval officers sometimes found John Fieldhouse a difficult personality to read. There was a story of an officer who went to see him about some difficulty and came away convinced he had an ally – "but it's only when you look round and your head falls off that you realise your throat's just been cut", he recalled.

Fieldhouse was promoted Admiral of the Fleet in August 1985 (the first submarine officer to reach that rank) and, in November, he took over as Chief of the

Defence Staff and Chairman of the Chiefs of Staff Committee. It was thought that his appointment out of turn was due to Margaret Thatcher's gratitude to the architect of the Falklands victory.

On stepping down in December 1988, he was unanimously elected chairman of the Military Committee of Nato; and he was in Brussels, being welcomed into his new post,when he suffered a burst aorta in his heart. He was appointed KCB in 1980, GCB and GBE in 1982, and created a life peer as Baron Fieldhouse in 1990.

John Fieldhouse enjoyed sailing, was a member of the Royal Yacht Squadron,and listed his recreations as "home, family and friends". Despite his eminence he was the most unassuming of men, being on christian name terms with the staff of his local supermarket.

He married, in 1953, Margaret ("Midge") Cull; they had a son and two daughters.

CAPTAIN
NIGEL CLOGSTOUN-WILLMOTT

Captain Nigel Clogstoun-Willmott (who died on June 26 1992, aged 81) was the original inspiration behind the Combined Operations Pilotage Parties, known as "Coppists".

He realised early in the Second World War that when the invasion of Europe eventually took place, the Navy would have to land the Army not in ports, but across defended beaches which had not been done since Gallipoli in 1915. The Coppists carried out covert surveys by submarine and canoe to chart offshore shoals and sandbanks, measure the depths of water and ascertain the gradients, textures, obstacles and defences of enemy-held beaches. Then they acted as navigation markers for the assault forces.

Clogstoun-Willmott made the first such survey early in 1941, when he was appointed navigating officer of Force X for the capture of Rhodes. A methodical man, he left nothing to chance and prepared himself for his mission by swimming 25 lengths every day in the Cairo Club baths. He landed from the submarine *Triumph* by folbot and swam in to explore the beach, getting as far as the garden of a seafront hotel. As he suspected, the charts were wildly inaccurate, some features represented as more than a mile from their true position. The assault of Rhodes was cancelled because of the need to evacuate the Army from Greece in April 1941.

He was Principal Beach Master at Port Raphtis in the Aegean where, in four hectic nights, he organised the embarkation of some 10,000 troops, although he never knew on any night which ships would arrive or how many; he also had to deal with incidents of disorder when drunken soldiers rushed the boats and fired at everything in sight.

Clogstoun-Willmott himself sailed to Crete in a commandeered caique with a crew of soldiers and went on to Alexandria, again under sail, in a 170-ton schooner. He was awarded the DSO. After the war the Admiralty sent him a bill for the loss of the caique.

In 1942 he formed and trained the first beach survey party. Codenamed "Inhuman", their first operation was Torch, the November landings in North Africa. But when they arrived in Gibraltar the Inhumans were coolly received. Many senior officers were sceptical about the need for them. And they were not allowed to land on the beaches, but had to survey them through the periscopes of submarines.

Five Inhuman parties took part in Torch. Clogstoun-Willmott himself embarked in the submarine P45 for the landing east of Algiers. Many things went awry. Some troops were put ashore miles from their correct beach, and it was as well the landings were unopposed. The need for beach surveys was proved. He was awarded the DSC. The Inhumans expanded dramatically and were officially named Combined Operation Pilotage Parties, with Clogstoun-Willmott as their CO and training bases at Hayling Island Yacht Club and later at Largs in Scotland.

In 1944 Clogstoun-Willmott carried out two surveys on the Normandy coast of what would be Gold, Juno and Sword beaches on D-Day; the first was by landing craft, for which he was mentioned in despatches, the second by midget submarine, for which he was awarded a Bar to his DSC. To his great regret, illness prevented him from taking part in the landings.

Herbert Nigel Clogstoun-Willmott was born on July 12 1910 at Simla, where his father was on the Viceroy's staff. Educated at Marlborough, he joined HMS Erebus as a cadet in 1928. As a midshipman he served in the battleship *Malaya* in the Mediterranean and the cruiser *Emerald* in the East Indies. He went back to the Mediterranean as a sub-lieutenant in the battleship *Revenge* and as a lieutenant in *Basilisk* during the Abyssinian crisis. In 1936 Clogstoun-Willmott was appointed navigating officer of the destroyer *Woolston*, and the next year he went out to

New Zealand to recommission the sloop *Wellington* in which he served until the outbreak of war.

Even apart from the Coppists Clogstoun-Willmott seemed to attract attention wherever he went.He was navigating officer of the destroyer *Faulknor* in the Norwegian campaign in 1940, covering the landing at Berjvik near Narvik by the French Foreign Legion. When *Faulknor* was damaged, and went home, he volunteered for the Norwegian merchant ship *Ranen*, which was fitted out as a decoy "Q" ship. Manned by sailors whose ships were sunk and by Irish Guardsmen, *Ranen* harassed enemy lines of communication in the fjords and carried out surprise attacks. Clogstoun-Willmott himself led a boarding party to "cut out" two troop barges and a tug, capturing them at pistol-point; he was mentioned in despatches.

In August 1940 he joined the cruiser *Glasgow*, and when she was torpedoed in Suda Bay in December he stayed in the Mediterranean to serve with the RAF's Long Range Intelligence Unit. In March 1942 he rowed ashore from the destroyer *Kelvin* in a dinghy to lead a Royal Marines raid on a radar station on Crete.

After sick leave in 1944 Clogstoun-Willmott went to the Plans Division in the Admiralty where he set up the first naval servicing craft organisation. A year later he established a radar plotting school at Sheerness.

In 1948 he took command of the frigate *Peacock* and supported the Arab Legion when the port of Aqaba in Jordan was threatened by Israeli attack. In 1952 he served on a Foreign Office sub-committee on subversion. His last appointment, in 1961, was as head of the newly formed Fleet Work Study Group with the difficult task of persuading the fleet that it was not a complete waste of time.

In retirement he farmed, worked for the Foreign Office and lived for some years in a 10-ton ketch, cruising between Biscay and the Minches. Latterly he was on Cyprus.

Clogstoun-Willmott was an outspoken man, not afraid to browbeat senior officers with his opinions, which were often unorthodox and far-sighted. He was a good captain; even the soldiers on Crete and the guardsmen in Norway said they would gladly serve under him again. When in the frigate *Peacock* in 1948 he demonstrated why it was sometimes necessary to launch seaboats by forcing a sceptical journalist to jump, screaming, overboard with him into the Red Sea. Clogstoun-Willmott was, above all, lucky: he was once court-martialled and reprimanded over the loss of a confidential book called *Communism and How to Combat It*, yet was promoted captain shortly afterwards.

He married three times, and had a son and two daughters by his first marriage.

VICE-ADMIRAL
SIR PETER GRETTON

Vice-Admiral Sir Peter Gretton (who died on November 11 1992, aged 80) was one of the greatest convoy escort commanders of the Second World War, during which he won the DSO and two Bars. He and a handful of others practised and perfected the art of convoy escort at a time when such duty was considered unfashionable.

In the early years of the war – Gretton recalled – the Home and Mediterranean Fleets had all the best officers, while Western Approaches had to make do with many of the failures from Scapa Flow, retired officers who had been recalled to service, and numerous incompetents. This situation no longer pertained by April 1943, however, when Gretton led his B7 Escort group – six ships he had trained to become expert U-boat hunters – in an epic battle around the outward-bound convoy ONS5. The conflict raged over nine days and nights and thousands of square miles of ocean; by May 6, 40 U-boats had been in contact and 12 merchant ships sunk.

Shortage of fuel forced Gretton's own destroyer, *Duncan*, to leave prematurely, causing him to miss what he called his "golden moment". But his remaining escorts, with a support group reinforcement, and long-range aircraft, sank six of the attacking U-boats; two more U-boats were lost in collisions. A total of 43 U-boats were lost from all causes in the month of May 1943 – losses which forced Admiral Karl Doenitz to withdraw his U-boats from the North Atlantic.

Convoy ONS5 and a series of other critical convoy battles in the spring of 1943 thus brought about the first defeat of the Atlantic U-boats. Though scarcely realised at the time – and rarely appreciated since – this was an important strategic victory for the Allies. Gretton himself was awarded the first Bar to his DSO.

A major's son, Peter William Gretton was born on August 27 1912 and joined the Navy as a cadet at Dartmouth, when he was nicknamed "Tishy". He had five first-class passes in his sub-lieutenant's courses and could have chosen any specialisation he wanted. Instead he elected to remain a non-specialist "salt-horse". He had yearned to serve in destroyers ever since an evening in the Mediterranean during 1930, when he stood as a young midshipman on the quarterdeck of the battle cruiser *Renown* and watched six flotillas – with nine destroyers in each flotilla – doing high-speed exercises together in close order.

Gretton served in the Royal Yacht *Victoria & Albert* for the summer season of 1934; in the aircraft carrier *Courageous*; and then in the cruiser *Durban* during the Abyssinian crisis and the Spanish Civil War. During the Arab Rebellion in Palestine in 1936 he and four sailors from *Durban*, with a two-pounder pompom gun mounted on a lorry, assisted the Army to protect convoys of trucks on the main road. Later he took a mixed platoon of sailors and stokers ashore to help the police to control the souk in Haifa. He was awarded the DSC.

To Gretton's horror, as the "least gymnastic officer in the Navy", he was then appointed seamanship and sports officer at HMS Impregnable, the boys' training establishment at Devonport. Next he spent two years as a house officer at Dartmouth.

During Easter 1939 Gretton did a week's anti-submarine course at the Portland A/S HMS Osprey, because he wanted to ride in the Cattistock and Blackmore Vale point-to-points, and Osprey offered free accommodation. This course was to shape his life. When war broke out Gretton was appointed first lieutenant of the destroyer *Vega*, escorting East Coast convoys; then, during the Norwegian campaign of 1940, he was first lieutenant of *Cossack*. She took part in the second battle of Narvik on April 13, when the battleship *Warspite* and her destroyer screen entered the fjord and briskly sank eight German destroyers and U-64. Gretton was mentioned in despatches.

His first command was the destroyer *Sabre* – "a beautiful ship with lovely lines", he recalled – in which he escorted several Atlantic convoys. In 1942 Gretton took command of the destroyer *Wolverine* which,during the Pedestal convoy to Malta in August 1942, rammed and sank the Italian U-boat *Dagabur*. Gretton was awarded the DSO.

In December he was appointed to lead B7 and when the U-boats returned to the North Atlantic in the autumn of 1943, he took it to sea from Londonderry on October 12. During the next 25 days, it steamed 6,700 miles and crossed the Atlantic five times. It supported five convoys and sank three U-boats, while not losing a single merchant ship in its company. Gretton was awarded a second Bar to his DSO.

From 1944 to 1946 Gretton was in the Plans Division of the Admiralty. He served as Naval Assistant to the First Sea Lord and commanded the cruiser *Gambia* before going to Washington as chief of staff to Admiral, the Joint Services Mission. From 1956 to 1957 he was commodore in command of the naval task group for Operation Grapple, the British atomic bomb tests near Christmas Island.

Gretton was Flag Officer Sea Training, from 1960 to 1961, then became Deputy Chief of Naval Staff and Fifth Sea Lord from 1961 until his retirement in 1963 through ill-health. Next he became domestic bursar and then senior research fellow of University College, Oxford. He also lived for a time on

Vancouver Island.

In 1964 he published his wartime memoirs, *Convoy Escort Commander*, with a codicil on convoy management and the convoy system which was once more unfashionable with the Naval Staff. His later books were *Maritime Strategy* (1965), *Former Naval Person: Churchill and the Navy* (1968) and *Crisis Convoy: the Story of HX231* (1974).

Gretton was vice-president of the Royal Humane Society (the testimonial of which he had received in 1940). He was appointed OBE in 1941, CB in 1960 and KCB in 1963.

Peter Gretton was a devout Roman Catholic. When joining one homeward bound convoy in 1943, he signalled to the convoy commodore that he had a particularly pressing engagement in the presence of witnesses at St Mary's, Cadogan Street, two days after they were due to arrive in Britain. The commodore replied that he himself had a golf match that same day, and would do his best. Both men kept their appointments.

Gretton's was with Leading Wren Judy du Vivier. They had three sons and a daughter.

CAPTAIN
ERIC NAVE

Captain Eric Nave (who died in South Australia on June 23 1993, aged 94) played a major part in breaking Japanese naval codes before and during the Second World War.

With his colleagues at the Far Eastern Combined

Bureau, the intelligence organisation in Singapore, Nave provided accurate information about Japanese intentions before the attack on the US Pacific Fleet at Pearl Harbor in 1941, which brought the United States into the war.

More than half a century later the precise effect of this intelligence on the outcome is still difficult to assess, because of the British government's continued refusal to release a single Japanese decrypt or intercept into the public domain. With hindsight, though, it is clear that code-breaking provided more than enough advance warning, which could have prevented the Japanese achieving such tactical surprise.

Theodore Eric Nave was born at Adelaide, South Australia, in 1899 and educated at the local state school. At 16 he passed the state civil service examination and joined his father in the accounts department of South Australian Railways.

Then, in 1916, he answered a Royal Australian Navy advertisement and joined as a paymaster midshipman the next year. His first ship was the cruiser *Encounter*. In 1919 he was due to sit his examination for sub-lieutenant, which required him to learn a foreign language. Nave chose Japanese because it was worth an extra five shillings a day whereas French and German only earned sixpence. He proved to have a natural talent for the language, and gained a first-class pass.

The Australian Naval Board sent Nave to Japan to improve his fluency, and in 1921 he sailed for Yokosuka in SS *Eastern* with 26 gold sovereigns as advance pay and expenses in a money belt strapped round his waist. He spent nearly two years living in a Japanese village, and passed his examination with 90 per cent.

In 1924 a Japanese squadron visited Australia and New Zealand as a gesture of thanks for their generosity after the disastrous earthquake of the previous year. Nave, who was serving in the cruiser *Sydney*, acted as interpreter with such success that the Japanese admiral commanding the squadron called him a genius.

The following year the Admiralty asked the Royal Australian Navy if they would loan Nave to the RN as an interpreter, based in Hong Kong. He joined the cruiser *Hawkins* on the staff of the C-in-C Station at Shanghai. His orders were to gather information about Japanese radio traffic and call signs, and to intercept signals for Naval Intelligence. He was quick to spot lapses by the other side. In December 1926, when the Emperor Yoshihito died and was succeeded by his son Hirohito, Nave realised that everything the new Emperor said would be relayed round the world. It was simple to match the coded text sent to embassies and naval headquarters with statements in the Japanese press.

By 1927 Nave had unravelled the entire Japanese naval radio organisation so that the Government Code and Cypher School (GC&CS) in London had a complete list of all their call signs and radio frequencies. After this success the Admiralty asked if Nave could be retained, and he arrived in London in 1928 to form the Japanese naval section of GC&CS, where his main task was the breaking of the Japanese naval attaché code.

He noticed that the Japanese naval attachés around the world liked to demonstrate their keenness to Tokyo by sending home articles on naval affairs. Again it was easy to compare the coded messages with likely articles of the same length. At that time the GPO routinely tapped telephones of all foreign embassies on behalf of GC&CS. Nave discovered that the Japanese were paying a quarterly retainer to a Labour MP, Cecil Malone, to pass information about defence matters; a British Army officer had also been recruited. It was decided to let matters continue rather than compromise GC&CS's ability to read the attaché code.

In 1930 the RAN, who evidently had no idea what Nave was doing in London, requested his return to Australia; but the Admiralty also asked for his services, and Nave formally transferred to the RN in December to be employed permanently by GC&CS. In 1931 he returned to Hong Kong to build up GC&CS's signal intelligence in the colony; he also led the cryptographic assault on a new Japanese general naval code.

Back in London in 1934, he finally broke the naval attaché code and the first Japanese machine cryptograph, known as the "Type 91" or "Red Machine", which was used for naval and diplomatic messages. When the international situation worsened in 1937, Nave was sent out to join the Far East Combined Bureau in Hong Kong, which needed a Japanese-speaking code breaker who understood specialist naval terminology. He fitted the bill perfectly.

On June 1 1939 the Japanese introduced Kaigun Ango-sho D (Navy Code D) known to the Allies as "JN-25". This transmitted the operational (as opposed to the diplomatic) signals about the attack on Pearl Harbor, and was the Japanese Navy's main operational code, used with periodic variations, for the rest of the war. JN-25 was, in fact, an old type of book code used by the US Army and Navy in the Spanish-American war in 1898 and long since discarded as insecure. Nave found it tedious rather than difficult, and had broken into it by the autumn of 1939.

In February 1940 Nave went back to Australia on sick leave, medically unfit for further tropical service. By now the RAN knew of his specialist expertise, and he found himself in the bizarre position of being loaned back to the RAN. He started a small cryptographic organisation which eventually grew into the Central Bureau, Australia's equivalent of the GC&CS.

Although still an RN officer, Nave headed the Australian delegation to the secret talks in London in 1946 which led to the Anglo-American Treaty whereby post-war intelligence and code-breaking information was shared around the world. He retired from the Navy in 1947 and joined the Australian equivalent to MI5, the Australian Security Intelligence Organisation, for which he worked a further 12 years.

In 1991 he was co-author with the imaginative James Rusbridger of *Betrayal at Pearl Harbor: How Churchill Lured Roosevelt into War*. The book did not justify its sub-title, and it contained many errors; though it gave fascinating insights into a code-breaker's life and work. It also revived Pearl Harbor studies among scholars, and showed that there was no consensus about what had happened.

Nave's long years in Intelligence made him almost compulsively secretive and he was a wary and somewhat disconcerting interviewee; a clean cut figure with a sharp mind, he would often break off in the middle of an answer to probe the questioner's motives. But he made a forthright contribution to a *Time Watch* programme on the intelligence aspects of Pearl Harbor, which was shown by BBC 2 in 1991.

Nave, who was appointed OBE in 1946, was twice married and had three children.

CAPTAIN
HENRY DENHAM

Captain Henry Denham (who died on July 15 1993, aged 95) was the naval attaché in Stockholm responsible for warning the Admiralty on May 20 1941 that "two large warships", escorted by destroyers and aircraft, had been sighted at sea in the Kattegat, off Gothenburg, that afternoon. They proved to be the German battleship *Bismarck* and the heavy cruiser *Prinz Eugen* about to sail on their sortie into the Atlantic.

Denham, who had a natural gift for making friends and keeping contacts, heard the news from the Norwegian military attaché, but doubted its authenticity. It seemed unlikely the sighting could have been reported so quickly, and he gave it only a modest reliability grading.

But the German ships had indeed been sighted and reported by a Swedish cruiser, and Denham's signal set in train the dramatic series of events which led to the chase and destruction of *Bismarck* on May 27. Next day Denham was gratified to receive an Admiralty acknowledgement of the crucial part the signal had played.

A year later, Denham's enhanced reputation had an unfortunate effect when he sent the Admiralty an accurate forecast of German naval plans in the north, which contributed to the tragic mistake made by Admiral Pound, the First Sea Lord, over the Arctic convoy PQ17.

On July 4, Pound learned through Ultra Special Intelligence that the German battleship *Tirpitz* was at sea. Such was Denham's reputation after *Bismarck* that when events seemed to be following his forecast – a convoy sighted at sea from the air, and German surface ships assembling in northern Norway – Pound decided that a surface ship attack was imminent. Although he had further intelligence that the German ships had not sailed, he ordered PQ17 to scatter. Deprived of their escort, many of the merchant ships were sunk by U-boats or the Luftwaffe.

Henry Mangles Denham was born on September 9 1897 and joined the Navy in 1910,going to Osborne and Dartmouth. He went to sea at the outbreak of war in 1914, joining the pre-Dreadnought battleship *Agamemnon* and served in her in the Dardanelles campaign, commanding a steam picket boat during the landings at Suvla Bay in August 1915.

As the campaign became bogged down he recorded how the loss of the ship's mascot, a jackdaw, contributed to the gloom. But Denham liked well enough General Birdwood, commander of the Anzac forces who chatted to him at the wheel even though he kept losing his sunglasses. After some dreary months at Salonika Denham was appointed to the coal-burning destroyer *Racoon* when it returned to the now deserted Straits. He was pleased with the accuracy of his gunnery in bringing down an aircraft until an infuriated Admiral Usborne, senior officer of the Dardanelles area, who had been on a reconnaissance flight, was fished out of the sea.

After service in the destroyer *Sylph*, Denham was one of the young officers sent by the Admiralty to Cambridge. He went up to Magdalene College in 1919 for what he recalled as one of the happiest years of his life. He did more rowing than reading, and was in one of the few "naval eights" to take part at Henley.

In 1920 Denham served in the battlecruiser *Renown* during Edward Prince of Wales's cruise to Australia and New Zealand. He then spent two years in the Rhine flotilla, commanding a small armed motor launch as part of the Army of Occupation. Next he served in the battleship *Centurion* in the Mediterranean before going to Austria to learn German. He was a divisional officer in the boys' training ship *Impregnable* at Devonport from 1924 to 1926, and was then invited by Admiral Sir Osmond Brock, C-in-C Portsmouth, to be his flag lieutenant.

In 1927 Denham went to the Mediterranean for what was to be more than five years, serving in the fleet flagships *Queen Elizabeth* and *Warspite* as boats officer and as "snotties' nurse", in charge of the midshipmen. During the Spanish Civil War and the Munich crisis he was executive officer of the new light cruiser *Penelope*.

Denham first joined Naval Intelligence in 1939, when he created an "information section", recruiting civilians from many walks of life, including the Librarian of the House of Commons and an assistant editor of the *Times*, to gather intelligence about potential enemy coastlines through such means as discreet surveys by yachtsmen and disguised fishing trawlers.

He was then appointed naval attaché in Copenhagen. When on April 7 1940 he heard of increased German minesweeping activity in the Great Belt, he went down to the coast to look; and was sitting on the beach with a pair of binoculars when the German cruiser *Blucher* and other ships passed by. Denham hurried to signal the Admiralty that it was probable the Germans were about to move against Norway. But his warning, like other intelligence pointing the same way, was ignored and the German landings, 48 hours later, caught the Home Fleet off balance.

When the Germans entered Copenhagen,Denham and the rest of the Legation staff went by special train to Ostend and thence to London, where he was appointed naval attaché in Stockholm.After a hectic, and often hilarious journey across northern Norway and Finland by ferry, seaplane, coaster, car, rowing boat, bus and train – sometimes only hours ahead of the Germans – Denham arrived in the Swedish capital early in June 1940 to find himself plunged into the midst of diplomatic furore.

The Swedish Navy had bought from Italy four destroyers which had reached the Faroes on their properly negotiated safe passage to Sweden when they were illegally seized and, worse still, looted by the British.Denham's delicate handling of the head of the Swedish Navy defused an incident which could have led to war between the two countries.The ships were allowed to proceed, although Britain had to pay one million kroner in damages.

Later in 1940 senior officers of the Italian Navy approached Denham, through a Swedish intermediary, with an amazing proposal to surrender the Italian fleet to the British. The offer was serious, and a Royal Marine colonel came out from Britain with "a bag of gold" to be given to the families of Italian sailors who "deserted" with their ships. Unknown to Denham, however, the British Minister started inquiries about the intermediary: the plot was leaked, and even the bag of gold was lost.

In January 1941 Denham played a part with the commercial attaché George Binney in organising a blockade-running operation by five merchantmen carrying special Swedish steel and ball and roller bearings vital for the British war effort. Another operation in March 1942 was less successful – only two out of 10 ships getting through – but more runs were made by motor-gunboats in 1943.

The Swedish government was always suspicious of Denham, and kept a close watch on him. At dinner in his flat one evening a noise was heard overhead. A man was discovered in the loft eavesdropping with a microphone. But the Swedes were much impressed when, in a dark period for the Allies, they heard that Denham had sent a telegram to England ordering a yacht to be built for him to sail after the war.

In 1945 he was appointed CMG, a rare award for a naval officer in the Second World War. He also received decorations from the Dutch, the Danes and the Norwegians. Even the Swedes – though they had tapped his telephone, bugged his flat and tried constantly to have him expelled as *persona non grata* – offered him an Order, which the British government refused him permission to accept.

After retiring in 1947 Denham was able to indulge his love of sailing every year from March to September, and he embarked on another career as a nautical travel writer. He published a series of "Sea Guides" on the Aegean; Eastern Mediterranean; the Adriatic; the Tyrrhenian Sea; the Ionian Islands to Rhodes; Southern Turkey, the Levant and Cyprus; and the Ionian islands to the Anatolian coast. These were a most readable blend of practical seamanship, navigational tips, history and mythology.

In 1981 he published the diary he had kept (contrary to regulations) as midshipman in the Dardanelles, containing caustic remarks about his senior officers, and in 1984 his memoirs, *Inside the Nazi Ring: a Naval Attaché in Sweden, 1940-1945*, came out.

Henry Denham married, in 1924, Madge Currie, who died in 1979; they had a son and two daughters.

REAR-ADMIRAL
GEORGE ROSS

Rear-Admiral George Ross (who died on July 30 1993, aged 92) made the first moves to obtain the Swiss-made 20mm Oerlikon anti-aircraft gun for the Royal Navy before the Second World War.

In 1935, when he was assistant naval attaché in Tokyo, Ross went to a Halloween party given by Prince Albert von Urach, the representative in Japan of *Volkischer Beobachter*, the Nazi newspaper. Among the guests were Richard Sorge, the spy, and a glamorous blonde whom Ross took on to the dance floor. She was Lola Gazda, and told him that her husband Antoine, a salesman for the Oerlikon Machine Tool Company, was in Tokyo to sell the manufacturing rights of the gun to the Japanese Navy.

Ross had never heard of the gun, but when Antoine Gazda told him that it was a completely new design with a high muzzle velocity and a rate of fire of 480 armour-piercing shells per minute, Ross asked why Gazda had not approached the British. Gazda said that when he had concluded the Japanese deal he intended to offer the British an improved version of the gun.

The two men remained friends, and when Ross was on leave in Austria in 1936 Gazda arranged a convincing demonstration of the gun at the Oerlikon factory in Zurich. In 1937 Ross took him to London to try to sell the Oerlikon to the Royal Navy, only to meet the entrenched opposition of Admiralty departments. Whitehall was prejudiced against a foreign invention and concerned to sustain the vested interests of Vickers, which manufactured the nearest British equivalent, the vastly inferior 0.5 machine gun.

Whereas the Oerlikon could be swing-laid by one man, firing from the shoulder as though swinging a shotgun after a pheasant, the Vickers needed a crew to lay and train it through clumsy gearing. Moreover, it vibrated so badly when firing that it could hardly be aimed. Gazda had a large number of meetings with Admiralty officials without progress.

Ross enlisted the help of his friend and Dartmouth term-mate Lord Louis Mountbatten. The combination of Mountbatten's lobbying and vigorous staff work by enlightened gunnery officers, such as Captain Stephen Roskill, finally led to orders being placed for the Oerlikon in 1939.

The son of Sir Archibald Ross, the Tyneside shipbuilder, George Campbell Ross was born on August 9 1900, and went to Osborne and Dartmouth. His first ship was the battleship *Warspite*, which he joined in 1916 just after the Battle of Jutland. After the war, he volunteered to become an engineering specialist and took a course at the Royal Naval Colleges at Greenwich and Keyham, Devonport.

He then went as a watch-keeper to the cruiser *Hawkins*, flagship of the China station. When *Hawkins* visited Yokohama after the earthquake of September 1923, Ross went ashore to salvage the contents of safes and strong-rooms belonging to British companies. He handled vast sums of money in yen, roubles, dollars and sterling, most of it in charred notes; later he was accused by a bank in Yokohama of stealing millions of yen, because he had been the last to handle them; they had crumbed in his hands.

In 1924 Ross went back to Keyham on the staff, and was serving there the next year when the Admiralty Board reneged on the promises given in the Fisher-Selborne Scheme of 1903. Under this all officers were to be "of one company", with equal training status and chances of promotion. At a stroke the Admiralty relegated engineer officers to non-military status, lowered their promotion ceiling and, as a final insult, ordered them to wear a purple-sleeve stripe of a brighter hue than in the past. Ross considered that the terms of the order announcing this "great betrayal"(as it was called) were so offensive that he considered resigning and delayed shipping his purple stripe for three years.

He served in the cruiser *Effingham*, flagship of the East Indies station, and then went to the dockyard in Chatham for two years. He was serving in the battleship *Rodney* during the mutiny in the Atlantic Fleet at Invergordon in September 1931. Ross recalled this episode as his worst period in the Navy in peacetime. He held the Admiralty entirely to blame for the unrest and wrote a critical report which had to be toned down before it left the ship.

When he arrived at Tokyo in 1933 the Japanese were growing openly more anti-western every year. But "Ross-San",as the Japanese called him,learned to speak Japanese and pulled off several intelligence coups. He reported on the new 24-inch oxygen-powered "Long Lance" torpedo, which was to prove such a devastating weapon in the war; but his report was dismissed in the Admiralty as unlikely.

When giving parties for Japanese naval officers he arranged with the local geisha house to send his guests' favourite geishas. Ross, too, had a favourite, Isochiyo-San, "an exquisite creature with eyes set in an oval face, altogether adorable". When she was performing a *Ginza no Boshi* ("My Ginza Hat") dance routine with a bowler hat in her hands after dinner, Ross rashly said he had seen it so often that he could do it. Two girls duly rushed him behind the stage curtain, and made him put on a kimono, powder his face white and put lipstick on one lip. He then came onto the stage to caricature the dance before deliberately falling down to rapturous applause. The incident became a legend in the

Japanese Navy; when he left Japan, Prince Fushimi Hirogaru, Chief of the Naval Staff, said to him: "I understand you are a great exponent of Japanese dancing."

Ross was the obvious choice to serve as liaison officer on the Japanese cruiser *Asigara* when she took part in the 1937 Coronation review at Spithead. He served in the cruiser *Manchester* on the East Indies station from 1937 to 1939 and then went to the Engineer-in-Chief's department in the Admiralty until 1941, when he was appointed Engineer Officer of the battleship *Nelson*. Ross took part in the Malta convoys and in the landings in North Africa and Sicily before becoming Staff Engineer Officer for Force H destroyers in Malta, where he was the first officer to go on board the flagship of the Italian fleet after its surrender in September 1943.

He went back to the Admiralty in the Aircraft Maintenance and Repair Department until 1947, and was ADC to the King the following year. His last appointment before retiring in 1953 was as Director of Aircraft Maintenance and Repair. He was appointed CBE in 1945 and CB in 1952.

Ross joined Armstrong Siddeley Motors and later transferred to Hawker Siddeley Aviation. With his languages – he also spoke French and German – he travelled widely and had four years with Blackburn Aircraft, when he tried to sell the Buccaneer to the Japanese. Then, in 1965, he joined the stockbrokers Grieveson Grant as a consultant. He finally retired on his 79th birthday, although he had recently taken a refresher course in Japanese and visited Tokyo on behalf of the firm.

George Ross was an entertaining raconteur, a keen

photographer (some of the 16mm colour film he shot during the war is now in the Imperial War Museum), and a fine skier who revitalised the Combined Service Winter Sports Association.

He married first, in 1929, Alice Behrens. He married secondly, in 1950, Lucia Boer; they had two daughters. He married thirdly, in 1975, Manolita Harris, who died in 1988.

———————

REAR-ADMIRAL
"BEN" BOLT

Rear-Admiral "Ben" Bolt (who died on March 25 1994, aged 86) played a crucial part as Fleet Observer Officer in the action between the Mediterranean Fleet and the Italians off Cape Matapan on March 28 1941.

Bolt, piloted by Leading Seaman "Ben" Rice, was catapulted in his Fairey Swordfish floatplane from the battleship *Warspite* to look out for the Italian fleet's guns. But the Italian ships, which were expected to appear over the horizon at any moment, were much further away than had been supposed, and Bolt remained in the air waiting for further orders. During the afternoon the battleship *Vittorio Veneto* was hit aft and had her speed reduced by one aerial torpedo.

The C-in-C, Admiral Cunningham, pressed on eagerly, hoping to finish his opponents off. Meanwhile, Bolt, who had been regularly reporting his dwindling fuel, seemed to have been forgotten. When Cunningham eventually learned that Bolt, whom he much liked and respected, had only 15 minutes' fuel left, he was furious, and wanted him to land beside a destroyer, which could pick him up and sink the aircraft. But the admiral's staff prevailed on him to change his mind, arguing that Bolt was a most experienced observer whose services might still be invaluable.

Rice then landed the Swordfish alongside *Warspite*, which was still making 16 knots, and taxied under her crane to be hoisted onboard. Bolt readily agreed to take off again to clarify conflicting reports of the whereabouts of the Italian fleet. Just after 6pm, he sighted *Vittorio Veneto* and broadcast a series of "copybook" enemy sighting reports. One of ABC's staff later said that "it was a classic example of air reporting, and the many hours spent on observers' training in peace would have been worth it for this hour alone."

Even the Italian admiral flying his flag in *Vittorio Veneto*, who soon received decrypts of Bolt's signals, admired their accuracy. "This aircraft's appreciation," he said, "was singularly exact." Guided by Bolt's reports, aircraft from the carrier *Formidable* attacked after dark, torpedoing one Italian heavy cruiser and stopping her dead in the water. Two heavy cruisers sent back to assist her were surprised, with their guns still trained fore and aft, and in the short but brutal night action were overwhelmed by the guns of *Warspite*, *Valiant* and *Barham*. All three cruisers were sunk, with heavy loss of life. When it grew dark the Swordfish had diverted to Crete where it taxied into harbour like a surface ship, using its own flares to create a landing patch.

Rice was mentioned in despatches and Bolt was

awarded a Bar to the DSC he had been awarded in 1940 for his work in DWI (Directional Wireless Installations). Wellington bombers specially equipped to sweep magnetic mines with external circles of coil 50 feet in diameter were energised from a generator inside the aircraft, whose magnetic fields detonated the mines.

It was very dangerous work because the Wellingtons had to fly as low as 50 feet over the sea; the detonation of one mine on the Goodwin Sands knocked Bolt off his seat, and temporarily stunned him. But the Wellington successfully swept mines in the Thames estuary, along the East Anglian coast, and later in the Suez Canal.

Arthur Seymour Bolt was born on November 26 1907 and attended the Nautical College, Pangbourne, before joining the Navy as a cadet at Dartmouth in 1921. His first ship as a midshipman was the battleship *Emperor of India*. He qualified as an observer in 1931 and served two commissions in the carrier *Glorious* in the Mediterranean and one in *Courageous* in the Home Fleet.

Although in the 1930s the Fleet Air Arm was still controlled by the RAF, and the Navy lacked modern aircraft, many wartime tactics – dive-bombing, torpedo attacks, night attacks using flares – were intensively exercised. In *Glorious* Bolt contributed to the first discussions of a plan to make a night torpedo attack on the Italian battle fleet in harbour. The plan was later brilliantly carried out by Swordfish crews, many of whom had served on *Glorious*, at Taranto in November 1940. Bolt was CO of 812 Naval Air Squadron in her from June 1939 until September, when he was invalided home for a tonsillectomy.

In 1942 he went to the Admiralty, where he served in the Naval Air Division, the Air Fields and Carrier Requirement department, and then as director of the Naval Air Radio department. He was to have commanded the escort carrier *Smiter* in the East Indies Fleet in 1945, but the war against Japan ended before he could take up the appointment.

Bolt was executive officer of the cruiser *Belfast* in the Far East from 1946 until promoted captain in 1947, when he took command of HMS Vulture, the Naval Air Station at St Merryn, Cornwall. His first sea command was the light fleet carrier *Theseus* in the Far East, which, in October 1950, took over from *Triumph* air operations along the west coast of Korea in support of the United Nations forces ashore. When she left the station in April 1951 *Theseus* had set a new light sea carrier record for the number of sorties flown in a day, and despite the bitter weather had managed to keep up a more intense rate of flying than larger carriers had achieved during the Second World War.

Bolt was awarded the DSO. Six of his officers were promoted off the ship, and *Theseus*'s air group won the Boyd trophy, awarded annually to the best feat of airmanship.

In 1951 he went back to the Admiralty as Director of the Naval Air Warfare Division and was involved in early plans to fit carriers with the angled flight deck and to equip the Fleet Air Arm with modern jet aircraft. From 1954 until 1956 he was chief of staff to Flag Officer, Air (Home).

His last appointment was as deputy controller of aircraft at the Ministry of Supply in 1957. He was appointed CB the next year. Bolt retired in 1960 after a career which had begun with 100mph Blackburn Ripon biplanes and ended with Mach 0.85 Blackburn Buccaneer turbojets.

Bolt became a tireless campaigner for the Fleet Air Arm, writing many magazine articles and letters to newspapers. The cancellation of the giant carrier CVA01 by the Labour government in 1966 was almost a personal affront.

He was most generous with his time, and always ready to give naval historians the benefit of his great knowledge of Fleet Air Arm history. When there was some correspondence in *The Sunday Telegraph* in 1980, disparaging the quality of the aircrews who had served in *Glorious* before the war, Bolt found out through the Second Sea Lord's office that those same officers had between them won five DSOs and 28 DSCs.

Ben Bolt was a keen and expert yachtsman and kept his own boat on the River Dart.

He married, in 1933, June Ellis; they had four daughters.

COMMANDER
CHARLES CUTHBERTSON

Commander Charles Cuthbertson (who died on April 1 1994, aged 87) was the corvette captain in the Battle of the Atlantic on whom Nicholas Monsarrat based Lieutenant-Commander Ericson, one of the main characters in his novel *The Cruel Sea*.

The two men first met after the tragic passage of convoy OG71, which had been outward bound to

Gibraltar in August 1941, when Cuthbertson commanded the Flower class corvette *Zinnia* and Monsarrat was first lieutenant of *Campanula*. The convoy, which Monsarrat afterwards called "my personal nightmare", was attacked by U-boats and lost several ships, including the *Aguila* which was torpedoed and sunk with great loss of life 470 miles west of Land's End on August 19.

In the early hours of August 23 *Zinnia* was hit amidships by a torpedo from U-564. She broke in two, and sank in seconds. Cuthbertson recalled that he remained in the water, "rapidly approaching complete exhaustion and ready to meet my Maker", until he was picked up, covered in oil, by a whaler from *Campion*.

He still had his binoculars on lanyards round his neck, and heard a sailor say:"Cor blimey, he must be an orficer, he's got a pair of glasses round his bleeding neck!"When he later applied to keep the binoculars as a souvenir, the Admiralty accused him of trying to steal them.

On *Campion*'s deck Cuthbertson could not stop himself shaking, but he took care to explain that this was not because he was frightened,"but because I was so bloody cold!" Later he was found collapsed on the deck of *Campion*'s bathroom "with blood and oil fuel coming out of me at both ends." He was one of only 15 survivors from a ship's company of 100.

At Gibraltar, Cuthbertson called on *Campanula*, where Monsarrat gave him gin and tonic ("the only stuff that would stay down") and questioned him closely on what it felt like to be torpedoed. In his memoirs Montsarrat wrote that Ericson's character "was based, so far as looks, achievement and reputation were concerned, on Lieutenant-Commander Cuthbertson."

Charles George Cuthbertson was born on September 3 1906 and went to *Worcester*, the training ship at Greenhythe on the Thames. He joined the Royal Naval Reserve as a probationary midshipman in January 1923, and the Union Castle Line as a cadet in September.

He served in Union Castle ships around the world, while continuing his annual naval training. In 1939 he was second officer of the liner *Caernarvon Castle*, with the rank of lieutenant-commander. For the first year of the war he commanded the flotilla of 70 anti-submarine trawlers on the east coast of Scotland. During the Norwegian campaign he volunteered for special service in the "Gubbins Flotilla". This was a mixed force of trawlers and "puffer" fishing boats which operated in the fjords, supplying General Gubbins's independent companies (forerunners of the commandos) with stores, personnel and ammunition. They came under frequent air attack, and Cuthbertson twice had his ship sunk under him.

In October 1940 he took command of the corvette *Hibiscus*, escorting Atlantic convoys, and was awarded the DSC for successfully attacking U-boats. Undeterred by his experience in *Zinnia*, he took command of *Snowflake*, another corvette, in October 1941, escorting Atlantic and Arctic convoys. He was mentioned in despatches for *Snowflake*'s part in defending convoy PQ11 in May 1942.

Cuthbertson then commanded the destroyer *Scimitar* until July 1943, operating in the North Atlantic; promoted commander, he took command of the new frigate *Helford* as senior officer of an escort flotilla. In 1945 *Helford* went out to the Far East to join the British Pacific Fleet, and Cuthbertson was again mentioned in despatches after escorting two floating docks under tow from Cochin in India to the fleet base at Manus in the Admiralty Islands. He was proud that when *Helford* came home after a two-and-a-half-year commission she still had the same ship's company with which she had sailed.

In 1946 Cuthbertson was commander of the Royal Naval Victory Parade Camp in Kensington Gardens, and marched at the head of the Navy's column. He returned to Union Castle, and was elected a Younger Brother of Trinity House and a member of the Honourable Company of Master Mariners. His last sea appointment was as master of *Sandown Castle* in 1948. He then came ashore and set up as a nautical consultant and assessor. In 1953 he was appointed a nautical surveyor in the Marine Survey Service of the Ministry of Transport and Civil Aviation.

Charles Cuthbertson was twice married, and had a son by his first marriage.

CAPTAIN
GORDON WALKER

Captain Gordon Walker (who died on April 20 1994, aged 100) was master of one of the "little ships" involved in the Dunkirk evacuation.

He commanded the cross-Channel ferry steamer *Maid of Orleans* which before the war had carried Southern Railway passengers between Folkestone and Boulogne; on May 26 1940 he made the first of five crossings to take men of the British Expeditionary Force off the Mole in Dunkirk harbour. Four days later the harbour was so obstructed by sunken ships as to be a navigator's nightmare. As he brought *Maid of Orleans* alongside, Walker said: "It's like a bloody fly crawling on a hobnail boot."

But *Maid of Orleans* took off 1,250 men in five hours, and was back again on June 1, when she lay alongside the Mole for six hours while two destroyers used her as a floating landing-stage to embark 1,000 men apiece. Looking at the soldiers packed below, and the crush on *Maid of Orleans'* upper deck, one Army officer said: "If we get hit we don't stand a chance with this lot." Walker replied: "If we get hit, we shan't stand a chance anyway. Let's take all we can get." He eventually sailed with 1,400 British and 400 French troops on board.

Maid of Orleans was leaving for Dunkirk again that evening when she collided heavily with the destroyer *Worcester*, and could take no further part in the evacuation. But by then she had evacuated more than 5,400 men. Walker and his chief engineer were both awarded the DSC.

The son and grandson of Trinity House pilots, Gordon Dyer Walker was born on August 3 1893. He went to sea in 1909, apprenticed to the Prince Line running between New York and South America, and gained his master's certificate in 1915. He spent the First World War trooping between Southampton and France before joining the Southern Railway. In 1925 he had his first command, the cargo ship *Deal*.

In March 1940 he volunteered to take *Biarritz*, sister ship of *Maid of Orleans*, to evacuate the British embassy and Dutch personnel from Rotterdam; and, before the Army started to fall back on Dunkirk, he took *Shepperton Ferry* into the port to pick up hundreds of refugees, many of them women and children.

After *Maid of Orleans*, Walker took command of the passenger ship *Canterbury*, which for a time was used as a target ship for Fleet Air Arm aircraft based at Stranraer. In 1943 she was converted into a landing ship for the Normandy invasion, and on D-Day Walker transported commandos to Juno Beach.

With the return of peace, Walker reopened the Golden Arrow service between Dover and Calais with *Canterbury*. In 1952 he was the first master of the new British Railways car ferry, *Lord Warden*, and commanded her for the rest of his sea-going career. Three years later he was appointed Commodore of the British Railways Cross Channel Fleet until his retirement in 1958.

Walker was twice married, and had a son and a daughter by his first marriage.

COMMANDER
JOHN HALL

Commander John Hall (who died on May 24 1994, aged 84) won a DSO for sinking two U-boats on successive days; he then staggered the Naval Staff by quoting from the Greek comic playwright Aristophanes in his report.

Hall commanded the Flower class corvette *Lotus*, which took part in the Torch landings in North Africa. On the night of November 12 1942, *Lotus* and her sister ship *Starwort* were escorting a convoy from

Gibraltar to Algiers when they detected and sank U-660.

After one attack Hall said: "It was obvious I'd hit him because there was this enormous bubble of air which came up from below and when you get that at night the light gets into the bubble and you can see through it." Characteristically, Hall felt sympathy for the U-boat survivors, including the captain, who were picked up. "I can't think of anything more horrible than to be depth-charged down in a tin box."

The next day, off Algiers, *Lotus* and another sister ship, *Poppy*, detected and attacked U-605. After several attempts with depth charges, *Lotus* used her "hedgehog" ahead-throwing weapons. Hall reported that though there was no visible evidence on the surface, his crew heard the sound of a submarine's hull breaking up under water, for which one of *Lotus*'s officers, who had been a classics master in civilian life, suggested the superbly onomatopoeic word *pompholugopaphlasmasin*, meaning "bubbling and boiling noises". The reference is to *The Frogs*, lines 246-9, which translate as:

Or when fleeing the storm, we went
Down to the depths and our choral song
Wildly raised to a loud and long
Bubble-bursting accompaniment.

The Naval Staff were so impressed by Hall's report that they circulated it as an example of how an anti-submarine attack should be carried out – but with suitable translations and explanations for less erudite officers.

The son of a marine superintendent, Harry John Hall was born on October 10 1909 and went to the training ship *Worcester* on the Thames, before joining the British India Steam Navigation Company as a cadet in 1925: he rose to second officer, with a master's certificate. In 1932 he joined the RNR, and six years later he went to work for the African Wharfage Company as superintendent at Lindi, Tanganyika. The territory had been a German protectorate, and Hall's first task when the Second World War broke out was to round up all his friends of German origin and intern them as enemies. Later he went to Zanzibar to command the Sultan's "yacht", the coaster *Al Hathera*, which had been converted to sweep mines in the Zanzibar Channel.

In August 1941 he was appointed in command of *Lotus*, building at Leith, and commissioned her as a Western Approaches convoy escort, based at Londonderry. In July the next year *Lotus* was part of the escort of the Arctic convoy PQ17. Whitehall ordered the convoy to scatter because of the threat of attack by the German battleship *Tirpitz*; having done so, it suffered grievous losses to U-boats and the Luftwaffe.

Acting without orders, and at a time when *Tirpitz* was expected to appear over the horizon at any moment, Hall turned back to pick up the master and crew of the American ship *Pankraft*, which had been bombed and abandoned on fire. He then tried to sink the ship with gunfire until her master told him she still had 5,000 tons of TNT on board.

Turning back to the north, Hall sighted "tall pillars of fire" reaching up to the sky; they were, in fact, smoke floats, lit by survivors of the convoy commodore's ship *River Afton. Lotus* picked up the commodore and more survivors. Hall was awarded the DSC.

In September 1943 he went to America to take command of the former US Navy Captain class frigate *Stayner*, which in June 1944 provided seaward defence for the Normandy landings. With the superb American surface radar, *Stayner* controlled a flotilla of MTBs in a series of night engagements against German E-boats along the coast of northern France. The night of June 7 *Stayner* and her MTBs were in action no fewer than seven times. On August 4, acting on Ultra Special Intelligence, *Stayner* and the destroyer *Wensleydale* intercepted and sank U-671, which had just left Boulogne, and once again picked up survivors. Hall was awarded a Bar to his DSC.

After the war he returned to civilian life and to Dar es Salaam, where some of the locals behaved as though he had been "on leave" for the previous six years. He again prepared the Sultan of Zanzibar's ceremonial barge, which had been presented by Queen Victoria, and trained a crew of oarsmen to take it to sea.

Hall was a gifted painter and produced accomplished oils and pastels, particularly of Zanzibar, until his eyesight failed. On his return to England in 1968 he became a practical and resourceful bursar of the Cathedral School at Salisbury.

He was often asked to contribute to wartime memoirs and programmes but preferred to stay a private man. He did give the occasional lecture on PQ17, but felt that the horrors of war outweighed any individual "successes" and said that the "enormity and miserable consequences of one's actions tend to generate humility and penitence rather than satisfaction."

His wife, Kitty, died a fortnight before him. They had one son.

ADMIRAL
SIR JOHN HAMILTON

Admiral Sir John Hamilton (who died on October 27 1994, aged 84) played a key role in the capture of the Suez Canal by British and French forces after its nationalisation by President Nasser of Egypt in July 1956.

Hamilton commanded the cruiser *Newfoundland* which fired the first shots in Operation Musketeer. Together with the destroyer *Diana* and other British warships, all darkened, *Newfoundland* entered the Gulf of Suez on the night of November 1. Their mission was to protect British ships in the Gulf and, if necessary, escort them out of trouble. Just after midnight Hamilton noticed something suspicious about the navigation lights of one ship among a number of merchantmen approaching from the north, and ordered it to stop.

It was the Egyptian frigate *Domiat*, escorting a convoy on its way to relieve Sharm al-Sheikh, which was under Israeli attack. Illuminated by searchlight, *Domiat* opened fire and hit *Newfoundland*, whose reply put *Domiat*'s forward gun out of action.

Domiat then attempted to ram *Newfoundland* until more shells knocked out her main engines and steering. The Egyptians kept on firing with 40mm guns until they were forced to abandon their sinking ship. *Diana* and *Newfoundland*, who had five men wounded and one killed, picked up 68 survivors, many of whom had been trained in Britain.Hamilton was mentioned in despatches, but thought the whole affair most unfortunate and unpleasant.

John Graham Hamilton was born on July 12 1910 and joined the Navy as a cadet at Dartmouth in 1924. He went to sea as a midshipman in the battleship *Ramillies*, and after service in the battlecruiser *Hood* and the destroyer *Ardent*, specialised in gunnery from 1936.

At the outbreak of the Second World War he was gunnery officer of the destroyer *Grenville*, in which he served until she was mined and sunk in the North Sea in January 1940. He then joined HMS Excellent, the gunnery school at Whale Island in Portsmouth, as training development officer. At that time merchant ships were being armed, and a large number of seamen had to be taught quickly how to fire guns aiming by eye, a technique known as "eye shooting". Excellent produced an *Eye Shooting Pocket Book*, illustrated by the *Punch* cartoonist Fougasse, and an instructional film for which Hamilton wrote and spoke the commentary, earning himself the sobriquet "the gunnery officer with the golden voice".

In 1942 Hamilton went to the Mediterranean as fleet anti-aircraft gunnery officer, and was then gunnery officer of the battleship *Warspite*, serving in Force H; he was mentioned in despatches when Force H was dissolved in November 1943.

Early the next year Hamilton went to the Admiralty to plan the ship bombardments in support of the Normandy landings. He ended the war with Force W in the East Indies Fleet. After the Japanese surrender Hamilton was senior naval officer at Sabang, Sumatra, going on to join the post-war resettlement staff at HMS Commonwealth at Kure, Japan.

His post-war career followed the "high-flier" pattern, alternating command at sea with service in the Admiralty. From 1946 to 1948 he commanded the sloop *Alacrity* in the Far East. He was Deputy Director Radio Equipment from 1949 until 1952, when he was appointed Captain (D) 5th Destroyer Squadron in *Solebay*, which he commanded at the Coronation Review at Spithead in 1953.

Hamilton was then Director of Ordnance from 1954 until 1956, when he took *Newfoundland* out to the Far East. Promoted rear-admiral, he was Naval Secretary to the First Lord of the Admiralty until 1960, when he was appointed Flag Officer Flotillas Home Fleet, flying his flag in the cruiser *Bermuda*.

After a spell as Flag Officer Naval Air Command, he was appointed C-in-C Mediterranean and Nato C-in-C Allied Forces Mediterranean. As C-in-C Mediterranean, a post created in 1792, Hamilton could number among his predecessors such men as Hood, Jervis, Nelson, Collingwood and Cunningham. But the station had lately declined in importance and had only a handful of ships; on June 5 1967 Hamilton was the last C-in-C to haul down his flag.

In retirement he became director general and then president of the Institute of Marketing. A devout Christian, he had an old-fashioned sense of honour and propriety. He was a strict disciplinarian, but recognised that the world and the Navy were changing, and adapted his style of leadership accordingly.

He was an energetic walker, and was fascinated by mountains. When in Japan he held the Navy record for the fastest ascent of Mount Fujiyama, and when his ship was in Scottish waters he zealously added to his total of "Munros" (peaks over 3,000 feet), of which he was reckoned to have made more than 200 ascents. He sent his sailors on shore expeditions, so that the starboard watch might be seen scaling one side of a mountain to place a Bofors gun on the summit, while the port watch (less the duty part) scaled the other side with the ammunition.

Hamilton enjoyed entertaining, and his after-dinner games were celebrated. On Malta senior Nato officers of various nationalities and their wives were often seen gathered around the table in Admiralty House to play Squails, a form of tiddlywinks mixed with shove-ha'penny.

Hamilton was an excellent photographer whose work was published in several magazines. He also loved reading and writing poetry. As president of the Newfoundland Association, he followed the careers of officers who had served under him and occasionally found them employment in civilian life.

Hamilton was appointed CBE in 1958, CB in 1960, KBE in 1963 and GBE in 1966. He married, in 1938, Dorothy Turner; there were no children.

CAPTAIN
BARRY ANDERSON

Captain Barry Anderson (who died on November 3 1994, aged 90) was Commodore of the Fishery Protection Squadron during the first "Cod War" in 1958.

The conflict began on September 1 that year, when Iceland extended her territorial waters from four to 12 miles. Two days later, some six miles off the coast, nine men from the Icelandic gunboat *Thor* boarded the Grimsby trawler *Northern Foam*, which at once radioed for help. Four Royal Navy warships were already off Iceland in case of trouble. The frigate *Eastbourne*, wearing Anderson's broad pennant, steamed through dense fog at 25 knots to arrive 10 minutes later.

Her sailors boarded the trawler and brought the Icelanders to *Eastbourne*. The captain of *Thor* refused to take back his men, so Anderson invited himself aboard to discuss the problem and avoid bloodshed. Captain Kristofferson agreed to him taking his men in *Eastbourne*; and, to save his face in Iceland, Anderson "captured"them while the trawler resumed fishing. The Icelandic government was very angry, but the sailors of the two crews became the very best of friends. Ten days later, the Icelanders were landed at night in one of *Eastbourne*'s whalers, which they were allowed to keep.

A qualified interpreter in Norwegian, Danish and Dutch, who also spoke a little Icelandic, Anderson handled matters with great diplomacy. But feelings ran high in Iceland, and the Icelandic gunboats became ever more hostile. Eventually the Icelanders made life so difficult that in 1961 the British reluctantly accepted the new limits,though two more "Cod Wars" followed over the next 18 years.

Anderson, who had had 42 different ships in his squadron at various times, received a message of congratulation from Harold Macmillan, the Prime Minister, and was appointed CBE in 1959.

Barry John Anderson was born on April 5 1904 and educated at George Watson's, Edinburgh, before going to sea at 15 in a Norwegian sailing ship in the North Sea and the Baltic. He then joined the Wilhemsen shipping company as an apprentice, sailing between Europe and the Far East, before gaining his master's ticket in Lamport & Holt ships sailing between Liverpool, Brazil and Argentina.

Anderson joined the RNR and in 1936 was offered a permanent commission in the Royal Navy. His first command, in 1939, was a wooden motor anti-submarine boat, with depth charges and a crew of six, sent to look for U-boats in the Irish Sea. "In fact," Anderson noted, "a U-boat would have been astonished to find such a small boat chasing him."

In May 1940 Anderson and his crew took part in the Dunkirk evacuation, during which they were strafed by enemy aircraft. His next ship was the cruiser *Mauritius*, serving in the Atlantic, the Indian Ocean and the Far East, where in 1941 Anderson was for a time a liaison officer with the US Pacific Fleet. He then returned to the Mediterranean, taking part in the landings on Sicily and at Salerno in 1943.

Anderson's next commands were the old destroyers *Vanessa* (acting as target for Fleet Air Arm aircraft in the Moray Firth) and *Vivacious* (which escorted convoys along the East Coast).Then,in May 1945, he took part in the liberation of Bergen, and was twice mentioned in despatches.

After the war he commanded the destroyers *Cockade* and *Jutland*, and was then executive officer of the cruiser *Newcastle* during the Korean War. On his return to England in 1954 he took up the post of Commander of the Royal Naval College, Greenwich, and, promoted captain, went to New Zealand as naval attaché.

In 1961 Anderson was Chief of Staff to the Flag Officer, Scotland,and Northern Ireland;the next year he was appointed Knight of the Order of St Olav following the King of Norway's visit to Scotland. After commanding HMS Lochinvar, the mine-sweeping base at Port Edgar, near Edinburgh, he formed Task Force 339,comprising 24 minesweepers, to carry out Operation Clear Road, a massive sweep through wartime minefields in the North Sea off Denmark and Holland, to enable the GPO to lay cables.

He was made a Younger Brother of Trinity House in 1958, and appointed ADC to the Queen in 1964, the year he retired. Anderson became Bursar of Barnard Castle School and then a JP in Torbay;he was Deputy Lieutenant of both Durham and Devon.

Barry Anderson married, in 1938, Marjory Gray, who died in 1971; they had two sons, one of whom followed his father into the Navy. He married, secondly, in 1972, Gwen Raine.

———

LIEUTENANT-COMMANDER JOHN MILLER, GC

Lieutenant-Commander John Miller (who died on December 15 1994, aged 91) won the George Cross for bravery and devotion to duty in mine disposal work during the London Blitz.

With his assistant, Able Seaman Jack Tuckwell, Miller disarmed 10 magnetic parachute mines during 1940 and 1941. Their GCs were awarded for the last of these, a mine which had fallen in the River Roding and was judged to be in a highly sensitive and dangerous condition.

It was a cold winter's afternoon and raining hard. Miller borrowed a canoe, which he and Tuckwell put on board a River Fire Service firefloat to take them to where the mine was thought to be, near a sewage outlet at Barking Creek. They dropped into their canoe and paddled towards the outlet until they sighted the top rim of the mine, nose down in the mud and sewage.

Wearing oilskins and gumboots, they waded out to it. Miller told Tuckwell to withdraw to safety, but Tuckwell pointed out that as Miller would be working under at least a foot of water he would need someone to hand him the tools. In any case, if anything were to go wrong Tuckwell preferred to share the fate of his boss.

Miller managed to remove one fuse but could not reach the second. Some crane drivers who had been evacuated from the scene had rashly come back to watch, and Miller asked them to help; they all volunteered. Miller and Tuckwell went back into the water and put ropes round the mine, which was lifted

by the crane out of the river and dragged carefully up
the bank and onto the wharf, where Miller removed
the second fuse.

John Bryan Peter Duppa Miller was born on May
22 1903 and educated at Rugby and Hertford
College, Oxford. He studied for the Anglican
priesthood but a fortnight before he was due to be
ordained surprised everyone by being received into
the Roman Catholic Church. Before the Second
World War he worked in local government education
in Hampshire and Northamptonshire.

In August 1940 Miller joined the RNVR. "I was a
yachtsman," he explained, "and thought my
experience might be of use." He was sent to HMS
King Alfred, the RNVR training establishment at
Hove, as an unusually elderly sub-lieutenant.

"I felt for humanitarian reasons that I didn't want
to shoot at the enemy," he said. "One day there was a
call for volunteers to dismantle mines, and I got my
chance of running risks without endangering others'
lives." So urgent was the need for mine disposal
officers that the officers on Miller's course received a
mere 48 hours of initial instruction at HMS Vernon,
the torpedo and mining school at Portsmouth, before
being summoned to the Admiralty for their first
assignments.

As they left each had to choose an assistant from a
row of sailors outside. "I had never seen such a
villainous-looking set of men in my existence," Miller
recalled. "As my eye passed along the line of faces
every jaw was moving slowly – every man was
chewing a quid of tobacco; all except one. As the
senior man I was given first choice and I chose the
only motionless jaw. It belonged to Able Seaman

Tuckwell, the finest fellow who ever put in 18 years service with the Royal Navy."

Years after the war Miller recalled that "we were always pretty terrified on the job; we were not some sort of supermen devoid of fear or human weakness. It was my normal practice standing by a mine to sign myself with the sign of the cross.If the mine was very bad I didn't do it, as fiddling of any kind seemed unnecessary."

His first mine had fallen on the railway viaduct outside London Bridge Station. It was lying on its nose against the wall of a signal box with the clockwork fuse on the underside and facing in towards the wall. Miller wriggled beneath it and lay on his back in a pool of water with his mouth and eyes six inches from the mine.

"The psychological reaction to lying beneath the mine at close quarters was distinctly unpleasant.It was obvious that if the clock started to run I could not hope to escape." He had hardly begun when he heard the "little fizzing sound" of the clock starting. He wriggled out and ran for his life. But nothing happened. On the second try he again heard the sound and again made a frantic flight.Again nothing happened.

Miller decided he would have to stay under the mine and carry on working. His luck held. Fuse and primer both fell out and rolled clear, and normal train service was resumed.

After disarming his 15th and last mine in Coventry, Miller was recommended for a second GC, but received a King's Commendation instead. Portraits of him and of Tuckwell by William Dring were exhibited in the National Gallery in 1941; the town of Ilford, where he had also disarmed a mine, commissioned a copy. Later the same year, Miller was appointed to the Torpedo and Mining Department in the Admiralty as secretary to a new committee supervising development of new anti-submarine weapons by naval officers, scientists and manufacturers. One of their early ventures became the "hedgehog" and "limbo" weapons.

After the war Miller was given the rank of brigadier – "It meant I didn't have to salute very often," he noted – and appointed deputy director of the Trade and Economic Division of the Control Commission in Germany, where he helped to liquidate German stocks of depth charges and other underwater weapons and to demolish factories capable of making munitions.

The rest of his life was spent in Africa. From 1945 to 1947 he was Inspector General of the Education Department in Emperor Haile Selassie's Abyssinian administration, and he helped to found Addis Ababa University. For the next 10 years he served in the Education Department in Kenya, where he was chairman of the European Civil Servants' Association and founding chairman of the Whitley Council.

During this time Miller became a close friend of Jomo Kenyatta, whom he assisted in founding the Kenyan African National Union; in the early 1960s he was also secretary to the Kenya Coffee Marketing Board and to the Coffee Board in Tanganyika.

As assistant secretary and marketing officer of the Ministry of Lands and Settlement in Kenya from 1963 to 1965, he was in charge of redistributing land to Africans in the former "White Highlands". He refused to stand for election to the new parliament, and after 1965 became an unofficial economic adviser to Robert Mugabe in Rhodesia.

In 1951 Miller published *Saints and Parachutes*, 17 essays describing his wartime mine disposal experiences and his progress from the Anglican to the Catholic Church. He also wrote a book on the attitudes towards Africa of post-war British politicians, which was not published as parts of it were judged to be defamatory.

He married first,in 1926,Barbara Buckmaster, who died in 1966; they had three sons, one of whom was to be the Conservative MP Sir Hal Miller. The marriage was dissolved; and he married, secondly, in 1944, Clare Harding, who also predeceased him. He married thirdly, in 1977, Greta Landby.

REAR-ADMIRAL GODFREY PLACE,VC

Rear-Admiral Godfrey Place (who died on December 27 1994, aged 73) won the Victoria Cross for his part in a daring attack by midget submarines on the German battleship *Tirpitz*.

The 44,000-ton *Tirpitz* rarely put to sea and used her main 15-inch guns in anger only once, against the island of Spitsbergen. But her presence in a heavily defended anchorage in Kaa Fjord, northern Norway, affected Allied ship movements around the world. Many attempts were made to attack her, but the first to do any damage was Operation Source, carried out by midget submarines (or X-craft) in September 1943.

The X-craft were 51 feet long, weighed 35 tons, and could dive to 300 feet. They had a speed of five knots and a crew of three officers and an engine-room artificer. Armed with two side charges which could be dropped under a target and set to detonate by clockwork time-fuses, they were towed to their target by "orthodox" submarines with a "passage crew" on board, an "operational crew" taking over for the actual attack.

Six X-craft took part in Operation Source: two to attack the battlecruiser *Scharnhorst*; one to attack the battleship *Lutzow*; and three to attack *Tirpitz* (X5, X6 and X7, which was commanded by Place). Towed by *Stubborn*, X7 left the depot ship *Bonaventure* in Loch Cairnbawn on September 11, and Place's operational crew took over on the evening of September 18, after a tow of nearly 1,000 miles.

The next night, 20 miles from the slipping point, X7 was on the surface charging its battery while the crew had supper when they heard an alarming noise from up forward. Place went on deck and saw that a German mine had caught in X7's towing wire and was bumping against its bow. He noticed that one horn was broken but, he recalled, "I didn't wait to examine it closely; keeping it off with my foot gingerly placed on its shell, I loosed its mooring wire from the bow and breathed deeply as it floated astern. When I got below I thought a tot would not do us any harm, so we toasted Minerva the mine with the crumpled horn."

X7 entered the fjord on September 21 and surfaced that evening to charge the battery. Place dived at 1am the next day and found a gap in the outer net. The submarine then ran into an anti-torpedo net at a depth of some 30 feet. The water was so clear that Place could see the mesh of the net through the periscope. X7 went full astern and then full ahead, flooded and then blew its ballast tanks, threshed and fought like a struggling salmon, and eventually broke through.

Place first sighted *Tirpitz* at 6.40am, at a range of about a mile. There was yet another net, in which X7 became stuck at a depth of 70 feet; but it penetrated it, and broke surface some 30 yards off *Tirpitz's* port beam. At full speed X7 struck *Tirpitz's* side at a depth of 20ft, slid gently under the keel, swung fore and aft in line with the ship and jettisoned the starboard side charge. X7 then went slow astern for about 200 feet further aft and dropped the port charge.

The charges had a time delay of roughly an hour, but this could not be relied on. Place tried frantically to penetrate the net again, but X7 was still stuck when the charges went off at 8.12am, and was blown clear of the net. X7 was now extremely difficult to control and broke surface several times, whereupon *Tirpitz's* guns opened fire, damaging her hull and periscope.

With all her high-pressure air exhausted, X7 sat on the bottom while Place considered the situation. He decided he must abandon the craft. X7 surfaced near a battle-practice target about 500 yards off *Tirpitz's* starboard bow. Place emerged, and began to wave a white sweater, but some water lapped into the submarine and, in her low state of buoyancy, she sank to the bottom. One officer escaped three hours later, but another and the artificer were drowned.

Place was taken on board *Tirpitz*, where he realised he cut a ridiculous figure on her quarterdeck –

"wearing vest, pants, seaboot stockings, and army boots size 12".Threatened with execution if he did not reveal where he had laid his mines,"I stated I was an English naval officer and as such demanded the courtesy entitled to my rank. I didn't say what rank – I had a fleeting vision of Gabby, the town crier in Max Fleischer's cartoon of *Gulliver's Travels*, shouting 'You can't do this to me, you can't do this to me, I've got a wife and kids, millions of kids!'"

X7's charges and those laid by X6 did so much damage that *Tirpitz* was not ready for sea again until April 1944. Place and Lieutenant Donald Cameron, X6's captain,who also became a prisoner of war, were both awarded theVC. X5, commanded by Lieutenant Henty-Creer, was lost with all hands.

Basil Charles Godfrey Place was born on July 19 1921 and joined the Navy as a cadet at Dartmouth in 1934. A midshipman in the cruiser *Newcastle* when war broke out, he joined the submarine service in 1941 and went out to the Mediterranean to serve in the 10th Flotilla in *Urge* and *Una* and as a liaison officer in the Polish submarine *Sokol*; he was awarded the Krzyz Walecznych (Polish Military Cross) in 1942.

As first lieutenant of *Unbeaten* he was awarded the DSC after she had carried out several successful patrols and sunk the Italian U-boat *Guglielmotti* off Sicily in 1942. Place was the only regular RN officer of all the early X-craft volunteers, and commanded the second experimental X-craft X4 before taking command of X7. He spent the rest of the war in Marlag-Milag Nord, where he played a part in the "Albert RN" escape, which employed a dummy.

After the war a tactless Admiralty bureaucrat

offered Place a humdrum submarine appointment because he had "lost" so much time as a PoW. So he turned his back on submarines to join the Fleet Air Arm. He qualified as a pilot in 1952, and served as a pilot and a squadron commander in the carrier *Glory* in the Korean War.

From then on his appointments were either in the Air Arm or in surface ships: on the staff of Flag Officer Flying Training; as commander of the destroyer *Tumult*; executive officer of the carrier *Theseus*, taking part in the Suez operation in 1956, and as commander of the destroyer *Corunna* until he was promoted captain in 1958.

He was then successively Chief Staff Officer to Flag Officer Aircraft Carriers, and Deputy Director of Air Warfare. He commanded the frigate *Rothesay*, as Captain (F) 6th Frigate Squadron; was captain of HMS Ganges, the boys' training establishment at Shotley, and commanded the commando-carrier *Albion* in the Far East until he was promoted rear-admiral in 1968 – by which time he was the only serving VC in the Navy.

Place's last appointments were as Director General Recruiting, and Admiral Commanding Reserves; he retired in 1970, when he was appointed CB.

In 1975 Place became the first ombudsman for complaints against solicitors. In his final report four years later he called for more vigorous action by the Law Society to reduce delays by solicitors acting as executors. When he found travel to London too tiring he bought and ran two leather goods shops and a saddlery near his home in Dorset.

Although his VC was for an act of outstanding courage, Place was an extremely modest man with an

almost self-effacing manner. He made a splendid
chairman of the VC and GC Association from 1971,
bringing together its highly individual personalities
into a unique fellowship.

He married 2nd Officer Althea Tickler, WRNS in
1943, weeks before the *Tirpitz* raid, with Henty-
Creer as his best man; they had a son and two
daughters.

COMMANDER
GRAHAM DE CHAIR

Commander Graham de Chair (who died on January
5 1995, aged 89) commanded *Venus* in Operation
Dukedom,the last Royal Navy destroyer action of the
Second World War, and one of the finest.

Venus and four other destroyers of the 26th Flotilla,
forewarned by Ultra Special Intelligence, "corner-
flagged" at high speed across the Malacca Strait in the
early hours of May 16 1945 to intercept the 10,000-
ton Japanese heavy cruiser *Haguro*, which was heading
for Singapore.

Venus was the first to detect *Haguro* by radar – at
the phenomenal range, for her set, of 34 miles. The
contact was dismissed as merely a rain storm; but
Venus's radar operator insisted,in de Chair's words,"to
the point of insubordination" that it was a true ship
echo. So it proved. *Venus* was also the first to attack,
though there was early disappointment.

"We could see the Japanese cruiser ahead with
night glasses," de Chair recalled, "and we were
obviously going to be in the perfect position to fire

torpedoes at very close range. When nearing the firing position I said to the sub-lieutenant, who was torpedo control officer, 'Are you ready, sub?' but received no answer.

"By this time the enemy was very close, her two funnels filled my glasses, and I repeated, 'Are you ready, sub?' He said in a quiet voice, 'We've missed it, sir.' He had angled the torpedoes ahead, in spite of my orders for straight running on the beam, and it was too late to alter the setting. Short of ramming the cruiser or possibly fouling one of the other destroyers somewhat astern of her, I had to alter to port, which I did under full helm to try and prevent the Jap from breaking out of our circle."

However, in a joint attack which they had exercised beforehand, the five destroyers surrounded their much larger and more heavily armed adversary and, after an exciting and confused night action, during which they thought at one point they had sunk their own flotilla leader, they dispatched *Haguro* with guns and torpedoes, some 45 miles south-west of Penang.

De Chair was awarded a Bar to the DSC he had won while in command of the long-range escort destroyer *Vimy* for sinking the large U-162 on September 3 1942. *Vimy*, *Quentin* and *Pathfinder* had been escorting the damaged battleship *Queen Elizabeth* to America and had just handed her over to an American escort. They were on their way to Trinidad when they made an Asdic contact with the U-boat. All three destroyers attacked with depth charges.

The U-boat surfaced and rammed *Vimy*, cutting her hull open, and *Vimy* retaliated with a charge set to explode at 50 feet depth, whereupon the U-boat heeled over and sank. The destroyers picked up the captain and 48 survivors.

Earlier still,on September 21 1941, while escorting convoy HG73 home from Gibraltar, *Vimy* attacked with two full patterns of depth charges and sank the Italian U-boat *Alessandro Malaspina*, which had been shadowing the convoy from astern.Though de Chair heard the booming underwater noises of the hull collapsing, he refused to claim the kill (which would almost certainly have won him the DSO) when he returned to Gibraltar, because there was no visible evidence except an oil slick on the surface, and because he was sure the Admiralty would claim on his behalf.

In fact no claim was made. When de Chair wrote to the Admiralty in 1951 setting out the facts they admitted his claim, but by then it was too late for any award.

Henry Graham Dudley de Chair was born on September 10 1905,the son of Admiral Sir Dudley de Chair and the older brother of Somerset de Chair, the author, soldier and MP who died the same day as him. Young Graham joined the Navy as a cadet in 1919,going to Osborne and Dartmouth.His first ship as a midshipman, in 1923, was the battleship *Iron Duke*. He then served in the destroyer *Wivern*, and in the sloop *Laburnum* in the New Zealand Squadron.In 1929 he became ADC to his father, then Governor of New South Wales.

After service in the battleship *Nelson* at the time of the 1931 Invergordon Mutiny, he began his long destroyer career with appointments to *Achates* and to *Venetia* in the Mediterranean during the Abyssinian crisis and the Spanish Civil War. His first command, in 1936, was *Wrestler* in the Vernon Flotilla based at Portsmouth.In December 1937 he took command of the destroyer *Scout*, intended for the China station.

But in January 1938, during gunnery trials in the Medway, *Scout* ran aground after the sub-lieutenant, who was officer of the watch, ordered the wrong course. De Chair was court-martialled and reprimanded. His career recovered and, after a spell as gas and ventilation officer and sports officer in the battleship *Royal Sovereign*, he was appointed to the destroyer *Thracian* in the Hong Kong Local Defence Flotilla in August 1938, as the Japanese were becoming ever more aggressive in the Far East.

Following the Second World War de Chair had appointments at HMS Rosneath, the combined operations base on the Clyde; in Hong Kong; as executive officer of the Royal Naval air station at St Merryn in Cornwall and of HMS Montclere and on the depot ship of the 3rd Submarine Squadron at Rothesay, by which time he was passed over for promotion. His last appointment was as commanding officer, Reserve Fleet Rosyth.

After retirement in 1955,de Chair commanded the Moray Sea School Outward Bound Training Schooner *Prince Louis* for four years.

Graham de Chair was a talented painter. His watercolour of *Haguro*'s last moments is in the Imperial War Museum. In 1993 he published his autobiography, *Let Go Aft: the Indiscretions of a Salt-Horse*.

He married first,in 1936, Patricia Gordon–Ramsey (marriage dissolved); they had a daughter and two sons. He married secondly, in 1960, Stella Harcourt.

CAPTAIN
GRAHAM LUMSDEN

Captain Graham Lumsden (who died on July 28 1995, aged 81) could justifiably be described as one of the luckiest officers in the Royal Navy. In six years as a navigating officer in the Second World War, which he spent almost entirely at sea, he survived several bomb and torpedo attacks, twice had a ship sunk under him, and was unharmed when his captain was killed next to him.

His navigation also survived defective compasses, officers of the watch who misunderstood their course orders, and lighthouses falsely lit by the enemy to deceive Allied ships. On the day his ship ran aground, he happened to be ashore.

Lumsden's war began quietly enough with a passage to Freetown, Sierra Leone, in the seaplane carrier *Albatross*. The climate and the boredom of life in West Africa were enervating, and when passing through Freetown two years later he was shocked to see the physical deterioration of his former messmates.

He was glad to be appointed to *Keith*, leader of the 19th Destroyer Flotilla. In May 1940, after the German invasion of Holland, *Keith* helped to evacuate the Dutch royal family from Ijmuiden, with a considerable amount of gold bullion. Later that month *Keith* and another destroyer, *Vimy*, went to Boulogne to take off as many as possible of the 6,000 men surrounded in the town, including Coldstream Guards and Royal Marines.

Both ships were subjected to accurate dive-bombing attacks while alongside, and small-arms fire from ashore made *Keith*'s bridge untenable. Lumsden was descending from it when a sniper's bullet passed over his head and killed the captain just behind him.

The first lieutenant, an RNR officer, asked Lumsden to take the ship to sea. "I had never conned a ship in a sternboard," Lumsden said, "and certainly not down a narrow and curving channel, peering through a small scuttle and with bullets hitting people between me and the men who would carry out my orders. I found myself replying, 'Of course I can, Number One!'" Lumsden successfully took *Keith* out to sea.

Under a new captain, *Keith* took part in the Dunkirk evacuation, and on May 30 embarked some 1,400 soldiers from the harbour Mole. Once again she was subjected to fierce air attacks and by the evening of May 31 had expended all her anti-aircraft ammunition. Early the next day *Keith* was dive-bombed and had to be abandoned. She was later hit again, and sank. Lumsden and other survivors were taken off by the tug *St Abbs*, which was herself soon bombed and sunk. Lumsden found himself swimming for his life.

"Thinking of something that would powerfully reinforce my will to swim on," he said, "I found myself picturing my wife's small but beautiful backside." He reached the shore, where French sailors gave him some dry clothes.

Back at Dover, Lumsden went to the castle, where his wife, a WRNS watch-keeper in the cypher room, had already seen the signal that *Keith* had been sunk and there was no news of survivors. She did not recognise her husband, with his oil-covered face, seaman's jersey and matelot's cap with pompom, and when she did she accused him of smelling of French perfume.

A grateful Queen Wilhelmina of the Netherlands awarded *Keith* the Order of Orange Nassau, with the rank of chevalier. *Keith*'s officers voted that Lumsden should receive it. He was also mentioned in despatches.

Lumsden was then appointed to the new light cruiser *Phoebe* for two hectic years in the Mediterranean: she escorted convoys from Alexandria to Malta; covered the Army's withdrawal from Greece in April 1941 (for which he was again mentioned in despatches); evacuated the Army from Crete in May (for which he was awarded the DSC); and took part in the Syrian campaign of June and July. On a trip to Tobruk in August 1941 *Phoebe* was badly damaged by an aerial torpedo. Repaired in New York, she took part in the Pedestal convoy to Malta in August 1942, one of the most spectacular naval operations of the war.

In October, when *Phoebe* was on her way to the Torch landings in North Africa, she was torpedoed by a U-boat off Point Noire in the Congo, and again had to leave for repairs. Lumsden was pleased by *Phoebe*'s farewell signal from Admiral Cunningham, commanding the Allied naval forces for Torch: "Romans Ch 16 verses i & ii". ("I commend unto you Phebe our sister . . . for she hath been a succourer of many, and of myself also.")

After a few months at HMS Dryad, the navigation school near Portsmouth, teaching "a course of young officers in the gentle art", Lumsden was appointed navigating officer of the cruiser *Sheffield*: he took part in operations in the Bay of Biscay in the summer of

1943, and gave bombardment support to the Salerno landing in September. On December 26 *Sheffield* took part in the battle off the North Cape of Norway when ships of the Home Fleet, led by Admiral Sir Bruce Fraser, flying his flag in the battleship *Duke of York*, pursued and sank the German battlecruiser *Scharnhorst*.

In a long and anxious day of manoeuvring in Arctic cold and darkness, *Scharnhorst* twice threatened convoy JW55B on its way to Russia, and was twice driven off by the cruisers *Belfast, Norfolk* and *Sheffield*. The sharp eyesight of Lumsden and the chief yeoman of signals enabled *Sheffield* to be the first to make the signal "enemy in sight" on both occasions. But during the pursuit *Sheffield* suffered a defect in one of her shafts and had to drop back, thus missing *Scharnhorst*'s final moments. Lumsden was awarded a Bar to his DSC.

In 1944 he was appointed navigating officer of the light fleet carrier *Venerable*, which joined the British Pacific Fleet and was present at the surrender of Hong Kong in August 1945.

Graham James Alexander Lumsden was born on November 24 1913 and joined the Navy as a cadet at Dartmouth in 1927. He served as a midshipman in the cruiser *Suffolk* on the China station, and as a lieutenant in the cruiser *Ajax* and the aircraft carrier *Courageous*, qualifying as a navigating officer in 1937.

Lumsden returned to Dryad on the staff after the war and then served in the cruiser *Superb*, and in the Admiralty Signal and Radar Establishment at Portsdown, near Portsmouth. In 1951 he relieved Prince Philip in command of the frigate *Magpie* in the Mediterranean. His last appointments before retiring in 1958 were in the Admiralty, in the Directorate of Navigation and Direction.

He married, in 1938, Daphne Sturrock.

CAPTAIN
STANLEY LEONARD

Captain Stanley Leonard (who died on August 1 1995, aged 70) was the subject of a celebrated helicopter search-and-rescue incident – the first in the Royal Navy's history – during the Korean War.

He was flying Hawker Sea Furies in 807 Naval Air Squadron, from the aircraft carrier *Theseus*. On October 10 1950 – *Theseus's* first day of operational flying during the war – Leonard was wingman to the air group commander on an armed reconnaissance some 70 miles behind enemy lines. While attacking a target, Leonard's Sea Fury was hit by anti-aircraft fire and he was forced to land in a paddy field. His spine was broken, and he was trapped in the wreckage of his aircraft. Although in great pain, Leonard threw his Mae West on to the wing of his aircraft to show that he was still alive, and fired his revolver at the encircling North Koreans.

Cannon fire from Sea Furies kept the North Koreans at bay, until an American helicopter carrying a medic arrived from Kimpo field, near Seoul. The medic, under intense rifle fire, had great difficulty in freeing Leonard, who was by now unconscious, so the pilot left the helicopter, its engine still running and its rotor blades turning, to help to carry Leonard into the cockpit.

The medic gave Leonard morphia and a blood transfusion during the return flight. He and the pilot were both later awarded the MC, and *Theseus's* captain sent them a bottle of whisky each.

Leonard, who had married a fortnight before sailing for Korea, was told by his doctors that he would be invalided from the Navy, would spend the rest of his life in a wheelchair, and would never be able to father children. He set out to prove them all wrong, and with the use of a stick, and cumbersome iron frame on his paralysed left leg, he was able to get around.

He persuaded the Admiralty to allow him to stay in the Navy, for limited non-flying shore duties. He then devised a special strap attached to his "good" leg, so that he could push and pull on an aircraft rudder bar. With the help of a friendly instructor, he began to fly in secret. Eventually, when his flying was formally tested, Leonard was given official permission to fly again – but not over water. It was thought that if he ditched, his iron leg would take him to the bottom.

He became flying instructor to the Northern Air Division at HMS Blackcap, the naval air station at Stretton, and was appointed MBE in the 1953 Coronation Honours.

Stanley Leonard was born on October 8 1924 and educated at Hawarden Grammar School, Deeside. In 1943 he joined the Navy as a trainee Fleet Air Arm pilot. His first squadron was 814, which flew accident-prone Fairey Barracudas; he later thought he was lucky to have survived. For the last few months of the war against Japan, Leonard was based on the carrier *Venerable* in the East Indies and British Pacific Fleets. He was present at the surrender of Hong Kong in August 1945.

Leonard left the Navy on demobilisation in 1946 but was offered a short service commission and rejoined the next year. He qualified as an instructor at the RAF Central Flying School and taught naval pilots until 1949, when he was awarded a permanent commission. When the Korean War broke out he was given a "pierhead jump" to *Theseus*.

From 1955 he had appointments on the staff at HMS Excellent, the gunnery school at Whale Island, Portsmouth. He was also Lieutenant-Commander (Flying) at HMS Goldcrest, Brawdy, and in the Admiralty in the Directorate of Naval Air Warfare.

Having persuaded the Admiralty that he could climb ladders, he was appointed Lieutenant-Commander (Flying) in the carrier *Hermes*, and obtained his bridge watch-keeping certificate in the frigate *Wakeful*. He was appointed OBE in 1964.

From 1964 to 1969 he was senior naval officer at RAF Linton-on-Ouse, where naval pilots underwent their initial flying training; he was Commander (Air) in *Hermes* in the Far East, and served on the staff of Flag Officer Naval Air Command.

Promoted captain in 1970, Leonard was Assistant Chief of Staff to the C-in-C Western Fleet at Northwood, and then Deputy Director of the RN War Course at Greenwich. His final appointment, from 1975, was in command of HMS Seahawk, the naval air station at Culdrose, Cornwall. This was the largest helicopter base in Europe and the centre of the Navy's air-sea-rescue service in southern England.

Disability was particularly bitter for Leonard. Before joining the Navy, he had played soccer as an amateur for Chester in the professional Football League, and he later turned down an invitation to join Everton. Until his accident he played soccer and rugby for the Navy, and was a fine cricketer and quarter-mile runner.

Nobody would have guessed from Leonard's outward manner, energy and enthusiasm that he suffered from such a severe handicap. However, in 1978, he decided to retire, slightly earlier than planned. Nearly 25 years of strenuous service had taken their toll. The paralysed leg needed constant painkilling treatment and was long overdue for hospital treatment.

In retirement Leonard was welfare consultant to the Royal British Legion Industries at Maidstone, to which he drove himself from his home at Rowlands Castle. He raised funds for the Churchill Centre project to improve the treatment and quality of life of the disabled.

He and his wife, Nancie, proved the doctors' gloomy prognosis quite wrong by having a son and three daughters.

CAPTAIN
"FISH" DALGLISH

Captain "Fish" Dalglish (who died on October 6 1995, aged 82) was the first executive officer of the Royal Yacht *Britannia*.

He was appointed in 1953, when she was building at John Brown's on the Clyde. In November that year the Queen and Prince Philip left for a

Commonwealth tour in the liner *Gothic,* and the Flag Officer Royal Yachts, who was also the captain of *Britannia*, accompanied them.

To Dalglish's great joy he was given the rank of acting captain and appointed in command of *Britannia*. The ship was still unfinished, and Dalglish faced a number of other problems. He had to keep the ship's name secret until the launch; to fend off senior officers and their wives who wanted to be shown around the royal apartments; to deal with Buckingham Palace staff; and to accommodate the royal Rolls-Royce, which was too long for the garage on board and had to have its bumpers removed whenever it was embarked.

Dalglish chose the royal yachtsmen, all volunteers, and weeded out those who thought it was going to be a soft number. He designed their working uniforms, taught them how to bow and how to help the Queen out of a motorboat. Everybody wore soft shoes, and Dalglish issued each man with a chamois leather.

Britannia's sea trials were accomplished successfully, despite some adventurous ship handling by Dalglish when negotiating buoys in Scottish harbours, a defective "singing" propeller and foul weather, with dragged anchors. During speed trials over a measured mile off Arran, Dalglish took the ship so close to shore that the navigating officer said he could see the spiders' webs on the bracken.

Silence had to be observed at all times. Denied a ship's broadcast for passing orders Fish devised a system using wooden pads, coloured red on one side (for Stop) and green the other (Hoist or Lower). Instead of the bugler sounding the customary note of

"G" as a signal for dressing ship, lowering boats or turning out booms, *Britannia* had flag "George", hoisted close up for "standby" and hauled down for "execute".

For her first royal duty, in April 1954, *Britannia* took on board a sandpit, a slide and extra milk before taking Prince Charles and Princess Anne out to Tobruk to join their parents, who were returning from their tour. As they sailed Dalglish signalled:"Just cleared Portland and on our way. Both royal children in cracking form. Sun shining and a following wind."

Dalglish then had to handle the Royal Yacht in the confined waters of Grand Harbour, Malta, with the eyes of the fleet and the world's media on him. He also had to receive his admiral (who did not always agree with the way Dalglish was doing things), attend a rush of social functions, and dine with the Royal Family – all with a broken bone in his foot,which he had incurred playing deck hockey.

Dalglish was confirmed in the rank of captain, and appointed CVO in the 1955 New Year's Honours.

A rear-admiral's son, James Stephen Dalglish was born on October 1 1913 and educated at Ampleforth Preparatory School before joining the Navy in 1927 as a cadet at Dartmouth. He became known as "Dogfish", later abbreviated to "Fish", a name which stuck for the rest of his time in the Navy. He went to sea as a midshipman in the battleship *Rodney* in 1931 and then in the cruiser *Enterprise* in the East Indies. After serving in the cruiser *Coventry* during the Abyssinian crisis and the battleship *Resolution* in the Spanish Civil War he specialised in gunnery in 1938.

Dalglish was appointed to *Faulknor* as gunnery officer of the 8th Destroyer Flotilla in the Norwegian

Campaign and then in Force H in the Mediterranean. After two years on the staff of the gunnery school at Chatham he joined the new cruiser *Swiftsure* as gunnery officer in 1943, and went out in her to the Far East to serve in the East Indies and British Pacific Fleet. He was mentioned in despatches.

In September 1945 Dalglish went back to HMS Excellent, the gunnery school at Whale Island, Portsmouth, in charge of the first post-war Long "G" course. It was a demanding job, which required him to frame a course syllabus that drew on all the gunnery experience of the war. Such was his devotion to duty that Dalglish went ahead with an important lecture despite knowing he had contracted mumps, and infected the entire front row of his class.

In 1947 Fish was appointed Staff Officer (Operations) to the Senior Officer Force "T", the Royal Navy element of the occupation force in Japan, and when that force was withdrawn he was squadron gunnery officer of the 5th Cruiser Squadron based at Hong Kong.

He was at Shanghai in the cruiser *London* in 1949 when the frigate *Amethyst* was fired on by Chinese communists and her captain was killed. *London* tried to go up the Yangtse to help but was badly damaged by Chinese gunfire and had to turn back. Dalglish discovered he had been nominated to take command of *Amethyst*, and try to extricate her. He was somewhat relieved when Commander Kerans came down from Nanking and eventually took *Amethyst* to sea in the celebrated "Yangtse Incident".

Dalglish then spent two years on the staff at the Royal Naval College, Greenwich, in charge of the junior officers' war course. In December 1952 he was given his first sea command, the destroyer *Aisne* in the Home Fleet. His next, in 1958, was in the depot ship Woodbridge Haven, known as "'Woo Ha", and the Inshore Flotilla of the 104th and 108th Mine-sweeping Squadrons in the Mediterranean.

His final appointment, in 1961, was in command of the commando carrier *Bulwark* in the Far East. He was appointed CBE in 1963 and retired the same year. For the next 10 years he was a respected and well-loved welfare officer to the Metropolitan Police.

Gunnery officers have never been noted for their sense of humour or their affability – indeed naval lore had it that they only became gunnery officers so that they would never have to serve with another gunnery officer. But Fish had a light touch. As captain of Excellent from 1959 to 1961 he was delighted to accept the title of "MooEe-Upta", or "Big Chief Thunderflash", when the Canadians, many of whom had trained at Whale Island during the war, presented the establishment with the carved totem pole Hosaqami. Dalglish donned a head-dress, smoked a pipe of peace, joined in a war dance and took part in an Indian feast of a whole pig roasted on a spit.

Fish Dalglish played rugger for the Navy and was Navy selector for many years. He much enjoyed amateur theatricals and played everything from Sophocles's Oedipus, King of Thebes to Marine Ogg in Ian Hay's *The Middle Watch*. He published his memoirs, *The Life Story of a Fish*, in 1992.

He married, in 1939, Eve Meyricke; they had a son and a daughter.

REAR-ADMIRAL
JOHNNY LEE-BARBER

Rear-Admiral Johnny Lee-Barber (who died on November 14 1995, aged 90) distinguished himself in command of *Griffin* from 1939 to 1942.

Griffin was in the 1st Destroyer Flotilla of the Home Fleet in the Norwegian campaign, which began in April 1940. On the 25th, while escorting ships carrying troops to Aandalsnes, *Griffin* captured the German trawler *Polaris*, which was wearing Dutch colours. *Polaris* proved a "treasure trove" for Intelligence; cryptographic material, mines designed to be laid by submarines, torpedoes, a 4-inch gun camouflaged as a boat and depth charges were found on board.

On May 2 *Griffin* took part in the evacuation of Allied troops from Namsos. General Carton de Wiart, VC, who was in command ashore, later wrote: "In the course of that last endless day, I got a message from the Navy to say that they would evacuate the whole of my force that night. I thought it was impossible, but learned a few hours later that the Navy do not know the word."

Later that month *Griffin* evacuated Polish troops from France, for which Lee-Barber was awarded the Polish Cross of Valour. She then carried out anti-invasion patrols off the British coast in the summer of 1940. Lee-Barber was awarded the DSO in July for his services in command since the outbreak of war, and was also mentioned in despatches for Namsos.

In the autumn *Griffin* went out to the Mediter-ranean, where she was in action at once. When the Italian submarine *Durbo* was attacked by destroyers and aircraft off Gibraltar on October 18, a boarding party recovered cypher and other operational documents before the submarine sank. This led two days later to the sinking of a second Italian submarine, *Lafole*, by *Gallant*, *Hotspur* and *Griffin*.

The Mediterranean destroyers were driven very hard by their Commander-in-Chief, Admiral Sir Andrew Cunningham (known to the Navy as ABC because his full name was Andrew Browne Cunningham). In March 1941, after escorting several convoys to Malta, *Griffin* was damaged by a bomb, which holed all her forward fuel tanks; she was left with oil only in the after tanks. Nevertheless, she sailed from Alexandria with the other destroyers on March 27 to escort the battleships *Warspite*, *Valiant* and *Barham* in the action with the Italian fleet off Cape Matapan the next day.

On the evening of the 28th, the Italian cruisers *Fiume* and *Zara* were returning to assist their stricken sister ship *Pola* – immobilised by a torpedo hit earlier in the day – when they were caught by surprise, their guns trained fore and aft, and overwhelmed by fire from the battleships.

Griffin was on the engaged side, nearest the enemy, when the action began, and hard though Lee-Barber tried to get clear she was illuminated by searchlights and found herself, as he said, "in the unenviable position of being smack in the line of fire when the 'battle boats' opened up and, received a very curt 'get-out of the way, you BF' from ABC"; *Griffin* and the other destroyers were later detached to search for the Italian destroyers and, in what ABC called "a wild night", sank two of them.

Griffin's subsequent movements, Lee-Barber said,

"were unfortunately very dull, as we saw nothing until we came upon the *Pola*, stopped and longing to surrender". *Pola*'s survivors were taken off, and she was dispatched by torpedo.

In April 1941 Griffin took part in the evacuation of the Army from Greece, and was always in the thick of the action: standing by the troopship *Pennland* after she had been bombed, and picking up her survivors when she sank; towing the damaged infantry landing ship *Glenearn* to safety in Suda Bay on Crete; recovering 50 men from a raft; embarking several hundred soldiers from the beach at Monemvasia; and towing the crippled submarine *Rover* from Suda Bay to Alexandria. Lee-Barber was awarded a Bar to his DSO.

In May *Griffin* escorted the Tiger convoy, bringing tanks to Egypt, and then taking part in the evacuation of the Army from Crete. So many of ABC's ships were hit by the Luftwaffe that he came under pressure to stop the evacuation. He replied that it had always been the Navy's job to re-embark the Army. "It takes three years to build a ship," he said. "It would take 300 to rebuild a tradition."

Griffin went on to escort every convoy to Malta in 1941, besides making 13 trips with troops, stores and ammunition to the besieged fortress of Tobruk. In October she towed the gunboat *Gnat* stern-first to Alexandria after she had been torpedoed by a U-boat off Bardia.

John Lee-Barber was born on April 16 1905, and joined the Navy as a cadet in 1919, going to Osborne and Dartmouth. He joined the destroyers *Vidette* as a midshipman, *Wessex* as a sub-lieutenant, and *Wakeful* and *Vimiera* as a lieutenant. From 1932 to 1933 he was first lieutenant of the river gunboat *Falcon* on the Yangtse. His first destroyer command, in 1937, was *Witch*, followed by *Ardent*.

When he left *Griffin* early in 1942 Lee-Barber was naval adviser to Southern Command Army Head-quarters, Home Forces. But in September he took command of *Opportune* in the 17th Destroyer Flotilla, escorting convoys to and from Russia. On December 26 1943 *Opportune* took part in the high-speed chase and destruction of the German battlecruiser *Scharnhorst* by ships of the Home Fleet in the Arctic. *Opportune* was one of the destroyers to apply the *coup de grace*, firing four torpedoes at *Scharnhorst*'s starboard side at a range of 2,100 yards and claiming one hit. She then turned for another run, fired a second salvo of four torpedoes at 2,500 yards and claimed a second hit. Lee-Barber was mentioned in despatches.

From 1944 to 1946 Lee-Barber was executive officer of HMS King Alfred, the RNVR officers' training establishment at Hove, then commanded the destroyers *St James* and *Agincourt* and the depot ship Woolwich. From 1950 to 1952 he was naval attaché in Santiago, Lima, Bogota and Quito and from 1954 to 1957 Commodore, Harwich, in command of the inshore flotilla.

His last appointment, in 1957, was as Admiral Superintendent Malta. It was a time of unrest, when the dockyard was being turned over to civilian ownership. Lee-Barber was attacked and had his leg broken by a brick-throwing mob. He returned in 1959, the year he was appointed CB.

Johnny Lee-Barber disregarded every rule of good health. He smoked 40 cigarettes a day into old age and enjoyed copious glasses of gin."I've never done a hand's turn of work all my life," he boasted. Like all the successful wartime destroyer captains he had tremendous physical stamina,and was able to stand on his bridge for hours on end and go for days without proper sleep. Some of his contemporaries cracked under the strain; Lee-Barber thrived on it.

On one bad day off Crete, *Griffin* endured 20 air attacks. Her sailors were enormously reassured by the sight of their captain, grinning under a salt-stained cap set at a jaunty angle, his faithful bull terrier Jamie at his side, watching the bombs leave the aircraft and giving helm orders to avoid them.Though a brilliant combat captain and shiphandler, he was entirely without vanity and abhorred self-advertisement.

In retirement he kept in touch with shipmates from *Griffin* and *Opportune* and was vice-president of the Russian Convoy Club.

He married, in 1939, Sue Le Gallais, who died in 1976.They had two daughters.

ADMIRAL "THIRTY-ONEKNOT" BURKE

Admiral "Thirty-one Knot" Burke (who died on January 1 1996, aged 94) was the last great American naval commander of the Second World War.

Though his *nom de guerre* suggested that he was a hell-for-leather destroyer skipper who went everywhere at full boiler-bursting steam, Arleigh Burke owed the sobriquet not to his ship's speed (destroyers could make 35 knots) but to an incident in the South Pacific during 1943. Burke was in USS *Charles Ausburne*, leading Destroyer Squadron 23, known as the "Little Beavers". When one Little Beaver, USS *Spence*, was reduced by lack of maintenance to a top speed of only 30 knots, Burke registered a protest by ending all his signals, "My speed 30 knots."

Eventually Burke ordered *Spence* to cross-connect her two machinery systems. This contravened Navy regulations, which laid down that the systems must be isolated to minimise the effect of action damage, but it gave *Spence* an extra knot. "My speed 31 knots," Burke signalled. Noticing the amendment, the fleet commander Admiral Halsey addressed his next signal, tongue in cheek, to "Thirty-one Knot Burke". War correspondents heard the story, and the name stuck.

In the Allied advances of 1942 to 1944, from Guadalcanal up through the Solomon Islands towards New Britain and New Guinea, the Americans had superior technology – except in torpedoes, where the Japanese had the formidable 40-knot oxygen-powered "Long Lance" – but they at first lost many ships because of rigidity in tactical control. Ships with the best radar were often wrongly placed in a formation, captains were not allowed to use their initiative, and the Japanese skill in night-fighting was grossly underestimated.

After studying other officers' actions, Burke devised his own tactics, splitting his divisions in two to surprise and confuse the enemy, and allowing his captains more flexibility. His plan worked brilliantly on the night of November 25 1943, Thanksgiving Day, off the southern tip of New Ireland. In an action later described as "nearly perfect", three Japanese destroyers were sunk, without a single casualty or hit on Burke's ships.

From the Battle of Empress Augusta Bay on November 2 1943 until the end of February 1944, Burke led the Little Beavers in 22 separate engagements; they were credited with sinking a Japanese cruiser, nine destroyers, a submarine and five other ships, as well as destroying 30 aircraft and carrying out 11 shore bombardments. The Beavers won a Presidential Unit Citation, and Burke was awarded the Distinguished Service Medal, the Navy Cross and the Legion of Merit.

On March 27 Burke was transferred at sea by wire jackstay from *Ausburne* to the aircraft carrier *Lexington*. He had been appointed Chief of Staff, with the eventual rank of commodore to Vice-Admiral "Pete" Mitscher, commander of the US Fast Carrier Task Force. Relations between the two men were at first icy. Mitscher had always had an aviator as his chief of staff and resented a non-flyer being foisted on him. Burke, for his part, furiously insisted that he was a destroyer man who knew nothing – and cared less – about flying.

At their first meeting Mitscher saw that Burke was exhausted, and told him to take a rest. Burke instead showered, sent for fresh khaki uniform from the officers' clothing store and was back on the flag bridge in half an hour.

Mitscher was impressed, and he mellowed further when he saw how Burke threw himself into "learning the birdman's lingo" and flying at every opportunity. Burke had a prodigious capacity for absorbing information about carrier operations, and his operational orders were always short and sharp, being written for the benefit of the men who were going to risk their lives, not for posterity.

Mitscher and Burke served together in an intense period of operations – the "Great Marianas Turkey Shoot" in the Philippine Sea in June 1944; the defeat of the Japanese Navy at Leyte Gulf in October; the marines' bloody assault on Iwo Jima in February 1945; the sinking of the battleship *Yamato* in the East China Sea in April; and the campaign in Okinawa from April to June. During these hectic and dangerous months the two men developed a deep mutual respect which ripened into a lasting friendship.

Burke was awarded Gold Stars in lieu of a second Distinguished Service Medal and a second Legion of Merit.He received a letter of commendation and the Silver Star after he had ignored personal danger to extricate men trapped by fire and smoke in a radio compartment beneath the bridge, when the carrier *Bunker Hill* was hit by a kamikaze suicide bomber off Okinawa on May 11 1945: more than 300 men were killed in the attack, including 14 of Mitscher's staff.

He was also entitled to wear the ribbons with stars for the Presidential Unit Citations awarded to *Lexington* and *Bunker Hill* and the Navy Unit Commendation awarded to *Enterprise* – all three Mitscher's flagships.

Arleigh Albert Burke was born on October 19 1901, at a "hardscrabble" farm near Boulder, Colorado. He went to the State Preparatory School, Boulder, and joined the Navy for a free higher education at the Naval Academy Prep School, Columbia, Missouri. At the US Naval Academy, Annapolis, he graduated 70th in a class of 412.

He served for five years in the battleship *Arizona*, specialising in Ordnance Engineering (explosives). After the Naval Post-Graduate School, Annapolis, and Michigan University, where he read engineering, he joined the cruiser *Chester* as assistant gunnery officer in 1932. His first command was *Mugford* in 1939.

When the Japanese attacked Pearl Harbor in December 1941 Burke was an inspector of gun-mounts at the naval gun factory in Washington, DC. Because few officers had his ordnance expertise his requests for sea duty were turned down. Finally he escaped by typing out his own orders, leaving Washington before anyone could stop him, and joining a troop ship to the South Pacific, where he arrived in February 1943.

With his motto "If it kills Japs, it's important. If not, it's not important", Burke became an outstanding combat captain. He knew that success at sea often hung by the narrowest thread. "The difference between a good officer and an excellent one," he used to say, "is about 10 seconds." He kept his sense of humour in his despatches and his signals. "Hold on to your hats, boys – here we go again!" he signalled the Little Beavers as they closed on the Japanese at Cape St George.

Although then as thin as a lath, with a face drawn by the strain of operations, Burke was physically tough. After the destroyer *Conway* was shelled by Japanese shore batteries in July 1943 Burke carried on with shrapnel wounds in his back, and two ribs dislocated, after the mast was hit and a signalman fell on him.

The end of the war found Burke back at a desk in Washington but, in 1946, he rejoined Mitscher, who

was C-in-C Atlantic Fleet, as his chief of staff. But
Mitscher died the next year. Burke's naval career
nearly came to a premature end in 1949 when he was
unfairly (and illegally) struck off the promotion list by
politicians for his part in the so-called "Admirals'
Revolt" over the controversial B-36 bomber for the
Air Force. Reinstated by President Truman, he went
out to the Far East as Deputy Chief of Staff to the
Commander, US Forces, and was awarded a Gold Star
in lieu of another Legion of Merit.

Two years later Burke was a member of the
Military Armistice Commission, playing a notable
part in the Panmunjon negotiations leading to the
end of the Korean War, and was awarded an Army
Oak Leaf Cluster in lieu of a fourth Legion of Merit.
In 1955 Burke was promoted over the heads of 92
admirals senior to him to become Chief of Naval
Operations, the professional head of the US Navy, a
post he held for an unprecedented three terms, lasting
six years.

Burke maintained the highest fleet readiness
through the Cold War crises, introducing guided
missiles, encouraging young blood in the Navy's
officer corps, promoting new designs in aircraft,
communications systems and anti-submarine warfare,
and sponsoring the project that became Polaris. He
worked 16 hours a day, and gave short shrift to the
stupid or idle. His summary sacking of one captain
made all the others sit up and take their feet off their
desks.

In contrast to the "anti-limey" attitude of Admiral
Hyman Rickover, Burke encouraged Lord Mountbatten, the First Sea Lord, over the Royal Navy's first
nuclear submarine. When Nasser nationalised the

Suez Canal in 1956 Burke determined that he had "to be shown that international thievery is unprofitable", recommended American support for Britain and France, and moved the US Sixth Fleet into the eastern Mediterranean. However, the political situation was so clouded by John Foster Dulles, the Secretary of State, that eventually its commander signalled plaintively to Burke "Which side are we on?"

Burke retired in 1961 to design and build his own cottage in Virginia. In 1976 he joined Japanese admirals to dedicate a garden of peace at the Admiral Nimitz State Historical Park at Fredericksburg,Texas. The next year President Ford conferred on him the Medal of Freedom, the nation's highest civilian award. In 1988 he attended the launch of the first of a new class of guided missile destroyer, *Arleigh Burke*.

"Thirty-one Knot" became one of the most venerated men in the American Navy. He was generous in giving interviews and corresponding with historians, and in 1986 published a slim volume of witticisms and reminiscences, *The Best of Burke*.

Arleigh Burke married "Bobbie" Gorsuch on the day he graduated from Annapolis in 1923.

LIEUTENANT
DOM MARTIN SALMON

Lieutenant Dom Martin Salmon (who died on February 10 1996, aged 76) became a monk of Downside Abbey after a mystical experience during an explosion aboard the destroyer *Arrow* in Algiers harbour in 1943.

Arrow went to the aid of a burning merchantman, unaware that its cargo was ammunition. First Lieutenant Salmon was checking the temperature in *Arrow*'s magazine when the merchantman exploded, sending itself to the deep, killing 36 of the destroyer's company and wounding all but 20 of the rest.

As he recovered consciousness in total silence and pitch dark (according to the dispassionate account he wrote years later) Salmon's lungs were filled with smoke and his head was bleeding profusely; he was uncertain whether he had died or had merely fallen from his bunk.Rising uncertainly, he kicked a bucket, which indicated that he was not in his cabin, and sat down again.

Taking comfort from the beads he wore around his neck like many Roman Catholic sailors, Salmon had started to recite the rosary when he felt a direct, though unspoken, command to get up. Only aware that it would have been discourteous to refuse, he followed the unknown presence up a ladder to the seamen's mess decks, then upwards by unrecognised hand and footholds until he reached blue sky. At that moment his invisible guide left – to his regret.

Salmon thought afterwards that he had come up through the ammunition hatch of the A gun, which had been blown overboard. He only knew that he had dived from the abandoned ship, and on being picked up had fallen into a 19-hour coma.

The son of a colonel and the grandson of Admiral of the Fleet Sir Nowell Salmon who won the VC during the Indian Mutiny, Christopher Nowell Salmon was born on February 3 1920 and brought up in Winchester – a few streets away from the future

Archbishop of Liverpool, Derek Worlock. He was educated at Dartmouth, where he was known as "Sleepy", and appointed a term cadet captain.

In 1938, young Christopher joined the battleship *Nelson* as a midshipman, serving in the North Sea, the Atlantic and in Malta convoys. After the *Arrow* explosion, he was in the light cruiser *Dauntless*, the cruiser *Chevron* (which was building at Linthouse) and in the landing craft *Sansovino* and *Silvio*.

After the war Salmon entered the Downside novitiate, taking the name Martin in religion. He was ordained priest in 1954 and read History at Christ's College, Cambridge, before settling down as a medieval history teacher and housemaster. Ever the efficient naval officer (who kept his grandfather's VC in his cell) he liked to begin his lessons with a five-minute test in which the boys made notes for full essays.

This enabled him to get even the most unpromising candidates through the two-year A-level syllabus in one year. As a housemaster, he was told at first that he was not beating hard enough, but he was soon running his house with firm discipline, leavened by a humorous awareness of how the clearest commands can go awry.

These tasks, however, did not prevent Dom Martin from maintaining a widespread correspondence on spiritual matters – with, among others, Siegfried Sassoon and Lord Hailsham, a close friend of his brother Hugo Salmon who was killed in the desert – as well as a vigorous apostolate through sport. Such was his dedication to the Colts cricket team, which he ran, that he once stood in the middle of his precious pitch to shoo away with an umbrella an aircraft which was attempting to land, and clipped a tree in making its escape. The hapless general on board had to land elsewhere and be driven to the school for his inspection of the Corps.

Dom Martin also organised numerous cricket and golfing fixtures during the holidays. The latter was such a passion that he once delayed his escape from a car whose engine had blown up to recover his clubs. On another occasion, when a bishop expressed unease about what he should say if his flock discovered that he was playing golf, Dom Martin replied: "My Lord, you are only on a course with handicapped priests."

BRIGADIER
ROY SMITH-HILL

Brigadier Roy Smith-Hill (who died on August 4 1996, aged 99) was the last surviving officer of the disgraced 6th Battalion Royal Marine Light Infantry, which served in Russia in 1919.

The seeds of potential unrest in the battalion were already there when it was formed in the summer of 1919, ostensibly to police the plebiscite being held in Schleswig-Holstein. Instead, the battalion was sent at short notice to Murmansk to join the Allied forces aiding the White Russians against the Bolsheviks. It included men who had already served for some time in France and were disgruntled by the unequal form of demobilisation being practised at home. There were also many young raw recruits who had expected to come home after the plebiscite, and a number of recently released PoWs who had just returned from Germany and had had no leave.

The battalion as a whole knew little and cared less about the war in Russia, and the situation was exacerbated by a vacillating British government, unable to make up its mind on policy. The men serving in the field were never sure whether they were formally at war or not. Eventually it was decided that the 6th Battalion would assist in holding the Lake Onega region, some 500 miles south of Murmansk, until the White Russians had been trained to defend the area themselves. But, from the moment the battalion arrived by train from Murmansk to join other already restive American, Italian and Finnish units, everything went wrong.

In the first engagement, on June 24, one company fired on another in an unfortunate "blue on blue" incident. Two other companies were ambushed by the Bolsheviks and severely mauled. An attack on a village held by the Bolsheviks was repulsed with losses. When Smith-Hill's company attacked the same village a week later, their Russian guide led them into a vulnerable position and then vanished. This left them exposed to machine-gun fire which caused several casualties, including the company's senior officers. Smith-Hill, who found himself in command, was ordered to retire.

This setback was too much for men who were already demoralised. Next morning, when Smith-Hill's company was ordered to attack the village again, they refused to obey their platoon commanders and retired to a friendly village nearby. Smith-Hill went after them and told them that if they did not fall in they would be court-martialled.

In the event, courts martial of 93 men of the battalion were held, but the proceedings and results have still not been released. Thirteen were sentenced to death; others received sentences of up to five years' hard labour. The death sentences were later commuted and the other sentences reviewed; all were reduced after angry questions in Parliament and a furore in the press.

The battalion continued to serve in the region until all British troops were withdrawn in 1919. Since then, there has never been another 6th Battalion.

Although Smith-Hill had behaved entirely correctly, and had done his duty in trying to maintain discipline, his CO later told him that he had incurred the displeasure of the Lords of the Admiralty. His request for a court martial was refused. He was, though, also told that Their Lordships' displeasure was not such a bad thing for a young officer since it meant he had been noticed. Certainly, it had no ill effect on his 35-year career in the Royal Marines.

Philip Royal Smith-Hill was born on May 5 1897 and educated at St Bees, Seascale. He joined the Royal Marines as a probationary subaltern in 1915 and during the First World War served in the battleships *Vanguard* and *Erin* in the Grand Fleet.

In the Chanak crisis of 1922, when British and Turkish armies faced each other across the Dardanelles, once again on the brink of war, Smith-Hill was serving in the light cruiser *Carysfort* and, unusually for a marine officer, regularly kept watch on the bridge at sea.

From 1924 to 1926 he served on the battlecruiser *Hood* as captain of Royal Marines and in charge of the 4-inch anti-aircraft gun batteries. After a two-year course at the Army Staff College, Camberley, Smith-Hill was seconded to the Army for four years, first on the staff at HQ Southern Command, and then as brigade major of the Devon and Cornwall Light Infantry Brigade (TA).

During the Second World War, Smith-Hill served on both naval and army staffs in Combined Operations. He was GSO1 to General Irwin for the ill-fated attack on Dakar in September 1940. For the assault on Algiers (Operation Torch) in November 1942, he was Staff Officer Assault, Planning, to the naval commander Admiral Burroughs. In July 1943 he was Staff Officer Liaison to the naval and military forces for the invasion of Sicily, then was on the staff of the Director of Combined Operations for the D-Day landings; later he was Brigadier General Staff to the Commandant General, RM, at the Admiralty.

Smith-Hill was appointed CBE in 1946.After the war he commanded the Infantry Training Centre at Lympstone, the RM School of Music and the RM depot at Deal.

He retired in 1950 and returned to his native Cumberland, where he was for four years county cadet commander. He became a Deputy Lieutenant for Cumberland in 1954, and was Area Civil Defence Officer of West Cumberland from 1957 to 1963.

He married Sybil Knight, who died in 1974.They had two sons and two daughters.

COMMANDER
DOUGLAS CRAVEN

Commander Douglas Craven (who died in Victoria, British Columbia, on August 15 1996, aged 94) was the senior British naval officer in Hong Kong when the colony was regained from the Japanese in 1945.

Craven had been the Naval Staff Officer (Operations) in Hong Kong before the Second World War, and became a prisoner of war when the colony was captured by the Japanese on Christmas Day 1941. As an officer, Craven was singled out for especially severe treatment by the Japanese, and he suffered years of beatings, malnutrition and disease. But his spirit never faltered, and he maintained his resistance to the Japanese to the end.

On the day Japan surrendered, August 14 1945, he and three colleagues were in Canton City jail, in the second year of five-year sentences on charges of espionage against the Japanese. The day after VJ Day, Craven was summoned to a meeting with the Commander-in-Chief of the Japanese Army in Southern China. But first he demanded, and received, new clothing to replace his prison rags.

He was told by the general that the Emperor had graciously granted an "armistice" to the Allies, "now that they had admitted their defeat by Japan". Not deceived by this claptrap, Craven returned to Hong Kong to become the naval member on the Executive Council set up to administer the colony by Franklin Gimson, who had been Colonial Secretary before the war, and who had just been released from internment. Craven had heard that Chiang Kai-shek intended to absorb Hong Kong into China, and so was surprised by the leisurely attitude of the British government towards the recovery of the colony.

A British naval task force under Rear-Admiral Cecil Harcourt, flying his flag in the aircraft carrier *Indomitable*, did not arrive off Hong Kong until August 29. A signal was sent to the Japanese commander in Hong Kong, informing him that a British aircraft would land at Kai Tak airfield at a certain time, and a Japanese officer must be ready to be flown back to *Indomitable* to receive orders about the British entry into the harbour. At first, the Japanese pretended that they had no powers to negotiate, but Gimson insisted, and asked Craven to be his representative. Craven was flown out to *Indomitable* with a Japanese naval officer who was wearing a samurai sword, and carrying charts showing the positions of Japanese minefields.

Several of *Indomitable*'s officers knew Craven from pre-war days, when he had been a brilliant amateur jockey, and they were as delighted to see him, pale and drawn as he was, among them again. Also on board was Captain Anthony Kimmins, Craven's Osborne and Dartmouth term-mate, who was Chief of Naval Information, British Pacific Fleet. Kimmins recalled that Craven had had difficulty in the past keeping his weight down, "but as he stepped out on to the flight deck of the *Indomitable*, almost straight from a long stretch of solitary confinement, he could have ridden as bottom weight anywhere. But in spite of being so weak, he braced his shoulders and saluted just as smartly as if he had been on parade at the gunnery school.

"Here was the moment he must have prayed for again and again during those interminable minutes, days, nights, weeks, months and years, but he never said a word of all that. He was back on the job, a staff officer with important information regarding future events. As I followed those two match-sticks of legs up the ladder to the admiral's sea cabin, there was something about the polish which he had given to what was left of his shoes that made me feel proud to belong to the same Service."

Craven recalled that Harcourt gave him a less than cordial reception: "He asked what the hell was I doing there?" Craven explained that, though he had no uniform worthy of the name, he was, indeed, Commodore in charge in Hong Kong. He said that the two million Chinese in the colony desperately needed rice, and there was a grave shortage of fuel. He also warned of Japanese suicide motor boats at Lamma Island.

Craven was flown back to Kai Tak the next day and had the pleasure of telling the senior Japanese naval officer that he was to move all his officers and ratings out of the dockyard in four hours. The Japanese obeyed, albeit with bad grace.

Harcourt shifted his flag to the cruiser *Swiftsure* and entered Hong Kong harbour at midday on August 30. The reoccupation was completed on September 1. Craven was appointed OBE for his bravery and endurance as a PoW.

Douglas Hugh Stuart Craven was born on November 21 1901 and joined the Navy as a cadet in 1915. He served in the battleship *Iron Duke* and the destroyer *Whitehall*, and was one of the young officers the Admiralty sent to Cambridge University in 1920. He specialised in navigation, serving in the cruisers *Colombo* and *Manchester* and was later Master of the

Fleet Mediterranean, in the battlecruiser *Hood*, and the battleships *Barham* and *Royal Oak*.

Craven rode his first winner when he was only 17. Riding in Gibraltar, Malta, Colombo and in Hong Kong, he won 99 races from 400 starts. Some of his favourite tack, including a race saddle weighing only a pound and a half, and a pigskin saddle with the names of all his winners written on it in Indian ink, were "lost by enemy action" in Hong Kong, and he never rode again.

After the war, when the Admiralty insisted he go to sea again, Craven resigned and emigrated with his family to Canada. He joined the Royal Canadian Naval Reserve and taught navigation at Royal Roads Military College. He was also sea training commander at Esquimalt until 1958. He sailed his yacht out of Sidney, British Columbia, until he was well over 80.

Although Craven became a Canadian citizen, he said, "I at no time felt that I was totally immersed in Canadian life", and that he had made no attempt to become fluent in the Canadian language. "PS I hate to be called Doug. Please don't do it."

Craven married, first, Avis Cox, who predeceased him. They had a son, who joined the Royal Canadian Navy, and a daughter. He married, secondly, Diana Lee.

COMMANDER
"RICHIE" McCOWEN

Commander "Richie" McCowen (who died on September 5 1996, aged 88) was one of the most distinguished members of that company of pre-war sportsmen and yachtsmen whose members abandoned their peacetime careers to join the RNVR on the outbreak of war.

McCowen served in Coastal Forces and won the DSO as senior officer of the 53rd Motor Torpedo Boat Flotilla when, in MTB693, he led an attack on an enemy convoy at the entrance to the Dutch harbour of Ijmuiden on the night of March 6 1944.

Other MTBs had operated off Ijmuiden the night before, but the enemy was still caught by surprise as McCowen's six MTBs slipped undetected between patrols and the convoy itself. McCowen sighted two merchant ships and detached two of his MTBs to sink them, while he led the rest to within 500 yards of the harbour breakwaters. Nearest to him was an unsuspecting gun coaster, with other ships in company. When he was almost on top of the enemy, McCowen turned broadside-on and opened a rapid fire with every gun.

"We held the stage for perhaps 15 seconds," McCowen wrote in his report, "and then the enemy opened a heavy and sometimes accurate, but mostly wild, fire on the unit from all directions, with the exception of the coaster, which was heavily hit by our initial burst." Having sunk five enemy ships without serious damage to his MTBs, McCowen withdrew southwards, leaving behind a confused situation, with enemy ships firing on each other. "It was most gratifying to see that the standard of shooting had improved considerably," he said. "Both sides seemed to be scoring a satisfactory number of hits."

McCowen's flotilla took part in the Normandy landings in June 1944, protecting the flanks from attacks by German E-boats. On the night of June 10, McCowen had Stanley Maxted of the BBC embarked when MTB693 lay in wait for E-boats off Cherbourg. In a violent action, McCowen cut off one E-boat, set it on fire and sank it, picking up six survivors. Maxted later described in his "Into Battle" broadcast how tenderly one of 693's gunners, a Scot, looked after an injured German stoker whom he had been doing his utmost to kill only minutes earlier.

Days later, just before the fall of Cherbourg, MTBs lay offshore, waiting for the German evacuation convoys. McCowen led three of them to intercept and sink what was probably the last vessel to try to escape. McCowen was awarded the DSC.

In October 1944, McCowen went to America with Captain Anthony Kimmins, the Navy's own war correspondent, for a six-week tour of factories and shipyards, giving lectures on Coastal Forces' achievements. Promoted commander in 1945, McCowen took command of HMS Beehive, the Coastal Forces base at Felixstowe where, on May 13 1945, he accepted the surrender of Rear-Admiral Karl Bruening, the German E-boat commander in Holland.

Donald Henry Ewan McCowen was born on February 26 1908, at Tralee, Co Kerry, into a local family, who owned businesses, a railway and extensive land. It was on their private beach in Tralee Bay that Roger Casement landed from a German U-boat in

April 1916. The McCowens' motor car, the only one in the area, was used to take him from Tralee police station to Limerick on his journey to the gallows.

McCowen went to Cheltenham College and then Pembroke College, Cambridge, where he was nicknamed "Richie" because, for an undergraduate, he was rich. He rowed in the college eight that won the Head of the River in 1931 and 1932, and in the Cambridge boat that beat Oxford in the 1932 Boat Race. He then took part in the Los Angeles Olympics.

In 1935, McCowen became a Lloyd's underwriter and founded the shipping firm of McCowen & Grosz. As a former leader of the University Air Squadron at Cambridge, he tried to join the RAF in 1938 but was turned down as too old for active service, and offered only an instructor's post; he joined the RNVR instead.

McCowen commanded the trawler *British Honduras* and then served at HMS Boscawen, the anti-submarine and minesweeping base at Portland, and at HMS Racer, at Larne, Co Antrim. Late in 1941, he went to HMS Skirmisher, the Coastal Forces base at Milford Haven, Pembrokeshire.

While McCowen was serving in the Navy, his partner Grosz kept the firm going, despite several war losses, including the MV *Derrymore*, sunk on February 13 1942 by the Japanese U-boat I-25, en route from Singapore to Batavia.

After the war, McCowen & Grosz converted two "Woolworth" aircraft carriers into merchantmen by cutting off their flight decks, but McCowen sold his interest in the firm in the early 1950s and became a farmer, breeding pedigree Hereford cattle and Dorset

Down sheep. He was a very good golfer (playing regularly for Old Cheltonians in the Halford Hewitt), and a keen yachtsman. He was also Commodore of the Royal Corinthian Yacht Club.

He skied until he was 65, when he took up langlaufing and curling. He once captained his hotel ski team, the Suvretta Corinthians, when they beat the Swiss National B team (who, over-confident, had had too good a lunch). Latterly, "Richie" McCowen lived in Bermuda.

He married, in 1934, Kitty Wilson; they had four sons and two daughters.

COMMANDER
TONY LAW

Commander Tony Law (who died on October 15 1996, aged 80) was the Canadian counterpart of Sir Peter Scott, combining gallant service in Coastal Forces during the Second World War with a long and distinguished career as an artist.

Charles Anthony Law was born on October 15 1916 in London, the son of a member of the Royal Canadian Regiment. He was educated at Upper Canada College, Toronto, and Lisgar Collegiate, Ottawa. He began to study painting after seeing an exhibition of the Group of Seven, which celebrated Canada's rugged landscape, and held his first show aged 21.

On being turned down by the Royal Canadian Naval Volunteer Reserve because there were no openings, he joined the Army, and was a captain commanding an ordnance ammunition company when war broke out. In a chance conversation with a naval officer on a skiing holiday in January 1940,Law learned that the Navy was looking for young officers to serve on loan to the Royal Navy in motor torpedo boats,and that he could transfer to the RCNVR if he wished. He came to England as an acting sub-lieutenant and went to HMS King Alfred, the RNVR training establishment at Hove.

After North Atlantic patrols in the armed merchant cruiser *Wolfe*, he joined Motor Gunboat 53 as first lieutenant in March 1941. His first command, MTB48, was based at Dover when, on February 12 1942, it was reported that the German battlecruisers *Scharnhorst* and *Gneisenau*, with the cruiser *Prinz Eugen*, were coming up the Channel, on their way from Brest back to Germany, strongly escorted by six destroyers and 24 E-boats, with a swarm of fighters overhead.

Five MTBs sailed at once to intercept and, although slower than all their opponents, achieved an attacking position on the enemy's bow. But, as Law said,"The E-boats kept close station, preventing any attempt to break through the screen.We were forced to fire from about 4,000 yards or more, a far from ideal range for us. But there was nothing for it but to try, so we fired away gamely, loosing the torpedoes from all five boats."

They scored no hits, and MTB48 was then chased close to the English coast by a German destroyer which Law only managed to shake off by steering straight for the Goodwin Sands. He was mentioned in despatches.

Law went back to Canada on leave in the summer

of 1942 and married a fellow artist, Jane Brumm Shaw, whom he had met when she was an art student five years earlier. He returned in the autumn to take command of MTB629, operating from Yarmouth. Again he was mentioned in despatches, after 629's part in a ferocious night engagement on October 24 1943, off Smith's Knoll in the North Sea, when an East Coast convoy was attacked by 32 German E-boats.

Early in 1944, Law had a new command, MTB459, and an appointment as senior officer, 29th MTB Flotilla, one of two flotillas of eight boats manned entirely by Canadians. The 29th went up to Holyhead to train for Operation Neptune, the naval element of D-Day. There, Law met Peter Scott, and the two became friends for life. Together they painted a mural on the walls of HMS Bee, the Coastal Forces base.

For the D-Day landings, the 29th's task was to protect the eastern flank of the invasion force against attacks by German E-boats and minelayers. They sank an enemy ship on that first night of June 6 1944, and then had one of the most hectic periods of operations ever experienced by Coastal Forces.

They were out almost every night, and met the enemy nearly every time. After two months of innumerable close-range engagements, 37 per cent of their personnel had been killed or wounded, and they had lost three boats, including Law's own which was hit in the engine-room by a shell that killed two men.

Law lost more than a stone in weight, but remained so imperturbable under fire that his sailors had the utmost confidence in him. "He was a quiet man," said one of his gunners, "but out there at night it seemed he'd put on another overcoat, and did the things that make people heroes. We loved him." Law was awarded the DSC.

He had another command, MTB486, and led the 29th off the Dutch coast in the winter of 1944. The following February, the 29th Flotilla was based at Ostend. On the 14th, Law was returning from taking 486 to Felixstowe for a new radar set, when he heard dreadful news. "The words fell upon me like a sentence of death," he said. "I found myself breathing hard, with every muscle in my body taut, and my throat choked with the horrible hurt."

While maintenance work was being carried out on the MTBs' engines at Ostend, quantities of petrol had been allowed to spill into the harbour, where a random spark ignited it. There was a huge fire, and the port was rocked by violent explosions for some minutes, as fuel in the MTBs' tanks caught fire, and ammunition and torpedoes "cooked off". Seven British and five Canadian MTBs were destroyed, with the loss of 64 lives, 26 from the 29th Flotilla, with another 65 wounded. It was the worst disaster in Coastal Forces history; it was also the end of the 29th Flotilla.

Law, who was known as the "painting commander", sketched and painted throughout his naval service. His work could show in a few lines the swish of a torpedo boat but also capture the quiet concentration of crews as they fended off mines while distant searchlights lit up the night sky. Towards the end of the war he became an official war artist. He wrote the 29th MTB Flotilla's history, *White Plumes Astern*, which was published with his own contemporary drawings in 1989.

In 1946 Law transferred to the RCN, and served in

the training cruiser *Uganda*, the carrier *Magnificent* and the icebreaker *Labrador*, which led him to do many of his finest paintings of the Arctic. He commanded the frigate *Antigonish*, the destroyer *Sioux* and the maintenance ship *Cape Scott*, and had appointments in Ottawa and Washington DC. He was awarded the Canadian Decoration in 1960, and retired in 1966.

Law then became artist-in-residence at St Mary's University, Halifax, and founded its art gallery, where he was the first curator. He also played a leading part in founding the Art Gallery of Nova Scotia.

His landscape work is represented in many galleries and museums, in the official war artists' collection, and (as he much preferred) in homes across Canada. In May 1996, St Mary's Gallery mounted a retrospective exhibition of his and his wife's work, to celebrate "Sixty Years of Painting in Nature". Shortly before he died, Law told a friend: "I don't need a tombstone. It's all on the walls."

Anthony Law was always something of an enigma. One naval officer, who served with him after the war, said:"I could never somehow equate this soft-spoken introspective man with the hero of those blazing, suicidal point-blank MTB battles."

His wife survived him.

ADMIRAL
SIR ANTHONY GRIFFIN

Admiral Sir Anthony Griffin (who died on October 16 1996, aged 75) proved himself as skilful in Whitehall as at sea. His main service to the Royal Navy, though he himself might perhaps have demurred at the suggestion, came in 1966 after Denis Healey, the Defence Secretary, cancelled the building of the giant aircraft carrier, CVA01.

The Navy had long planned for the project and lobbied hard for it against intense opposition from the RAF. Its demise prompted mass Navy Board resignations. Griffin was a newly promoted rear-admiral, only a few weeks into his appointment as Naval Secretary, when the resignations of the First, Second, Third, Fourth and Fifth Sea Lords, the Vice-Chief of Naval Staff and the Deputy Chief of Naval Staff, arrived on his desk.

Griffin had to work out the implications of resignations on such a large scale, which not only involved restructuring the appointments of all flag officers but reached far down into the captains' list. He pointed out that the inevitable result would be that he, Griffin, would be promoted First Sea Lord in 1969. "All agreed," he said, "that this would be an unacceptable blow to the Royal Navy." In the event only the First Sea Lord, Admiral Sir David Luce, took early retirement.

The new First Sea Lord, Admiral Sir Varyl Begg, appointed a working party to consider a revised structure for the Fleet, and to report in six months. Griffin was a member. The working party was unanimous that it was vital for the Navy to retain its own air power. Griffin had a personal reason to know this:his uncle,Admiral SirTom Phillips, was lost when flying his flag in the battleship *Prince of Wales* after she and the battlecruiser *Repulse*, lacking air cover, were sunk by Japanese aircraft in the South China Sea in 1941.

The working party recommended a large "command ship", capable of operating helicopters and V/STOL aircraft. Knowing that in the political climate of the time, the very mention of the words "aircraft carrier" would alarm Whitehall and Westminster, Griffin suggested the ship be called a "through-deck cruiser". Begg, a gunnery officer of the old school, rejected the proposal out of hand; he accused the working party of lack of professional integrity, and brutally ended the career of its chairman, an officer of exceptional ability.

However, the concept of the command ship did survive, and eventually arrived in the fleet in the shape of the Invincible class,although the case for one of the working party's main recommendations, the need for Airborne Early Warning, was lost. For this, as Griffin said, "*Sheffield* paid the price off the Falklands in 1982."

Anthony Templer Frederick Griffith Griffin was born on November 20 1920 and went to Dartmouth as a cadet in 1934. His first ship was the cruiser *Gloucester* in which he narrowly escaped with his life when he was near the captain who was killed on the bridge by a direct hit from an Italian bomber; his calmness, at 19, in taking control of the ship until a more senior officer could assume command, greatly impressed the chief yeoman of signals who was present.

In 1941 Griffin, as a sub-lieutenant on his way to join the destroyer *Hereward*, was a passenger in the liner SS *Britannia* when she was sunk off Freetown, Sierra Leone, by the German commerce raider *Thor*. Griffin's lifeboat had 57 survivors – women, priests, lascars,civilians and a naval draft.Subsisting on a daily ration of half a cup of water and one and a half biscuits spread with condensed milk, they were picked up after three days, and taken to Montevideo. "Luckily," Griffin said, "the government was on Easter hols, and we weren't interned."

He then joined the destroyer *Fury* as navigating officer, taking part in the Pedestal convoy to Malta in August 1942 and in several Arctic convoys, including the ill-fated PQ17 in July 1942.He was mentioned in despatches.

In 1943 Griffin was appointed first lieutenant of the destroyer *Talybont*, which picked up survivors from the cruiser *Charybdis* and the destroyer *Limbourne*, sunk by German destroyers in the disastrous Operation Tunnel off the north coast of France. The following year he specialised in navigation, and joined the carrier *Implacable* as "2nd N" for operations off Norway. He then went to the East Indies Fleet as navigator of the escort carrier *Empress* and was mentioned in despatches a second time after carrying out a survey of the Malay peninsula, in preparation for the Zipper landings in September 1945.

Griffin was already marked out as a high-flier. He went to HMS Dryad, the navigation school, in 1946, and served as a navigation and direction officer until 1952, when he was appointed Application Commander at the Admiralty Signal and Radar

Establishment, developing new types of shipborne radar.

His next appointment was as executive officer of the aircraft carrier *Eagle*. She was a somewhat accident-prone vessel, and her officers and ship's company greatly benefited from Griffin's calm leadership over two years which included Operation Musketeer, the Anglo-French action to regain the Suez Canal.

Deservedly promoted out of the ship, Griffin spent two years at the Admiralty, and then in 1959 he and his wife went to Malta for "a splendid married accompanied job, our first", as Captain, Inshore Flotilla, in command of the depot ship Woodbridge Haven. But within a month Woo Ha, as she was known, was ordered to Singapore because of trouble in Laos. "We arrived to find there was no job, no base and no one at all pleased to see us. We happily made our own base and explored Thailand, Borneo and Vietnam, dealing with some interesting piracy and sweeping up the odd Japanese mine."

Griffin was now on the classical path to high rank, his appointments alternating between Admiralty and sea: Deputy Director of Plans; command of the carrier *Ark Royal*; ACNS (Warfare); Flag Officer, second in command, Far East Fleet; and Flag Officer, Plymouth, and Admiral Superintendent, Devonport, jobs that had been combined, he said, "because a predecessor had told the Secretary of State that he was too busy playing polo."

In 1971, Griffin was appointed Controller of the Navy and Third Sea Lord, responsible for the Navy's ships and *matériel*. He was five years in the post, and the Navy as it appears today, with its mix of small carriers, anti-submarine and anti-air-warfare frigates, and nuclear submarines, is very largely the result of his handiwork. Griffin was appointed CB in 1967, promoted to KCB in 1971 and to GCB in 1975, when he retired from the Navy to become chairman-designate of British Shipbuilders. In three years, he reduced the losses due to industrial disputes to the lowest on record.

As a leader Tony Griffin had a priceless talent of inspiring lasting loyalty. On the tumultuous day of the CVA01 resignations in the Admiralty, Griffin found the officer who had been secretary to his predecessor clearing his desk prior to what he thought was an inevitable move to another job. Griffin asked if he would mind staying for another 24 hours "until the dust settled". Those 24 hours became 10 years and developed into a warm and lasting friendship.

Griffin was a co-founder of the British Maritime League and British Maritime Charitable Foundation. He was chairman of the Governors of Wellington College from 1980 to 1990, president of the Royal Institution of Naval Architects from 1984 to 1986, and Vice-Admiral of the United Kingdom in 1988.

In his 70th year, he was presented with a Royal Humane Society Award for Bravery for diving into the Thames, near Richmond Bridge, after hearing cries for help. He spent 30 minutes in the river trying to save a young Jamaican who disappeared and drowned. Griffin himself was rescued by a policeman in a dinghy and taken to hospital suffering from exposure.

Latterly he was much involved in the design of an engine which used water as fuel, converting his garage into a labyrinth of tubes, bubbling vats of water and electric wires. He believed himself to be on the verge of a breakthrough.

He married in 1943 Rosemary Hickling, daughter of a Captain RN, who was then a Leading Wren plotter in Devonport. They had two sons, one of whom followed his father into the Navy, and a daughter.

———————

COMMANDER "RAGS" BUTLER

Commander "Rags" Butler (who died on October 23 1996, aged 75) won the DSC as a 19-year-old midshipman RNR in the armed merchant cruiser *Jervis Bay* in 1940.

On the afternoon of November 5 *Jervis Bay*, commanded by Captain Fogarty Fegen, was in the mid-Atlantic as sole escort of the 37-ship convoy HX84, homeward bound from Halifax, Nova Scotia, when the smoke and masts of a strange ship were sighted on the horizon to the north-east. The stranger proved to be the German commerce-raiding pocket-battleship *Admiral Scheer*, which rapidly came over the horizon, closed the convoy and opened fire.

Jervis Bay had seven 6-inch guns, made in the reign of Queen Victoria, with a problematical range of about 10,000 yards, and it was very unlikely that she would ever get within range of the enemy. Nevertheless, Fegen hauled out of line and headed straight for *Scheer*, while the convoy scattered under cover of smoke.

One eye-witness said later: "I can only describe the

way the *Jervis Bay* engaged that ship as magnificent.
She just turned away as though she was protecting a
brood of little chickens from a cat coming over the
fence."

It was not a fight, but a massacre. *Scheer*, whose
main armament was six 11-inch guns with a range of
over 17 miles, hit *Jervis Bay* with her third salvo,
setting the forward bridge on fire and shattering
Fegen's right arm. Butler's action station was on the
after bridge, where he directed the after guns with a
Dumaresq, a primitive gunnery instrument which
gave the rate of change of the target's range and the
deflection.

Butler left a vivid account of the scene when the
after bridge was hit:"There was a blinding flash and a
ripping rending sound like a thousand gongs. The
man beside me literally burst into pieces. I felt my
face warm and wet and looking down saw my hands
and my coat red with blood, and stuck on it some
utterly revolting pieces of flesh and gristle."

Jervis Bay was hit repeatedly on her superstructure.
Her hull was holed in several places, and major fires
started down below. But her guns continued to fire
for some time. Her after battle ensign was shot away
and, in an episode of Elizabethan drama, Butler
helped a sailor climb the flagstaff and nail another
ensign in place.

Captain Fegen came aft and gave the order
"Abandon ship", telling Butler to make sure that
everybody aft heard it. Butler remembered how "his
arm, shattered from just below the shoulder to the
forearm, was cranked slightly across his body. The
blood running down the arm glistened, showing red
where it ran over the four gold stripes on his sleeve."

Fegen then went back to the remains of the forward bridge. "We did not see him again," said Butler.

Jervis Bay did not sink until almost 8pm, nearly three hours after *Scheer* first attacked. This precious delay undoubtedly saved the convoy from annihilation, as *Scheer* could only round up and sink five ships. One lifeboat and two rafts got away from *Jervis Bay*. Butler swam to a raft and found himself the only officer in it. The Swedish *Stureholm*, which was in the convoy, returned in the early hours of November 6 to look for survivors, and picked up 68 of *Jervis Bay's* people, three of them already dead. One hundred and ninety-one officers and men, including Fegen, were lost.

When the survivors reached safety and told their experience, the story of *Jervis Bay's* self-sacrifice thrilled the free world. King George VI immediately awarded Fegen a posthumous VC.

Ronald Alfred Gardyne Butler, known as "Rags", was born on June 28 1921 and went to Pangbourne Nautical College, joining the RNR as a midshipman in 1939.

After *Jervis Bay*, Butler served in the destroyers *Boadicea* and *Active* and then, in 1942, joined the destroyer *Intrepid* as gunnery officer. *Intrepid* took part in Arctic convoys, the Pedestal convoy, and the Sicily and Salerno landings. Late in 1943, she was involved in a disastrous campaign in the Dodecanese, when the lessons of air power at sea, so painfully taught off Norway and Crete, were ignored. *Intrepid* was one of several ships lost; after being bombed by the Luftwaffe in Leros harbour, she capsized on September 27.

Butler became a prisoner of war, but escaped and stole a motor launch, only to be recaptured when it was sunk. He escaped again, stole another launch and was again recaptured. He succeeded at the third attempt, in another stolen ship, and reached Beirut, where he caught a plane for Cairo, which crashed on landing.

He accepted a year's accelerated seniority in lieu of a Bar to his DSC, and, in 1944, was appointed gunnery officer in the fast minelayer *Apollo*, taking part in the Normandy landings. Subsequently he went on to serve in the British Pacific Fleet.

After the war Butler, having accepted a regular commission in the Royal Navy, took part in trials in the ex-German destroyer Z–38 (recommissioned and renamed *Nonsuch*); served as flag lieutenant in HMS Tamar in Hong Kong, and as new entry training officer at Portsmouth; and then joined the staff of Simonstown dockyard, South Africa.

In 1965, he laid a wreath on the war memorial at St John's, Newfoundland, to mark the 25th anniversary of the encounter with *Admiral Scheer*. His last job before retiring in 1967 was as an inspecting officer in the Naval Ordnance Department. He then worked on oil rigs in Australia and in the Pacific for Burmah Oil Company.

Butler had two daughters by his first marriage, which was dissolved, and one daughter by his second.

CHIEF PETTY OFFICER
"LOFTY" ROGERS

Chief Petty Officer "Lofty" Rogers (who died on January 17 1997, aged 86) was a member of the ship's company of *Li Wo*, which fought a gallant battle against a vastly superior Japanese force in the Java Sea in 1942.

Owned by the Indo-China Steam Navigation Company, *Li Wo* was a 700-ton, coal-burning, flat-bottomed, shallow-draught passenger steamship, built in 1938 for service on the upper Yangtse. She was requisitioned by the Admiralty in December 1941, after the outbreak of war against Japan, and commissioned under the White Ensign as an auxiliary patrol vessel.

Armed with one old 4-inch gun, two machine guns and a depth charge thrower, she was commanded by her peacetime captain, Tam Wilkinson, who was given the rank of temporary lieutenant, RNR. On Friday February 13 1942, two days before the fall of Singapore, *Li Wo* was ordered to Batavia in Java, and sailed from Singapore that day. She had embarked 84 officers and men, including regular RN ratings such as Rogers (whose own ship, the battlecruiser *Repulse*, had been sunk) as well as men from army and RAF units, and one civilian. They had on board 13 rounds of 4-inch ammunition, and some rounds for the machine guns.

By the afternoon of February 14, when *Li Wo* was in the Java Sea, she had survived four air attacks, one of them by 52 Japanese aircraft, and had been considerably damaged. Two Japanese convoys were sighted, escorted by Japanese warships, including a heavy cruiser and some destroyers. These were the advance guard of the Japanese invasion fleet, heading for Sumatra.

Wilkinson had never had a day's naval training in his life, but he proved to be a natural leader. When the ships had been identified as Japanese, he called his scratch ship's company together and told them, in the presence of the enemy, that rather than try to escape he had decided to engage the convoy and fight to the last, hoping at least to inflict some damage. As recorded later in Wilkinson's citation, in words worthy of Hakluyt, this "drew resolute support from the whole ship's company".

At first, the Japanese could not believe what was happening – that a small, grubby-looking steamer, all alone and belching clouds of black smoke, was coming out to fight them. This allowed *Li Wo* to close with the nearest Japanese ship (a large transport) and open fire. The crew of the 4-inch gun, captained by Rogers, had never exercised together before, but their shooting was splendid. By the time their 13 rounds had been expended, they had reduced the enemy's superstructure to wreckage and set it on fire.

"The damaged ship was now approaching the *Li Wo* still firing," Rogers recalled. "We had expended all our 4-inch ammunition, so the CO decided to ram her. We hit her at top speed amidships and became interlocked, our bows being buckled back – we were now really at close quarters."

A furious point-blank gun duel now began, with one of *Li Wo*'s machine guns, manned by an RAF flight sergeant, being particularly accurate. Wilkinson went astern to disengage, and *Li Wo* at once came under fire from the Japanese warships. With her twin rudders, *Li Wo* was extremely manoeuvrable, despite her buckled bows, and Wilkinson was a superb ship handler.

Dodging and jinking, he kept her in action against the Japanese heavy cruiser for more than an hour. But the end was inevitable. *Li Wo* was hit several times and Wilkinson ordered "Abandon ship". He and his scratch ship's company had fought a naval action in the highest traditions of the service.

"The last sight I had of the *Li Wo*," Rogers said, "as she started on her last voyage to the bottom was something I shall never forget – her ensigns were still flying and the captain was standing on the bridge; although listing to port, she was still under way. Then, suddenly, she disappeared."

The Japanese fired on *Li Wo*'s people in the water, and only 10 of them were eventually captured. Rogers was one of them, but not Wilkinson. Only some of the 10 survived the horrors of Japanese PoW camps to come safe home in 1945.

When the survivors told their story, Wilkinson was posthumously mentioned in despatches, and then, a year later awarded a posthumous Victoria Cross. There were 12 other awards to *Li Wo*'s officers and ship's company, including Rogers, who was mentioned in despatches.

Charles Halma Rogers was born on June 20 1910 into a naval family. His great-great-grandfather served in *Victory* at Trafalgar, and his father was wounded at Jutland in 1916. He joined the training ship *Impregnable* at Devonport as a boy seaman in 1925. Then he qualified as a gunnery rating and served in the battleships *Empress of India*, *Rodney*, *Royal Sovereign* and *Revenge*, and in the destroyers *Whitehall* and

Diamond, before joining *Repulse* in 1939.

His action station in *Repulse* was in the after director tower, operating the range-finder for the after 15-inch guns, and he was one of the last to get away from the ship when she and the battleship *Prince of Wales* were both sunk by Japanese aircraft in the South China Sea on December 10 1941. Rogers was picked up by a destroyer and taken to Singapore where he took part in operations along the west coast of Malaya to recover troops cut off by the Japanese advance. He was mentioned in despatches for the first time.

Rogers left the Navy in 1950 and was for a time a porter at Swindon Technical College. He was a staunch supporter of Swindon Royal Naval Association.

He left a wife, Daisy, and a son.

LIEUTENANT
ANTHONY DANIELL

Lieutenant Anthony Daniell (who died on January 30 1997, aged 79) was one of the Navy's most successful Second World War submarine captains until a tragic "friendly fire" accident in the Mediterranean in 1943 ended his career.

He went out to the Mediterranean late in 1942 to take command of the U-class submarine P43 in the 10th Flotilla. Based in Malta, and strategically placed across the Axis supply routes to North Africa, the 10th fought one of the longest and most effective submarine campaigns of the war. Losses were very high.At one time, the chances of a 10th Flotilla boat surviving were put at no better than even money. But, superbly led by Captain "Shrimp" Simpson,they took a steady toll of supply and troop ships bound for the Afrika Korps, and eventually sank more than 650,000 tons of enemy shipping, having a major influence on the Eighth Army's campaign in the desert.

The 10th often used guns as well as torpedoes. Daniell himself particularly favoured gun actions, not least as morale boosters for his ship's company. In February 1943,P43 sank a German ship off the north African coast which, Daniell recalled,"blew up with a very spectacular Guy Fawkes night display, with lots of noise, plenty of stars going up – quite a satisfactory 'do'. Normally, with an ordinary torpedo attack, the ship's company didn't see anything, hear anything or know what was going on; pretty dull stuff. But in a gun action everybody joined in, as well as getting some fresh air through the boat during the day, a very unusual occurrence."

Later that month, after Churchill decreed that all submarines should have names instead of numbers, P43 became *Unison* (replacing its sailors' unofficial name of *Ulysses*). In July, during Operation Husky, the invasion of Sicily, *Unison* anchored off Cape Passaro, the south-eastern tip of the island, to act as a navigation beacon for ships carrying the assault troops of the 51st Highland Division.While waiting, Daniell watched gliders pitching into the sea only a mile away, but had to make the hard decision not to move out of position to look for survivors in case he misled the incoming convoy.

Unison was supposed to shine an infrared light along the bearing, which the convoy would pick up with suitable receivers. But the weather worsened, and Daniell only sighted the first ships when it was too late to shine the light. "So I strung together as many short Anglo-Saxon words as I could think of," he said, "and got the reply in suitably phrased Scots."

As the campaign in Sicily got under way, the great increase of surface and air traffic across the waters west of Malta made the chances of a "blue on blue" incident, when a British submarine was mistakenly attacked by friendly forces, all the more likely. As a safeguard, submarines returning from the Straits of Messina were routed far to the north of Sicily and then west of known minefields and south to Bizerta, where they would join a Malta-bound convoy.

Unison and another submarine, *Unrivalled*, left Bizerta on August 2 to join a convoy. But the convoy had not been adequately warned about their presence, and *Unison* had no sooner taken up its position as "tail-end Charlie" just before midnight when the nearest ship, an American tanker, took it for a U-boat and opened fire. One shell hit the pressure hull forward, penetrating the torpedo stowage compartment where off-watch sailors were asleep. Miraculously, nobody was hurt. The other shell hit *Unison*'s bridge, exploding on the forward periscope standard.

Daniell and the lookouts were all badly injured. The first lieutenant, John Haward, below in the control room, heard the commotion and went to the bridge ladder, where he saw blood dripping from above, followed by a blood-spattered lookout, who had fallen down the ladder. Haward took command and headed the boat back towards Bizerta, escorted by the Polish destroyer *Slazak*. The doctor on *Slazak* was sent across to *Unison*, but he could do nothing for the officer of the watch, Lieutenant King, RNR, who died of his wounds that night and was buried at sea the next morning. Daniell suffered horrific injuries in his hip, thigh and left leg. He lost four toes, his spine was permanently affected, and pieces of shrapnel in his body were still "surfacing" 50 years later.

Unison had made 14 war patrols and was credited with sinking 18,000 tons of enemy shipping. In September 1943, when he was still in hospital, Daniell was awarded the DSO. He was invalided out of the Navy in 1945.

Anthony Robert Daniell was born on February 23 1917 and went to Dartmouth as a cadet in 1930. His first ship as a midshipman in 1935 was the cruiser *Devonshire* in the Mediterranean. He joined the submarine service in 1938, and in 1939 served as a sub-lieutenant in the minelaying submarine *Porpoise*, whose CO was "Shrimp" Simpson. His next submarine was H50, and in 1940 he joined *Upright* as first lieutenant.

Upright was one of the most successful boats in the 10th Flotilla (although the flotilla did not officially become the 10th until September 1941), and Daniell was awarded the DSC in 1941 after *Upright* sank a 5,000-ton cruiser in a night attack east of Sfax in Tunisia on February 25. Daniell went home late in 1941 to take the submarine COs' qualifying course. His first command in 1942 was the ex–American "Lend Lease" boat P552, which he brought across the Atlantic; next was P216, later renamed *Seadog*.

Daniell looked after his sailors, and they in turn respected and trusted him. Many ship's companies would have been daunted and depressed by what happened in the convoy that night, but *Unison's* took it as the fortune of war. The esprit de corps which he inspired in *Unison* was marvellously well expressed by their coxswain, Petty Officer "Happy" Day, who had both his legs shattered. As he was being lowered over the side on a stretcher, Day exclaimed, "Let's break open a jar of rum and blame the spillage on this shambles!"

Daniell always made light of his disability. He farmed in Suffolk, and was a keen shot and a sailor. He was one of the principal sponsors of *The Fighting Tenth*, the history of the flotilla, written by John Wingate, who himself served in the flotilla. He also initiated a memorial to the officers and men of the 10th in St Paul's Cathedral, Valletta, Malta.

Anthony Daniell married, in 1940, Ann Chamberlain, who died after a riding accident in 1966; they had two sons and two daughters. He married secondly Diana, widow of Admiral Sir William Beloe.

CAPTAIN
JOE BAKER-CRESSWELL

Captain Joe Baker-Cresswell (who died on March 4 1997, aged 96) was the destroyer commander whose capture of a U-boat in 1941 led to a sensational intelligence coup which changed the whole course of the Second World War.

Late in 1940, Baker-Cresswell was appointed captain of the destroyer *Bulldog*, leading the 3rd Escort Group. On May 9 1941, his ship was in the

Atlantic, escorting convoy OB318, outward bound from Liverpool, when she was attacked by U-110, commanded by Kapitän Leutnant Julius Lemp, the ace who had sunk the liner *Athenia* on the first evening of the war.

Lemp sank two ships in the starboard columns of OB318, but his periscope was sighted by the nearest escort, the corvette *Aubrietia*, which gained a firm Asdic (ultrasound detection) contact and dropped a pattern of 10 depth-charges. *Bulldog* and the destroyer *Broadway*, who also had firm Asdic contacts, were about to join the attack when all eyes were caught by a sudden, violent water turbulence, almost directly between the ships. The patch of strange broken water, containing eerily large bubbles, spread very rapidly and then, before anybody could react, a U-boat surfaced in the middle of it, with men already pouring out of the conning tower.

Having just lost two ships in his convoy because of this sinister black shape, Baker-Cresswell "saw red" for a moment and steered to ram, but then collected himself and turned away again. It seemed that the U-boat sailors were manning their gun, so *Bulldog* opened fire with all weapons down to small arms. *Broadway* joined in, and for a minute or so there was bedlam.

The U-boat survivors (Lemp was not among them) were picked up by *Aubrietia*. Baker-Cresswell was quick-witted enough to realise that the U-boat crew would assume their boat had been sunk. Their captain was certainly dead. So they were quickly hustled below decks where they saw, and were told, nothing. Meanwhile, OB318 steamed onwards and out of sight, thus removing possibly awkward eye-witnesses from the scene.

U-110 was boarded by a party from *Bulldog* which methodically stripped the boat of all the equipment they could remove – binoculars, sextants, books, logs, charts, diaries, pictures, tools, and instruments. A telegraphist noted down the tuning positions of all the radio sets in the wireless office. *Bulldog*'s engineer officer came over to try to start some machinery, and her whaler had to make several trips back and forth, loaded with treasures.

Baker-Cresswell realised there was a good chance of saving this U-boat and of keeping any information gained from it secret from the Germans. He decided to take U-110 in tow. This was achieved shortly after 4pm and, at first, *Bulldog* made good progress, although the U-boat was noticeably down by the stern. But the weather worsened overnight, and *Bulldog* had to heave to. Next morning, U-110 suddenly put its bows up in the air, until the hull was nearly vertical, and then sank.

It was a bitter disappointment when Baker-Cresswell lost his prize, but the cryptanalytical gains from U-110 were beyond price – far more valuable than the U-boat itself. Experts from Bletchley Park went up to Scapa Flow to meet *Bulldog*, taking with them small briefcases, expecting only a few papers.

When they saw two large packing cases, they could hardly believe their eyes. They handled the contents like men in a daze. Here were items they had only dreamed of, including U-110's Enigma cypher machine, with the settings for May 9 still on its rotors, the special code settings for high-security *Offizierte* (officer only) traffic, and the current code book for U-boats' short-signal sighting reports.

Baker-Cresswell was awarded the DSO, and his engineer officer, Lieutenant-Commander Dodds, and the boarding officer, Sub-Lieutenant Balme, were both awarded DSCs.

Addison Joe Baker-Cresswell was born on February 2 1901, into an old Northumbrian family. He went to Gresham's School, Holt, and joined the Navy in 1919. His first ship, as a midshipman, was the battlecruiser *Tiger*.

He then served in the cruiser *Castor* at Queens-town, during the Irish troubles, and in the sloop *Veronica* in the Far East, based in New Zealand. He specialised in navigation in 1927 and was appointed to the minelayer *Adventure* and the battleship *Nelson*. There followed three happy years as navigating officer of the battleship *Rodney*, when he was twice commended by Their Lordships for his skill in piloting that famously unwieldy ship in and out of harbour.

At the outbreak of war he was in Cairo, on General Wavell's planning staff, and was involved in missions to Turkey and Greece. His first command, in 1940, was the destroyer *Arrow*. After *Bulldog*, Baker-Cresswell joined the Joint Intelligence Staff at Storey's Gate in London, and was then appointed Training Captain Western Approaches, in command of Tom Sopwith's yacht *Philante*, working up Atlantic escorts in Lough Larne.

Late in 1943, he was appointed Chief of Staff to the C-in-C Western Approaches, Admiral Sir Max Horton, but after a volcanic clash of personalities he asked to be relieved, and went out to command the East Indies Escort Force until the end of the war. In Ceylon, he had to solve administrative as well as operational problems – for instance, the feeding of Hindu crews of Royal Indian Navy ships. He converted an old minesweeper into the Royal Navy's only specialist goat-carrier, and sent it around ports to embark the animals.

In 1946, Baker-Cresswell commanded the cruiser *Gambia* for a two-year commission in the Far East. For his last three years in the Navy, he was Deputy Director of Naval Intelligence. He retired in 1951, and was appointed ADC to King George VI the same year.

In retirement, Baker-Cresswell went back to his native Northumberland. He farmed near Bamburgh, became a JP and chairman of the bench, and was High Sheriff in 1962. He was devoted to fishing, and was an honorary naval member of the Royal Yacht Squadron.

The story of U-110's capture was kept secret for many years. The formal letter the Admiralty sent Baker-Cresswell on his retirement, summarising his naval career, did not mention it. The official naval historian Captain Stephen Roskill, who published his first volume on the Second World War in 1954, knew nothing about it then; but in 1959 he brought out a full account, *The Secret Capture*, dedicated to Baker-Cresswell and the officer and men of the 3rd Escort Group.

On that one day in May 1941, Baker-Creswell had more effect on the progress of the war than any other single naval officer. U-110 yielded code-breaking information which was to have major influence, not only on the Battle of the Atlantic, but on the land campaign in Africa. As King George VI said when he invested Baker-Cresswell with his DSO, U-110's capture was perhaps the most important single event in the whole war at sea.

Baker-Cresswell married in 1926, Rona Vaile, of Auckland, whom he met when he was serving in *Veronica*. They had two daughters, one of whom predeceased him, and a son.

COMMODORE
GEOFFREY MARR

Commodore Geoffrey Marr (who died on March 4 1997, aged 88) was the last captain to command the giant passenger liners *Queen Mary* and *Queen Elizabeth*; of the two, his favourite was the *Elizabeth*, although she was not completed until 1940 and lacked some of the lavish internal decoration of the *Mary*.

Marr made headlines in 1967 when he docked *Queen Elizabeth* at Pier 92 in New York without tugs, turning her in a tideway and in a space not much wider than the length of the ship. He made it sound easy:"I had to bring her up the river, swing her above the berth, bring her down and then wait for that precise moment to come down, stemming the flood tide and then turn her into the pier and hope that I got her around before the ebb started and carried me on to the other side."

He told the press photographers, newsreel and television cameramen who swarmed on board that they were "a lot of blasted ghouls, hoping I'm going to hit that pier". Despite them,things went very well: "We actually docked just as quickly as we normally do, in about 30 minutes."

In 1971, Marr took *Queen Elizabeth* to Hong Kong with a Chinese crew after she had been bought by CY Tung to be refitted as a floating university and cruise liner. He was saddened when he was woken early one morning in January the following year and told that she had caught fire – almost certainly due to sabotage – and capsized.

"I got the impression," Marr said, "that she was so much bigger, so much more complicated than anything the Chinese had dealt with up to that time, that they were rather afraid of her, as one is afraid of something you don't really understand."

Geoffrey Thrippleton Marr was born on August 23 1908 and went to *Conway*, the training ship on the Mersey. He joined Elders & Fyffes as an apprentice in 1924, his first ship being the SS *Greenbrier* (formerly the First World War German raider *Moewe*). He gained his master's ticket in 1933 and, three years later, heard there was a vacancy at Cunard, and joined them as the first new officer they had engaged for eight years.

He served in the smaller Cunard liners until 1938 when he joined the *Queen Mary* as junior third officer. In February 1940 he was appointed as a lieutenant, RNR, to contraband control at HMS Fervent at Ramsgate. Three months later, he took part in the evacuation of the British Expeditionary Force from Dunkirk, commanding the steam drifter *Lord Collingwood*, which brought more than 300 soldiers home from the beaches.

Marr joined the new battleship *King George V* when she was commissioned in October 1940, as the assistant navigating officer. He was on board for the chase and destruction of the German battleship *Bismarck* in the north Atlantic in May 1941. His action station was in the emergency conning position, a secondary bridge about two-thirds of the way up the after funnel, from which he had a grandstand view of the final stages on May 27.

"It was a sight I shall remember to my dying day," he recalled. "As daylight strengthened, we saw these magnificent ships, *King George V* and *Rodney*, running before the gale, decks cleared for action, their big silk battle ensigns streaming from every masthead, like knights in armour riding out to meet their adversaries on the jousting field." He watched *Bismarck*'s final throes. "She was a holocaust of flame, on fire fore and aft; through my binoculars I could see her crew running along the deck, jumping overboard. We had reduced her to a floating ruin."

From *King George V* Marr went as navigating officer to the sloop *Ibis*, based at Londonderry with the 41st Escort Group, bringing convoys through the Atlantic and to Freetown, Sierra Leone. In August 1942 he was appointed to the escort carrier *Activity*, again as navigating officer. She provided air cover for convoys to Russia, anti-U-boat patrols in the Western Approaches for the D-Day landings, and then joined the East Indies Fleet for the rest of the war.

Ferrying replacement aircraft to Australia for the British Pacific Fleet, Marr took a route through the Torres Straits, between Australia and New Guinea, and then inside the Great Barrier Reef to Brisbane, a rare pilotage feat for a ship as large as *Activity*. In February 1945, the American Liberty ship *Peter Silvester* was sunk by a U-boat 1,100 miles west of Fremantle. Air and surface searches failed to find all her boats.

Activity was on passage in the Indian Ocean at the time, and from local currents and wind directions Marr worked out where the boats were likely to be. *Activity* duly found one boat, three weeks later, and nearly 600 miles from where the ship was sunk.

Marr was awarded the DSC for his service in *Activity* in the New Year of 1946.

He returned to Cunard after the war and had his first command,the small cargo-liner *Andania* in 1952. His first passenger liner command was *Ascania* in 1955, and he went on to command the liners *Carinthia*, *Caronia* and *Mauretania*.

Marr was captain of the *Queen Mary* in November 1965, and his final appointment was as the senior Cunard captain, in command of the *Queen Elizabeth* with the rank of commodore, from January 1 1966. *Queen Mary* was withdrawn from service at the end of 1967, and *Queen Elizabeth* a year later.

Marr published *The Queens and I* in 1973. His wife Dorothie predeceased him; they had a son and a daughter.

CAPTAIN
GERRY SOUTHWOOD

Captain Gerry Southwood (who died on March 13 1997, aged 84) won the DSC as engineer officer of the submarine *Regent* for his part in one of the most bizarre incidents of the Second World War.

On April 27 1941, when the Germans were advancing into Yugoslavia, *Regent* sailed from Malta, bound for the Dalmatian port of Kotor, to embark

Ronald Campbell, the British Minister to Yugoslavia, and his staff. Having passed unknowingly through two enemy minefields, *Regent* arrived at Kotor five days later, flying a large White Ensign.

After an exasperating two-hour wait, a Yugoslav naval officer and a civilian pilot came off in a boat and said that an armistice had been agreed between the Yugoslavs and the Axis, the whole area was now in Italian hands, and furthermore Mr Campbell was not there; he was in another village down the coast.

The pilot went ashore to telephone Campbell and ask him to go to another small harbour, where there was a jetty. When *Regent* arrived, there were several Italian officers on the jetty, but no Campbell, and a long and increasingly acrimonious negotiation began, shouted across the water. For hours, *Regent* lay off the jetty, in water too shallow to dive, while Italian aircraft circled overhead. It was, as the Admiralty's official communiqué later said, "a tense and farcical situation".

Farce was to turn to tragedy. Two aircraft, which turned out to be German, attacked with bombs that exploded close alongside, damaging *Regent*'s main battery. The captain's first concern was for his ship. He decided to abandon the mission and put to sea, leaving *Regent*'s officer behind, but taking a hostage with him.

Regent was attacked again, with bombs and machine-gun fire, and the captain, the first lieutenant, and the lookout were all wounded by shrapnel. As the only unwounded officers, Southwood and the sub kept watch and, despite a main battery in a delicate state that made diving risky, they reached Malta safely.

Regent's officer was later repatriated. Campbell and

his staff were also evacuated, through normal diplomatic channels.

On an earlier patrol, *Regent* had had to surface in daylight because of a defect in the forward hydroplanes. When Southwood volunteered to crawl between the pressure hull and the casing to make repairs, the captain made it quite clear to him that if a ship or an aircraft appeared he would have to dive the submarine and leave him trapped. Southwood went ahead regardless, and was mentioned in despatches.

Horace Gerald Southwood was born on April 19 1912 into a naval family. He never knew his father, who was lost in the cruiser *Good Hope* off Coronel on November 1 1914. He joined the Navy as a boy artificer in the battleships *Resolution* and *Barham*. He then went to the Royal Naval College, Greenwich, as an acting sub-lieutenant (E) in 1936.

He joined the submarine service in 1938, and served in *Regent* on the China station, and then in the Mediterranean after the outbreak of war. In 1942 he went to the Engineer-in-Chief's department, and was then appointed engineer officer of *Amphion*, the first of the new A class of submarine, building at Vickers, Barrow. He saw it through its trials and early commission, when several serious stability problems were rectified.

After the war, Southwood was senior engineer of the light fleet carrier *Vengeance* and then Commander (E) of the carrier *Glory*. From 1954 to 1958, Southwood was deputy manager of HM Dockyard Portsmouth, and from 1959 to 1962 chief engineer of HM Dockyard, Singapore. His last appointment, from 1963 until he retired in 1967, was as manager of the engineering department of Portsmouth Dockyard.

He was then on the shortlist for promotion to rear-admiral, but chose instead to become general manager of Devonport Dockyard, as a civil servant employed by the Ministry of Defence. As a dockyard manager, Gerry Southwood was refreshingly different. He would walk round the yard every morning, to talk to the men in the various workshops, and would spend evenings with union officials, drinking pints of beer and playing skittles.

From 1974 to 1978 Southwood was managing director of Silley, Cox & Co, Falmouth Docks, and from 1974 to 1979 chairman of the Falmouth Group, mainly doing complex conversions of North Sea oil tankers, US turbine ships and *Lowestoft*, the first warship to be repaired in a commercial yard since the war. The Falmouth workforce were surprised to find their new chairman standing at the dockyard gate to wish them good morning when they came to work.

Southwood played rugger and boxed for the Navy. In the 1960s, he ran the United Services Portsmouth rugger team and was for some years a Navy selector. He was appointed CBE in 1967.

Gerry Southwood married, in 1936, Ruby Hayes; they had two sons and a daughter.

CAPTAIN
NICK BARKER

Captain Nick Barker (who died on April 7 1997, aged 63) commanded *Endurance* the Antarctic ice-patrol ship, survey vessel and Falkland Islands guardship, during the conflict of 1982.

Barker and his ship's company in *Endurance* (known as the "Red Plum", from her hull colour) played notable parts in the conflict. But his later career was drastically affected by the resentment of Whitehall officialdom after it was publicly disclosed that, as early as four months before the invasion of the Falklands, he had given repeated, and well-founded, warnings of Argentina's aggressive intentions. These had been ignored, discounted or derided by those same Whitehall officials.

When he was appointed captain of *Endurance* in May 1980, this was a much more important command than it appeared. Although armed only with two 20mm guns and two Wasp helicopters, *Endurance* was the sole regular bearer of the White Ensign south of the Equator. Her presence had great symbolic significance for the Falkland Islanders as highly visible evidence that they were still British and still mattered to the United Kingdom.

Thus her captain had to be a diplomat as well as a sailor, acutely sensitive to the special political, historical, scientific and navigational aspects of the Antarctic. Barker rose to this challenge superbly. Rex Hunt, Governor of the Falklands, became his friend for life, and he also did his best, in difficult circumstances, to be on good terms with the British Embassy staff in Buenos Aires.

With his knowledge of the Antarctic, Barker was only too well aware of the catastrophic political effect on the whole region of the announcement in John Nott's 1981 defence review, that *Endurance* – which Nott described as "foundering, and falling to pieces" – was to be scrapped without relief, to save money.

With the assistance of Lord Shackleton, Barker began a campaign to try to save the ship until he was called to Northwood headquarters to be severely reprimanded by the C-in-C Fleet, Admiral Sir John Fieldhouse, and ordered to desist from his campaign – an order, he was told, which came from 10 Downing Street.

Endurance's removal appeared to the Argentine junta to be the final green light, showing that the Foreign Office's efforts, over several years, to get rid of the Falklands were at last being realised and that the United Kingdom was no longer interested in the islands. Invasion plans were brought forward and the diplomatic climate rapidly deteriorated. When *Endurance* paid a courtesy visit to the southernmost Argentine port of Ushuaia in January 1982, the atmosphere there was what Barker called "distinctly frigid".

He was told that he was now in "the Malvinas war zone". When he asked who the enemy was, the answer was: "You." An Argentinian admiral, while enjoying Barker's hospitality in *Endurance*, said: "I will tell you there is to be a war against the Malvinas. I do not know when, but I think soon."

Barker passed these and other warnings on, but Whitehall and Northwood assumed they were merely Barker's further attempts to save his ship, and he was again ignored. In March 1982, Barker was fully vindicated when Argentine "scrap dealers" and marines landed illicitly on South Georgia and raised their national flag. After the main Argentine invasion on April 2, *Endurance*'s first concern was to avoid the Argentine Navy, which she did by hugging the coast of South Georgia, "hiding behind a rock by day, pretending to be an iceberg," Barker said, "not easy for a red-painted ship."

When Barker telephoned Northwood by satellite to clarify the rules of engagement, should he encounter an Argentine missile destroyer around the next iceberg, he was told "to phone back after two o'clock as the particular staff officer was at lunch".

Later in April, *Endurance* took part in Paraquat, the operation to recapture South Georgia, which, in Barker's opinion, was "in military terms, a monumental cock-up", although it was ultimately successful. *Endurance*'s helicopters joined in harrying the Argentine submarine *Santa Fe* (whose captain was a friend of Barker's) with missiles until it ran itself aground.

Endurance's final operation, in June, was Keyhole, the re-occupation of Thule, in the South Sandwich Islands, where the Argentinians had had an illegal garrison since 1977. By then, it was public knowledge, having been broadcast on radio and television, that Whitehall and Northwood had both ignored Barker's warnings.

Endurance was in the South Atlantic longer than almost any other ship – Whitehall's punishment, her sailors believed, for her captain's indiscretions.When she eventually returned,to a large press gathering,she was first met by two MoD minders, who warned Barker:"Your future in the Navy depends more upon Friday's press conference than anything you have ever done." In the event, Barker was admirably non-committal.

Officialdom would have much preferred a low-key return for *Endurance*, but the people of Chatham and the Medway towns would have none of that, and turned out in their thousands to welcome the "Red Plum" home.

Barker was appointed CBE in October 1982, and his ship's company were awarded two DSCs, a DSM, an MBE, four BEMs, eight mentions in despatches and 11 C-in-C's commendations.

Nicholas John Barker was born on May 19 1933, in Malta, and was christened on board his father's ship, the destroyer *Arrow* – the ship's bell being used, in traditional Navy fashion, as the font. His father, Lieutenant-Commander John Barker, DSC, was killed while commanding the destroyer *Ardent* when she and *Acasta* were both sunk trying valiantly to protect the aircraft carrier *Glorious* in an action with the German battlecruisers *Scharnhorst* and *Gneisenau* off Norway in 1940. Lieutenant-Commander Barker and Commander Glasfurd, *Acasta*'s captain, were both recommended for, but not awarded, posthumous Victoria Crosses.

Young Nicholas went to Canford School, and joined the Navy as a National Serviceman, being selected for a permanent commission in 1953. After service in the frigates *Termagant*, *Chichester* and *Loch Fyne*, he had his first command, the fishery protection vessel *Squirrel*, in 1963. He went on to command the minesweeper *Brereton*, and the frigates *Jupiter* and *Nubian*.

He was Deputy Commodore, Contract Built Ships, from 1973 to 1975 and then stood by the Type 21 frigate *Arrow*, the eighth ship of her name in the Navy, building on the Clyde. He commissioned her in Sunderland in 1976, and commanded her at the Spithead Silver Jubilee Review in 1977.

Barker also held appointments at HMS Ganges, the

boys' training establishment; at HMS Osprey, the naval base at Portland; and in the Naval Secretary's Department in the Admiralty. After *Endurance*, Barker spent a year on a Defence Fellowship at Churchill College, Cambridge, and from 1984 to 1986 commanded the Fishery Protection Squadron.

By then, he was not optimistic about promotion to flag rank, but his hopes were raised when he was given command of the Type 22 frigate *Sheffield*, building at Swan Hunters. However, he only commanded her for a few weeks after she was commissioned in June 1988, and then retired from the Navy.

In retirement, Barker gave his time generously to the Sea Cadets and the Royal British Legion, and was Honorary Colonel of the Royal Marine Reserve unit on Tyneside. He was a Freeman of the City of London, a Younger Brother of Trinity House, a Fellow of the Royal Geographical Society and of the British Institute of Management, and a Member of the Nautical Institute. He managed the Sea Safety Centre and North East Marine Service in Sunderland, and was gazetted Deputy Lieutenant of Tyne and Wear a month before he died.

Barker wrote novels, including *Red Ice*, a thriller set in the South Atlantic, and also *Beyond Endurance*, his account of the Falklands War. As a captain, Nick Barker had a swashbuckling disregard of rules and regulations which was bound to annoy bureaucrats.

Endurance came home for a short refit in 1981. After John Nott's pronouncements, so little notice was taken of her that when she sailed from Portsmouth in October, on what was ostensibly her last voyage south, there was not even a crane driver available to lift away the heavy ship-to-shore gangway. Barker waited a decent time, then ordered the wires to be slipped, and moved off, leaving the gangway to fall into the water.

He always took pains to look after his sailors, and his sailors loved him in return. At the height of the war, he arranged for one sailor to telephone home from South Georgia because his mother was very ill. This was when Whitehall fury over Barker's revelations was at one of its periodic fever pitches. The sailor came to thank him, and to say:"Me Mum says you're in the shit again, sir!"

Barker was not bitter after his experience. He gave as one of his recreations "championing lost causes". But he had a sharp tongue. When a fresh inquiry into the Falklands was mooted, he remarked:"We should let sleeping dogs lie. Most of those who might be found culpable have been knighted, promoted or decorated – or all three."

Barker returned to the Falklands in 1992 for a BBC television programme. His comments had a sad refrain."It was such an unnecessary war. Once again, the armed forces had to save the politicians' necks."

Nick Barker married first, in 1967, Elizabeth Redman; they had two sons and two daughters. After the marriage was dissolved, he married secondly, in 1989, Jennifer Jane Cayley, daughter of Commander Cayley DSO and two Bars, CO of the submarine *Utmost*, which was lost with all hands in the Mediterranean in 1942.

SIGNALMAN
GUS BRITTON

Signalman Gus Britton (who died on July 21 1997, aged 74) made an outstanding contribution to the history of the submarine service. After 15 years as a signalman in the Royal Navy, including four years of wartime submarine patrols, Britton became involved in the Royal Navy Submarine Museum at Gosport, Hants, in its early days. He was then for many years until his death the museum's archivist.

From his little office in the museum, Britton answered queries about submarines from all over the world, from press and television, naval historians, serving and retired submariners and their families.His knowledge was so encyclopaedic and his friendships so widespread that, whenever there was any question about submarines, the cry would go up:"Ask Gus, he knows everything and everybody." His help was gratefully acknowledged in the forewords of innumerable books about submarines, and he was always ready to render invaluable advice for submariners' obituaries in *The Daily Telegraph.*

His quarterly "Fore Ends News" in the *Submarine Old Comrades' Association News* and his eccentrically typed Ditty Box newsletters contained a hilarious mixture of gossip and anecdote; queries about the present whereabouts of long-lost shipmates; tributes to deceased submariners; ribald references to submarine coxswains, chief stokers and Royal Marines, as well as his own brand of rhyming slang.

Ernest Charles Britton was born on September 9 1922, the son of a chief petty officer who served in the light cruiser *Caroline* at Jutland, and later in submarines. At the age of 11, he was sent to the Royal Hospital School, Holbrook, whose boys wore naval uniform and, in addition to normal subjects, were taught seamanship and respect for service life and discipline.

He then went as a boy seaman to HMS Ganges, the training establishment at Shotley, in March 1938. It was there he acquired the nickname Gus, after a newspaper comic strip character Gus the Ancient Briton, much preferring it to the name Ernest. He was a boy signalman in the battleship *Nelson* when war broke out, and later served in the cruiser *Fiji* and the destroyer *Beverley*, one of the 50 ex-US four-stackers which served as convoy escort in the Atlantic.

Britton had found "big ship" life in *Nelson* irksome, and volunteered for submarines in March 1941, thus achieving his ambition to follow "in my dear old dad's footsteps". He carried out 17 operational war patrols, mostly in the Mediterranean, in *Trident* and *Uproar*.

He survived severe depth-charging (a "bollocking", he called it) in *Trident* off the island of Capri in November 1942. "I heard for the first time," he recalled, "the spine-chilling cheeping notes of an Asdic transmission in contact, followed by the rumbling of an express train going overhead and shattering explosions of a pattern of depth charges going off right above us."

When *Uproar* was acting as a navigational beacon for the Anzio landing in January 1944, Britton stood on the bridge shining an Aldis signalling lamp out to sea to guide the incoming assault. After the war, he served in the submarines *Tapir*, *Acheron*, *Seascout* and

Truculent, which he left shortly before she was sunk in collision with a Swedish tanker in the Thames Estuary in January 1950;many of his friends were lost in the accident. He then served in the submarines *Totem, Scythian* and *Telemachus* before leaving the Navy in 1953.

Although a man of well above average intelligence and capability, Gus Britton was never promoted; but then his career was by no means unblemished. In 1943 his conduct was rated "Fair",which he said "was the lowest assessment apart from being discharged. Maybe it was because in that year I spent a week in cells on the submarine depot ship Maidstone alongside the wall in Algiers", (for celebrating too enthusiastically the return of another submarine from patrol).Actually, he said,his cell,although spartan, was a great deal more comfortable than the fore end of a U-class submarine.

Outside the Navy, he had a variety of jobs. He was a deckhand in an unsuccessful expedition with Commander "Buster" Crabbe to recover Armada gold from Tobermory Bay. He was a barman and bouncer at the French Pub in Soho, and a redcoat and chief lifeguard at Butlins. In 1957, he joined the City of London Royal Marine Reserve Special Boat Section and qualified as a parachutist.

After a spell at the museum, Britton went to the Ecole Thérèse d'Avila, a girls' convent near Lille, where he was swimming and PT instructor for 10 years, amazing the nuns and the girls with both his French and his English. He kept in touch, and spent a holiday every year with his friends in France.

A strong swimmer since Ganges, Britton held the Navy records for 100 and 200 metres freestyle and backstroke. At the age of 65, he swam across the Solent to the Isle of Wight and back in five hours, to raise money for the Submarine Old Comrades' Association. In September 1993, in his 71st year, he made a sponsored parachute jump into the Solent to raise money for the Submarine Memorial Fund.

Gus Britton held that apart from one notorious incident – the machine-gunning of SS *Peleus's* survivors by U-852 – the U-boat arm had fought the war with honour, and he had close links with their old comrades' associations. He was a member of the association of U-616, which *Uproar* had narrowly missed sinking during the war. The only submariners he would not countenance were the Japanese, whom he considered had disgraced the good name of all submariners with war crimes.

Gus Britton was appointed MBE in 1996, which delighted submariners around the world, and it was typical of him that he invited Charles and Agnes de Baccre, his long-standing friends from France, to attend his investiture at Buckingham Palace. He never married.

CAPTAIN
BILL McVICAR

Captain Bill McVicar (who died on August 9 1997, aged 83) accomplished an epic feat of seamanship in the Second World War when he sailed a lifeboat more than 1,500 miles to land.

He was third officer in the Anchor Line passenger steamer *Britannia* when she encountered the German commerce raider *Thor* some 600 miles off Freetown, Sierra Leone, on the morning of March 25 1941. *Thor* approached close to *Britannia* and shelled her for more than an hour, doing great damage to her lifeboats, upper deck and superstructure. In all, 122 crew and 127 passengers (service personnel bound for the Mediterranean and India) were lost.

When the order was given to abandon ship, McVicar manned No 7 lifeboat, starboard side aft, near the ship's single gun, which had been hit and disabled early in the action by a shell which also smashed the nearby No 8 lifeboat. By the time No 7 was clear of the ship and had picked up other survivors, there were 64 lascars and 18 Europeans, a total of 82, in a lifeboat designed for 56.

The boat's hull was riddled with shrapnel holes, the survivors had to bail furiously for some hours, and the following morning it was out of sight of the other boats. The holes were repaired by Sub-Lieutenant Ian McIntosh, one of *Britannia*'s passengers, who hung over the side, held by the legs, while he applied makeshift patches made of bits of blanket and pieces of tin.

They hoisted the mainsail and tried to sail eastward towards Africa, but could make no progress against the fresh north-east trade wind. McVicar had a note of *Britannia*'s position when she was sunk, and an RNR lieutenant on board had pre-war knowledge of the positions of the ports in Brazil.

From this McIntosh sketched a "chart", with which he and McVicar (the only one who had any experience of handling a boat under sail) decided they should sail to Brazil instead. They had on board about 16 gallons of water, 48 tins of condensed milk, and two tins of biscuits. Calculating that it would take 24 days to reach Brazil, they fixed the daily ration at a third of a dipper (a little less than an eggcupful) of water each and one biscuit.

Two tins of milk were issued each day, being doled out by dipping a boxwood spoon into the milk and cleaning it on the palm of each man in turn, so that he could lick it off. They saw four ships during the first week and tried frantically to attract attention by burning flares, but in vain.

After about 10 days, they passed through storms and caught rainwater, increasing the ration to an eggcupful. Later still, the ration was doubled as more water was caught and the numbers in the boat decreased. Some of the Indians drank seawater, despite warnings, and eventually died.

Soon everyone suffered from saltwater sores, boils and abscesses, aggravated by the overcrowding and the constant rolling of the boat which threw them against each other. It was impossible to sit, lie or even stand in comfort, and they took it in turns to lie down for an hour at a time on a thwart cleared for the purpose. The hardship and privation began to tell, and men died at the rate of three or four a day.

They sailed due west to longitude 33 degrees west, and then south-west. After three or four days of shifting winds, they picked up the south-east trades. Though steering by sun and stars, and a compass 20 degrees out, the navigation was excellent. They could sniff the "earthy" smell of land after three weeks, and sighted the green of shoal water.

In fact, they were only two degrees of latitude and three of longitude in error, when the 38 survivors waded ashore near São Luis in Brazil, after a voyage of 1,535 miles in 23 days. Other boats from *Britannia* were picked up, and there were 235 survivors in all. McVicar and McIntosh were appointed MBE.

A son of the manse, William McVicar was born on May 12 1914 at Southend, Mull of Kintyre. He went to Campbeltown Grammar School before joining the Anchor Line as a 17-year-old cadet.

After the open-boat navigation, his war adventures were not over. He was serving in the Anchor Line passenger ship *California*, sailing in a small troopship convoy, when they were attacked by Focke-Wulf Kondor long-range bombers off the Portuguese coast on July 11 1943. The Canadian Pacific *Duchess of York* was sunk; *California* was set on fire and had to be sunk by the destroyer *Douglas*. The Canadian destroyer *Iroquois*, the frigate *Moyola*, and *Douglas* picked up all but 57 of those on board both ships.

McVicar stayed with the Anchor Line after the war, and was the senior Master when he retired in 1976.

He married, in 1941, Nina Tawse; they had three daughters.

Vice-Admiral Sir Ian McIntosh wrote: The RNR lieutenant became very ill (malaria, I think) and died before we made land, so that all the time Bill was the only real seaman with me. We shared the sailing, navigation and the general repair and maintenance of the boat and its rigging as well as control of our general living arrangements.

You can imagine how valuable it was to have a quiet, undemonstrative reliable seaman as one's companion in such circumstances. Bill must have been 26 or so to my 21, but we seemed more like twin brothers. I did become very worried in the last few days before we made land for Bill developed a really nasty poisoned foot which caused him intense pain and restricted his movements – though he still took his trick on the helm.

CHIEF PETTY OFFICER
FRANK MILES

Chief Petty Officer Frank Miles (whose death, aged 87, was reported on September 23 1997) was one of the veteran submarine coxswains who bore much of the brunt of the underwater war from 1939 to 1945.

In a submarine, the coxswain, after the captain, is the most important man on board,and Miles was one of the best. His first boat as coxswain was the 1919-vintage H31, running from Gosport in 1937. The following year, he was coxswain of *Regent* in Hong Kong and was still serving in it when it went to the Mediterranean in 1940, after the start of the war against Italy. From 1941-42 he was coxswain of *Tribune*, first at Blyth,in Northumberland,and later in the Mediterranean.

Miles had such long submarine experience that there were few events or emergencies he had not witnessed before and, as the boat's regulating officer, there were few sailors' excuses for being late off leave he had not heard before. He was the boat's medical officer, with a simple code of practice. For ailments above the waist: aspirin; below the waist: a Number Nine laxative "depth-charge", guaranteed to move the bowels of the earth.He was also the boat's caterer, providing such delicacies as "train smash" (skinned, tinned tomatoes), "babies' heads" (a particularly glutinous kind of steak-and-kidney pudding), "figgy duff", and a variety of brown sauce fierce enough to polish bright-work.

The coxswain took the helm when a submarine entered or left harbour, so it was Miles who steered *Regent*, commanded by the celebrated Lieutenant-Commander "Hairy" Browne, into Kotor harbour in April 1941 to pick up the British Minister in Yugoslavia. The attempt failed, and *Regent* was bombed and machine-gunned by enemy aircraft, wounding the captain, the officer of the watch and the lookout.

The coxswain controlled the after hydroplanes, at diving stations or during an attack. In an earlier patrol in February, *Regent* fired a salvo of six torpedoes at an enemy convoy. The water compensating tanks failed to work properly and *Regent*, suddenly relieved of the weight of six torpedoes, lost trim and shot to the surface in front of an Italian destroyer.

An emergency dive took the submarine back down to 300 feet, with a bows-up angle of 25 degrees. All the water in the bilges rushed aft, together with all loose gear such as buckets, plates, cups and saucers, making a noisy racket easily heard by the ship above, which carried out an unpleasantly close depth-charge attack.

Throughout the incident, Miles went on calmly reporting the boat's depth and angle from the gauge and inclinometer in front of him. *Regent* later surfaced and escaped.

Miles was awarded the DSM for eight war patrols in the Mediterranean in *Regent* from October 1940 to August 1941.

Frank William Miles was born on January 31 1910 and went to HMS Ganges, Shotley, as a boy seaman in 1925. He joined the submarine service in 1932 and served in L71 and *Otway* at Gosport, and in *Phoenix* and *Parthian* on the China station. After *Regent* he joined the instructional staff at HMS Elfin, the base at Blyth, and the depot ship Wolfe at Trincomalee, in Ceylon.

After the war, Miles was the personal coxswain to the Admiral Submarines, at HMS Dolphin, Gosport, and president of the chief petty officers' mess. He left the Navy in 1950 and became a cinema manager for the ABC chain. Latterly, he was a stalwart of the Basingstoke Submarine Old Comrades' Association.

His wife predeceased him. They had a son.

LIEUTENANT
GINGER LE BRETON

Lieutenant Ginger Le Breton (who died on October 4 1997, aged 90) was the only sailor to take an active part in the mutiny of the Atlantic Fleet at Invergordon in September 1931 and then to go on to be commissioned as an officer.

Le Breton was an able seaman torpedoman in the cruiser *Dorsetshire* when, as a result of the financial crisis of 1931, drastic cuts were announced in public sector pay. In the Navy, one shilling (5p) a day was to be cut from everyone's pay.

A shilling meant little to an admiral. But to an able seaman on four shillings a day it was a cut of 25 per cent. Many sailors, who had wives and young families and rents to pay, faced ruin. An incompetent and insensitive Board of Admiralty, who had failed utterly to present the Navy's case to the Government, also bungled the announcement of the cuts, so that the first the sailors at Invergordon heard of them was through rumour and the newspapers, followed by bald statements on the ships' noticeboards.

At that time, there was no effective means of airing lower-deck grievances. The so-called "normal channels" were known to be useless. Le Breton and thousands of other sailors had to choose between patriotism and justice. They chose to stand against injustice. Thus, as the sailors had decided the previous Sunday, early on the morning of Tuesday September 15, when the fleet was due to put to sea for exercises, crowds of defiant sailors, in moods of mixed exhilaration and trepidation, mustered on the fo'c'sles of their ships and began to cheer.

Echoing Spithead in 1797, the cheering swept down the lines of warships, as the signal for the mutiny to begin. It was a very polite affair, more of a sit-in than a mutiny. There was no violence. The sailors bore their officers no ill-will. Their grievance was with the Government and the Admiralty.

In *Dorsetshire*, Le Breton was among 100 sailors who sat down on the mess deck and refused to fall in for work. "Eventually the commander came forward to speak to us," he recalled. "He started talking about what we were doing *wrong*, and letting down the Navy, and then eventually he said '*Right*, everybody on deck.'

"He gave us an order. And we just sat there. Did nothing. Just looked at him. And he looked at us, and his face went red. So angry. You could see the anger on his face. Then he said: 'All right then, if you won't go aft, then go down on the lower mess deck,' where we would have been battened down. We just laughed."

Dorsetshire's torpedomen chose Le Breton as their delegate to make their case to the torpedo officer who was, according to Le Breton, "understanding and sympathetic". He continued: "There was then a pipe that the captain [Arthur John Power, a much loved and respected officer] would talk to us on the fo'c'sle. He strolled along, with no other officers, his cap under his arm. This was a great piece of leadership and psychology. He more or less staked his career."

"We liked him. We trusted him. After a few sensible words, saying the admiral had gone down to London, there was nothing more we could do, and the situation was in hand he said that he had work to do, and was going aft, and he hoped we would do the same. Putting his cap on, he walked aft. The bugler sounded 'Fall In'. And that is just what we did – walked aft."

The mutiny in *Dorsetshire* was over, but in some ships it lasted until the Friday, and eventually ended in a partial victory for the lower deck. The shilling a day was scrapped, and sailors' pay cut by only 10 per cent. Le Breton and his fellow mutineers had sent a seismic political and financial shock around the world and helped to force Britain off the gold standard. The home naval ports were soon swarming with MI5 and Special Branch agents, looking for mutineers and evidence of communist influence in the Navy. About 100 "ring-leaders" were rounded up.

Some of them, on mere hearsay evidence provided by their own shipmates, were subjected to "physical training", which was unpleasantly close to punishment, and then, although most had character and conduct assessments of "Very Good, Superior", summarily discharged from the Navy "SNLR" – Services No Longer Required.

Two of *Dorsetshire's* torpedomen, friends of Le Breton, suffered this fate, on the word of another torpedoman whom the commander had asked to watch out for "ringleaders". Le Breton himself was very fortunate not to be picked out as a prominent mutineer. Apart from his distinctive ginger hair, he was well known onboard, playing football for the ship, and,as the only lower deck member of the ship's cricket team being personally acquainted with many of the officers. So he was relieved to see that his next annual assessment was still "Very Good, Superior".

Meanwhile, a humiliated and vengeful Admiralty Board, who had themselves been entirely responsible for the debacle, searched for scapegoats and found them in the officers, many of whom had their careers permanently blighted, merely because they had been serving in ships which had mutinied. The torpedo officer who had been so sympathetic to Le Breton was only promoted to commander years later, when he was on the Retired List.

Herbert William Le Breton, known from his earliest days as Ginger, was born on June 22 1907 and joined the training ship *Impregnable* at Devonport as a boy seaman, 2nd class, in 1922. His first ship was the battleship *Resolution*, in which he gained accelerated advancement to ordinary seaman, aged $17\frac{1}{2}$. He qualified as a torpedoman at HMS Defiance, the Devonport torpedo school, in 1926 and gained a first-class pass in the Higher Educational Test for warrant rank the next year.

After two and a half years in the destroyer *Vanquisher*, he joined *Dorsetshire* for her first commission in 1930, and remained with her in South Africa (during which time he ran the ship's illicit bookmaking business). Five years later he became chief quartermaster in the aircraft carrier *Glorious* in the Mediterranean, at the time of the Abyssinian crisis. He came home to undergo the course for torpedo gunner, qualifying and being promoted to warrant rank on July 1 1937. "I was now Mister Le Breton," he said, "a very big day in my life."

He was the Gunner (T) in the destroyer *Basilisk* from 1937 to 1939, and then joined the destroyer *Hasty* for a hectic first 20 months of the war: capturing the German merchant ship *Morea* off the Portuguese coast in February 1940; taking part in the Norwegian campaign in April; the sinking of the Italian cruiser *Bartolomeo Colleoni* off Crete in July; and joining with *Havock* to sink the Italian submarine *Berillo* off Egypt in October.

By the time Le Breton left *Hasty* early in May 1941, she had been engaged in the night action off Cape Matapan in March when three Italian heavy cruisers and two destroyers were sunk, and in the evacuation of the army from Greece in April.

Until June 1943 he commanded the trawler *Redwing*, *Defiance*'s torpedo target and recovery vessel in Looe Bay. He was then appointed to the fast minelayer *Ariadne*, serving with the US 7th Fleet in the Pacific until 1945. His last appointment before retiring in 1948 with the war service rank of lieutenant was as *Defiance*'s mining and explosives instructor.

After 26 years in the Navy, Le Breton then spent 24 years in the licensed trade, becoming a well-known figure in Old Portsmouth as landlord of the Dolphin Hotel in the High Street.

To the end of his life, Ginger Le Breton was unrepentant about his part in the mutiny. In the programme *Mutiny* in the BBC series "The Call of the Sea" earlier in 1997 he said:"I'm in no way sorry about Invergordon. I look on it with pride. Otherwise I wouldn't be telling you, if I felt I'd been a traitor. I wasn't. I was doing the right thing."

He and his wife Phyllis,whom he married in 1940, had a son.

CAPTAIN
GEOFFREY STANNING

Captain Geoffrey Stanning (who died on October 9 1997, aged 85) was the only officer of the Paymaster Branch to take charge of one of HM ships in action against the enemy; consequently he was the only paymaster lieutenant to be awarded the DSO, after one of the most celebrated naval actions of the Second World War.

During the Norwegian campaign of 1940, Stanning was serving in the flotilla leader *Hardy* as secretary to Captain Warburton-Lee, commanding the 2nd Destroyer Flotilla. On April 9, the flotilla was detached from the Home Fleet with orders to go up the fjords to attack German transports, which were believed to have landed troops at Narvik.

On the way,Warburton-Lee learned that at least six

large German destroyers had been seen going up to Narvik, and that the enemy was therefore in much greater strength than had been reported. Nevertheless, he signalled:"Intend attacking at dawn high water."

Hardy arrived off Narvik at 4.30am on April 10, after a most hazardous passage in pitch darkness,thick mist and blinding snow squalls.There were, in fact, 10 large German destroyers there or nearby, and some two dozen enemy merchant ships.

Hardy and her flotilla mates *Hunter, Havock, Hotspur* and *Hostile* achieved complete surprise, and made three gun and torpedo attacks in the harbour. They finally left it in a chaotic confusion of smoke, fires and sporadic gunfire, with criss-crossing torpedo wakes streaking through the water. Two German destroyers were sunk and two damaged, and six merchantmen were also sunk.

Withdrawing down the fjord towards the open sea, the flotilla encountered the remaining five German destroyers and a running battle took place in which three more German destroyers were damaged; but *Hunter* was lost. *Hardy* had just hoisted the signal "Keep on engaging the enemy", when a 5-inch shell hit her bridge, killing or wounding everybody on it.

Stanning, who had been at the rear of the bridge recording events, was thrown bodily into the air by the force of the explosion and fell sprawling and dazed on the gyro compass binnacle. When he recovered his senses, he found his left leg was lifeless. He also had shrapnel wounds in his back from which he was to suffer for the rest of his life.

Looking around the shambles of the bridge, Stanning saw he was the only one on his feet.There was no-one in command of the ship, which was by now careering down the fjord at some speed, with a rocky shore close on the port side.

Paymasters were non-executive officers, not trained or expected to take part in fighting or control of a ship. Stanning, like all captains' secretaries, was nicknamed "Scratch". But, showing great initiative, he now took charge of the ship. There was no reply or any sound from the wheelhouse below, so dragging his shattered leg behind him, he went down and took the wheel from the lifeless hands of the coxswain until relieved by a sailor, when he struggled back to the bridge.

More shells had hit *Hardy*'s engine room, so that she began to lose speed. The torpedo officer, Lieutenant Heppel, arrived from aft in time to approve the order Stanning had just given, to run *Hardy* ashore before she sank. Stanning even had the presence of mind to remember to throw the weighted confidential and code books over the side before the ship grounded.

Hardy's survivors waded through the icy water to the shore. Here they were fed and looked after by the Norwegians until British destroyers arrived three days later. Warburton-Lee, mortally wounded, was floated ashore on a raft, but died on the way. He was awarded a posthumous Victoria Cross, the first of the war.

Geoffrey Heaton Stanning, a clergyman's son, was born on April 13 1912. He was a foundation scholar at Marlborough before joining the Navy as a paymaster cadet in the training ship *Erebus* in 1930. He served in the cruisers *Norfolk* in the Home Fleet and *Ceres* in the Mediterranean, and in the battleship *Barham* in 1934 as secretary to the captain, Max Horton.

In 1935-36 he was in the cruiser *London* in the Mediterranean during the Abyssinian Crisis and the Spanish Civil War. Stanning qualified as an interpreter in German in 1937, and again served under Horton, who was the admiral commanding the Reserve Fleet, flying his flag in the cruisers *Hawkins* and *Effingham*.

It took Stanning more than a year to recover from Narvik, but he later joined Admiral Sir Bertram Ramsay's staff at HMS Odyssey, the Combined Operations headquarters. In 1944, by then promoted commander, he received a formal Letter of Praise for his part in the planning of Operation Neptune, the invasion of Normandy.

He then joined the cruiser *Bermuda*, serving in the British Pacific Fleet and taking part in the reoccupation of Shanghai and Tsingtao after VJ Day. When the Korean war broke out in 1950, Stanning was in the cruiser *Belfast*, as secretary to Rear-Admiral W G Andrewes, the Flag Officer Second-in-Command Far East, who took command of the Commonwealth warships.

It fell to Stanning to organise, virtually from the start, the logistics of providing fuel, ammunition and other supplies from the fleet base at Sasebo, on the southern Japanese island of Kyushu, which was more than 1,000 miles from Hong Kong. Stanning was mentioned in despatches. He remained as admiral's secretary in Bermuda when Andrewes was C-in-C America and West Indies in 1951, and then at SACLANT HQ, in Norfolk, Virginia, when Andrewes was Deputy Supreme Allied Commander Atlantic, from 1952-54.

After a year as supply officer of the aircraft carrier *Ocean*, Stanning was loaned to the Royal New

Zealand Navy in 1955 as third Naval Member of the NZ Naval Board, responsible for personnel. He came home in 1958 to be Director of Supply Officers' Appointments. His last appointment, in 1961, was as Director of Administrative Planning.

Stanning retired in 1963 to take up the post of bursar at his old school, where he proved a most able administrator. At that time, every prep school headmaster was imploring the Master of Marlborough to "do something"to improve the food. It was Stanning who introduced cafeteria feeding. He made a point of attending every school function – social, religious, dramatic, musical, artistic, sporting – but was reticent about his wartime record. He came to know the members of the council so well that he could write the minutes of meetings before they were held.

He was chairman of the Public Schools' Bursars' Association from 1972 to 1975 and,after he retired in 1976, was president of the old boys' Marlburian Club in 1986.

Geoffrey Stanning took a prominent part in local and church affairs,in Marlborough and in Mildenhall, where the village fête was held in his garden every year. He married, in 1942, Mary Kinnear; they had a son and two daughters.

CAPTAIN
DICKY COURAGE

Captain Dicky Courage (who died on February 27 1998, aged 88) was probably the Royal Navy's most successful jockey of all time. He was the only serving naval officer ever to own and ride the winner of the Grand Military Gold Cup, known as the "Soldiers' Grand National", at Sandown Park.

Though he had a long and distinguished career in the Navy, and was twice decorated as a signal officer, he was especially proud of his racing victory at Sandown Park in 1935, when he and his horse Young Cuthbert won a keenly-contested race by two lengths in a field of 19. Sadly, the horse finished lame and never won again.

Richard Henry Courage, known as Dicky or sometimes Tufty, was born on November 14 1909, the son of Commander A V Courage, who had two runners, owned and trained by himself, in Golden Miller's Grand National in 1934. Dicky Courage, who was on loan to the Royal New Zealand Navy and serving in the cruiser *Dunedin*, listened to the race commentary on a radio provided by the ship's signal officer. One of the horses finished sixth, the other fell. Courage himself had previously won on both horses at Sandown, and had completed a double on the two at Lingfield.

Courage had gone to Dartmouth in 1923 and as a cadet had his first public ride at Hambleton Hunt point-to-point in 1926. As a midshipman, he rode on the flat in Malta and Greece and against barelegged Polynesian natives with spurs in Samoa. In the late 1920s he served for three and a half years in the

Mediterranean, where, as a four-goal polo player, he was an outstanding member of Mountbatten's team, the Shrimps.

Courage chose to specialise as a signal officer, thinking that would give him more chances to go racing, although, as he said, "the Navy always came first, and no mistake". So it was appropriate that he qualified at HM Signal School, at Portsmouth, in the year he won the Grand Military. When pressed by his Army racing rivals to transfer, Courage said: "No fear. I absolutely love the Navy and, anyway, I only do it to beat the Army!"

In fact, as a qualified signal officer, Courage had very much less time for racing. As Squadron Signal Officer to the 1st Cruiser Squadron, he served in the cruiser *London* under Rear-Admiral Max Horton during the Abyssinian Crisis and the Spanish Civil War. From June 1939 until November 1941 he was Fleet Signal Officer, East Indies Station. He was appointed OBE in 1942.

Courage was appointed Fleet Signal Officer, Home Fleet, in August that year. He soon had his baptism of fire in the anti-aircraft cruiser *Scylla*, flagship of Rear-Admiral Bob Burnett, during the passage of the convoy PQ18 which sailed from Loch Ewe on September 2.

PQ18, consisting of 40 ships, had a hard passage to Archangel, losing three ships to U-boats and 10 to the Luftwaffe. Maintaining communications between *Scylla*, the convoy commodore, the "fighting escort" of destroyers and the carrier *Avenger* put a heavy load on *Scylla*'s communications staff. More than once, Courage himself went 24 hours without sleep, but he and his staff never faltered under the most extreme pressure. He was awarded the DSC.

He was on the flag-bridge of the battleship *Duke of York*, as Fleet Signal Officer to Admiral Sir Bruce Fraser, the C-in-C, when ships of the Home Fleet hunted down and sank the German battlecruiser *Scharnhorst* off the North Cape of Norway on December 26 1943.

In his light-hearted account of that long and anxious day of searching in Arctic cold and darkness, Courage described the moment *Scharnhorst* was illuminated by starshell and *Duke of York* opened fire: "It was a dramatic moment, especially as the C-in-C nearly became a casualty. A large 'kitchen' clock was hung on the bulkhead of the admiral's bridge – essential for timing changes of course when zig-zagging. Normally before a full calibre firing such items are taken down but in the long-drawn-out run-up to the action this had been overlooked. With the first salvo it fell with a loud crash between the C-in-C and myself. That was our most dangerous moment, and also the only time either of us saw the *Scharnhorst*."

When the fleet arrived back in Scapa Flow, the ships' companies had the Christmas dinners they had missed at sea. At *Duke of York*'s somebody said:"Dicky ought to arrive at the Admiralty carrying the despatches on a horse." Arrangements were made with the Metropolitan Police to provide a horse for Courage who would fly south and bring the good news,not from Hendon (which was too far) but from Charing Cross.

But the aircraft landed at Hornchurch because of bad weather. Courage was relieved. "I'm sure I would have capsized on the way from Charing Cross station to the Admiralty," he said."I was in no state to ride a sharp two furlongs across Trafalgar Square in the blackout."

When, in 1944, Fraser was appointed C–in–C, British Pacific Fleet, he asked Courage to be his Fleet Signal Officer. The British ships were to operate with the US Navy and it was Courage, based in Australia, who, despite some opposition from home, successfully carried out the difficult and complicated task of changing the fleet's signalling methods and practice to the American system.

Courage came back to Britain in 1946 to serve as Communications Officer on the staff of Flag Officer Air (Home) and, from 1948 to 1949, as executive officer of *Illustrious*, the training and trials carrier in home waters. He then went to the Signal Division of the Admiralty before getting his first and only sea command, the sloop *Flamingo* in the Persian Gulf during the Iranian crisis of 1950-51.

His last appointment from 1951 until he retired at his own request in 1958 was in command of HMS Blackcap, the Royal Naval Air Station at Stretton, near Warrington. While there, he had his last race, at the age of 42, finishing third in the 1951 Liverpool Foxhunters on his own mare, Prudent Glen.

This must have been the first time a serving naval officer in his forties finished in the frame at the Aintree Grand National meeting. "Of course," Courage said, "they were real Captain Becher fences in those days. The winner picked up £600 and we got £41 2s.6d. That works out at five bob a fence and seven shillings and sixpence for Becher's!"

On leaving the Navy, he went to work for the family firm of Courage, the brewers, being careful to ensure that the maximum number of pubs were named after horses and that their signs and pictures were accurate. He liked to navigate in strange territory with nautical terms, saying such things as "promising property on the port bow".

In 1954 Courage applied for a permit to train. One question on the form was: "Is your head lad permanent?" Courage's reply was:"I hope so, it's my wife, Philippa!"

On his retirement, he moved to Petworth, in Sussex, within driving distance of seven racecourses. He acted as steward at local jump meetings and had horses in training with John Dunlop at Arundel.Until arthritic hips somewhat reduced his mobility, he and his wife regularly went racing more than 90 times a year. Even in a wheelchair, he was ever-present at Goodwood, and he was at the party at Sandown in 1990 to celebrate the 150th running of the Grand Military.

He had five hip replacement operations, and donated his hips to medical research.

Dicky Courage was excellent company, the most genial of men, who seemed to know everyone in the Navy. He established a real rapport with the sailors in every ship he served in. He was an authority on horses and racing, which he loved, but he was also very willing to draw on his own experience and give invaluable help to naval historians on a wide variety of subjects, from the sinking of *Scharnhorst* to the history of the Signal Branch.

He married, in 1937, Philippa Standish, whose forebear, Sir Frank Standish, owned the winners of three Derbys in the 1790s. They had a son and a daughter.

LIEUTENANT-COMMANDER
NINIAN SCOTT-ELLIOTT

Lieutenant-Commander Ninian Scott-Elliott (who died on March 24 1998, aged 86) had a distinguished wartime career at sea, and then went to live on a tropical island, enjoying the way of life of a character in a Joseph Conrad novel.

Ninian Scott-Elliot was born on August 29 1911, the son of the black sheep of an ancient Scottish family and a Hungarian princess. He went to Eton before joining the training ship *Erebus* in 1929. His first ship as a midshipman was the cruiser *Sussex*. He went out to the China station as a lieutenant to serve in the river gunboats *Falcon* and *Gannet* on the Upper Yangtse.

After command of the gunboat *Scorpion* in 1940 he came home to serve in the cruiser *Penelope* in the Mediterranean, before joining the Tribal class destroyer *Zulu* as first lieutenant in January 1942. In March, *Zulu* took part in the Second Battle of Sirte, when light cruisers and destroyers under Rear-Admiral Philip Vian defended a Malta convoy against a much more powerful Italian force which included two heavy cruisers and the battleship *Littorio*. By bold manoeuvring, adroit use of smoke screens as well as feinted and actual torpedo attacks, Vian's ships held off the enemy until dusk. Scott-Elliot was awarded the DSC.

In September 1942, *Zulu* took part in Operation Agreement, an ill-conceived attempt to storm the fortress of Tobruk and destroy its defences and port facilities. Everything possible went wrong. A heavy RAF bombing raid intended to subdue defences ensured that all the defenders were awake and at their posts. Few of the troops, carried in MTBs, or the Royal Marines, embarked in *Zulu* and *Sikh*, got ashore. *Sikh* was hit by shore fire and sank while *Zulu* was towing her. *Zulu* herself was bombed, badly damaged, and sank while under tow by the Hunt class destroyer *Hursley*.

Scott-Elliot was one of the 550 officers and men who became PoWs, though he was later mentioned in despatches for his work in *Zulu*, when he returned to England after his escape from a moving train which was taking him to Germany. He lifted the floorboards in his truck and dropped on to the track, where he lay while the train passed over him. He walked across the Alps,pausing for some skiing on the way.

Late in 1944, Scott-Elliot took command of the sloop *Amethyst*, one of five ships in the 22nd Escort Group, who sank U-482 in the North Channel off the Mull of Kintyre, on January 16 1945. On February 20, in the Irish Sea, *Amethyst* made a sharp 10-minute attack, one of the shortest of the war, on U-1276 and sank it;Scott-Elliot was awarded a Bar to his DSC. She then went out to the Far East to join the British Pacific Fleet. She was present when the Japanese forces in the Bismarcks, the Solomon Islands and New Guinea signed their surrender on board the carrier *Glory* off Rabaul in September 1945.

After the war, Scott-Elliot had two more destroyer commands: *Zambesi* from 1947 to 1949, and *Savage* from 1950 to 1952, when with difficulty he persuaded the Admiralty to let him leave the Navy.

Memories of the lush Solomon Islands he had seen in 1945 remained in his mind, and he decided to go there. Late in 1953 he set off in the 80-foot ketch *Sorengana* on a five-month voyage to the northern Solomon island of Rendova, where he landed on April Fool's Day 1954.

His companions hacked a clearing in the forest and pitched his tent. They sensed that he was impatient for them to go. So they sailed away, leaving him a case of gin, food, books (including novels by Conrad) and the bagpipes he had played almost every evening across the Atlantic and the Pacific.

There was a plantation on the island, derelict since the war. Scott-Elliot revived it, although his first crop, a variety of cocoa recommended by the Government, failed. "They didn't know whether it was Christmas or Marble Arch," he said. His estate of 2,000 acres grew coconuts and cocoa, with labour recruited from neighbouring islands.

Eventually he employed more than 50 men, giving them living conditions and terms of employment they had never dreamed of – their own houses with private gardens, a school, a church, a superannuation scheme, and paid holidays.

The Commander, as he was known, ran a taut ship. In a population which grew to more than 300, he knew everybody and everything about them, their marriages, their love affairs, their debts and superstitions, their hopes and their worries. He gave them all a cow at Christmas, milk for the babies, hurricane lamps for each house, and a bottle of oil a week.

He sent the pregnant women (the "bubbly Marys", in pidgin) to hospital. Once a month, on the evening of pay day, the children fell in outside his house and sang "London Bridge is Falling Down" and "Where

Are You Going, My Pretty Maid?"

The Commander had porridge, sausages and Cooper's Oxford marmalade for breakfast; scones and raspberry jam for tea. His shoes were made by Lobbs, and he had a pigskin diary from Asprey's every year. When the moon was full, he played Mozart, and Gracie Fields singing "Land of Hope and Glory", on a wind-up gramophone. Each evening after dinner, he drank brandy and smoked a cigar, looking out to sea from the verandah. On Trafalgar Day, he opened a bottle of champagne.

He liked being an anachronism, and abhorred visitors, especially almost naked Australian women tourists in yachts which would anchor in his lagoon. "Stone the crows," he said. "I suppose they like that sort of thing!"Into this Eden, a serpent was bound to arrive. In 1978, the Solomons became independent. The Government decreed no foreigner could own land. The Commander's freehold became a 75-year lease, with all manner of restrictions.

At the whim of an official in the capital, Honiara – someone "who doesn't know a frangipani from a beetroot" – decided that the Commander could be told what to do on his own plantation and have it confiscated if he transgressed. Disgusted, Scott-Elliot sold up and left.

He tried growing coffee in Costa Rica, but did not like the Costa Ricans. He spent his last years in Devon. Scott-Elliot's attitude to life was summed up by himself when *Amethyst* was pursuing a U-boat very close to shore and his navigating officer said, "Sir, I don't think this is very wise." "Pilot," said Scott-Elliot, "you'll never get anywhere in this life if you do only what is wise."

Attached to his will was a request:"Please send my two whale's teeth to the Fijian High Commission," and a note:"I just want to disappear; no notice in the papers or anywhere else, no stone, no plaque, no flowers, no obituary notice – just nothing. Cremation: and throw the ashes in the river."

In fact,the ashes went back to the Solomons,where the Commander is still held in the greatest respect and affection.

VICE-ADMIRAL
SIR PATRICK BAYLY

Vice-Admiral Sir Patrick Bayly (who died on May 1 1998, aged 83) was one of the Royal Navy's pioneer Combined Operations beach masters in the Second World War, during which he won a DSC and Bar; he earned another Bar in the Korean War.

Bayly was Principal Beach Master for Operation Husky, the invasion of Sicily in July 1943, and Operation Avalanche, the landings at Salerno in September. Although there have been famous amphibious operations in naval history, notably Quebec and Gallipoli, the Navy's traditional pre-occupation had always been to keep ships off beaches. The great series of amphibious operations of the Second World War therefore demanded a drastic change in attitude and proper specialist training.

He joined Combined Operations in October 1941 as Principal Beach Master on the staff of the Senior Officer (Landing), 101 Force, at Expeditionary Force Headquarters at Largs, Ayrshire. He was responsible for much of the early development of beach parties. A talented artist, he drew sketches of exercise landing areas as navigational aids for landing-craft coxswains. These were the forerunners of the models, based on aerial photographs, used for the Madagascar landings in May 1942 and ultimately for the D-Day landings in 1944.

Some of the earlier operations, particularly the disastrous Dieppe raid in August 1942, showed the need for specialist headquarters ships, and for landing-craft to be properly guided to their beaches; obstacles needed to be cleared before tanks could be landed, and stranded vehicles to be recovered.

In 1942 Bayly was appointed training officer for the Beach Commandos, as they were called, at HMS Armadillo, the training centre at Ardentinny on the shores of Loch Long. In 1943 he went to North Africa to take over "M" Beach Commando for Husky. Their task was to put the 51st Highland Division ashore at Portopalo Bay, the south-eastern toe of Sicily.

There was no immediate opposition, but Bayly found that "the beach in the sandy bay was not suitable for the larger landing craft. However the rocky beach on the northern shore was soon made suitable for all types of craft by pulling down walls and pill-boxes to fill crevices. This enabled us to discharge the landing craft in record time – so much so that the soldiery asked us to slow down, but I refused. Our aim was to clear the vulnerable landing-craft before the enemy could cause damage." Bayly was awarded the DSC.

Back in Tripoli, Bayly commandeered a motorcycle but was injured when he was forced off the road by an Army convoy. His arm was in a sling for the landing at Salerno by the London Division. This time there was enemy resistance and some landing craft beached in the wrong places, but Bayly deployed his beach commandos so as to get most of the assault troops ashore safely, although he was injured again in a road accident.

Some weeks later, he carried out an extremely hazardous survey of possible landing places in enemy-held territory, prior to a crossing of the River Volturno. He was awarded a Bar to his DSC.

As an experienced beach master, Bayly would have expected to take part in the Normandy landings, but by some quirk he was sent instead to the cruiser *Mauritius* as first lieutenant and fo'c'sle officer. When he joined early in January 1944, *Mauritius* was in a very delicate state of discipline. The ship had just called at Plymouth, where her sailors expected to go on long leave. When she was ordered to return to the Mediterranean, numbers of the ship's company refused duty. On the fo'c'sle, Bayly had to weigh anchor with the help of a few petty officer volunteers.

Thus, on June 6, Bayly was not on the beaches but in *Mauritius* bombarding them. The blast of her forward guns wrecked the ship's own electric capstans. Sailors who had refused to weigh anchor were glad of the chance to come up into the fresh air and do the task by hand, while the Royal Marine band stood on top of a turret playing "Anchors Aweigh".

Some time later, when Admiral Sir Bertram Ramsay, the Allied naval commander, visited *Mauritius*, he asked Bayly his name and where he had got his two DSCs. When Bayly said, "Sicily and Salerno as Principal Beach Master", Ramsay exclaimed, "Not *the* Bayly!"

Patrick Uniacke Bayly was born on August 4 1914 and went to Dartmouth as a cadet in 1928. He served as a sub-lieutenant in the cruiser *Amphion* on the South Africa station, as a lieutenant in the gunboat *Cicala* on the China station and in the cruiser *Durban*.

After the war, Bayly returned to the Mediterranean and to *Mauritius* as Staff Officer (Operations) to the Flag Officer 1st Cruiser Squadron, when the ship took part in anti-immigration patrols off Palestine. Following appointments in the Admiralty, he went to the Far East in 1951 to command the sloop *Alacrity* and then the destroyer *Constance* in the Korean War, operating on both the west and east coasts of Korea.

In February 1952, *Alacrity* had closed the eastern shore to engage a locomotive on the coastal railway line when a 45mm tank gun opened fire at 3,000 yards range and scored seven hits before *Alacrity* could get clear. Damage was negligible and there were no casualties, although one shell narrowly missed Bayly himself. He was awarded the US Legion of Merit for *Alacrity* and a second Bar to his DSC.

Bayly came home in 1953 and was Staff Officer (Operations) to the C-in-C The Nore. Promoted captain in 1954, he went to the Admiralty as Assistant Director of Plans and in 1957 took command of *Cavendish* as Captain (D) 6th Destroyer Squadron. He then had appointments on the staff of the Nato Supreme Allied Commander Atlantic, at Norfolk, Virginia, and as Chief of Staff to the C-in-C Mediterranean.

As a rear-admiral, Bayly was Flag Officer Sea

Training at Portland from 1963 to 1965, and then President of the Royal Naval College, Greenwich, until his promotion to Vice-Admiral in 1967. His final appointment (1967-70) was in Malta as Chief of Allied Staff Naval Headquarters Southern Europe.

In retirement Bayly was director for 17 years of the Maritime Trust, founded in 1969 by Prince Philip and the Duke of Westminster. During that period, ship preservation became organised nationally. Bayly's advice was sought on almost every aspect of vessel preservation, restoration, building, sailing and access to the public. He was concerned with the restoration and preservation of the *Mary Rose*; the clipper *Cutty Sark*; the Victorian battleship *Warrior*; Sir Francis Chichester's yacht *Gipsy Moth IV*; the steamship *Great Britain*; *Belfast*; Sir Alec Rose's *Lively Lady* and Scott's *Discovery*, as well as a range of small craft.

In June 1984 Bayly witnessed the launch of the space shuttle Discovery in Florida, when Captain Scott's telescope from RRS *Discovery* was taken into space. He kept his close association with the shuttle programme for many years. He attended the International Congress of Maritime Museums and opened the new Sydney Maritime Museum in 1988. He was a founding member of the Falkland Islands Appeal and Trust, and opened the new swimming pool in Port Stanley in 1990. He was also an honorary member of the International Association of Cape Horners, patron of the RN Commando Association and a trustee of the British Korean Veterans Association.

Patrick Bayly was adept at running off appropriate verse at the drop of a hat to suit any occasion. In Malta, he did extensive research into St Paul's shipwreck on the island. He was an expert carpenter and a keen golfer, regularly playing in the Admirals v Generals match.

He was appointed CB in 1965, and KBE in 1968. In 1945, he married May Jardine; they had two daughters.

VICE-ADMIRAL
SIR ROY TALBOT

Vice-Admiral Sir Roy Talbot (who died on June 16 1998, aged 88) had a 44-year naval career which was a hectic affair of chances: two sinkings and two DSOs, a near fatal air crash, war wounds, an ankle injury and official disapproval followed by promotion.

Towards all these vicissitudes Roy Talbot maintained a philosophical attitude. As he remarked in his memoirs *Old Rope*: "That's life, you can't please everyone all the time."

Arthur Allison Fitzroy Talbot was born on October 22 1909 into a naval family. His father was a distinguished captain and two of his cousins were admirals. At 12, he plucked up courage and said he "would much prefer to go to Sandhurst and the Cavalry than go to sea. The result was more or less a crack over the head with an empty bottle, and that was that."

Talbot went to Dartmouth as a cadet in 1923 and passed out tenth from bottom of his term. He and the cadet who finished ninth from bottom were the only two of their 56-strong term to achieve flag rank. As a midshipman, Talbot joined the battleship *Royal Oak* in the Mediterranean, where he witnessed the *Royal Oak* court martials, the great naval scandal of 1928. The affair was sparked off by a rear-admiral's rebuke to the Royal Marine bandmaster over the "unsuitable" music played at a wardroom dance.

The upshot was damage to the careers of the rear-admiral, *Royal Oak*'s captain and commander and the C-in-C, who did not, as expected, become First Sea Lord. Leaving *Royal Oak* with the discouraging report – "This officer's only redeeming feature is his sense of humour" – Talbot went out to join the cruiser *Cumberland* on the China station. "To qualify as a China Bird at that time," he said, "it was necessary to visit the Great Wall of China, face North and relieve yourself. We all passed this test with flying colours."

As a sub-lieutenant, Talbot joined the light cruiser *Centaur*. But he soon grew bored of pacing the quarterdeck and, to the intense disapproval of his commodore, his father and his grandfather, volunteered for flying. Early in 1932, Talbot was about to land his Avro 504N at RAF Leuchars when another aircraft flew into him. He remembered saying, "Good God, I believe I am crashing", before he landed on the shore at St Andrews, near the Royal and Ancient Golf Club. He suffered a permanent ankle injury.

The following year, Talbot was appointed first lieutenant of *Bryony*, the C-in-C's despatch vessel. *Bryony* was a social ship, as was made clear in the briefing which her captain "Wash" Warburton-Lee, who was to win a posthumous VC at Narvik, gave Talbot: "Your main duties will be to run the stables, and provided you keep the ponies fit and the groom sweet, and the senior officers are handed the right length polo stick on the right pony, you will be doing all right. Got it?" For two years Talbot "got it"to such a degree that he was given his first command, the small 1918-vintage coal-burning minesweeper *Stoke*.

Talbot was next appointed first lieutenant of the new destroyer *Imperial* and returned to the Mediterranean at the time of the Spanish Civil War. In October 1939 he was given command of the 10th Anti-Submarine Striking Force – actually four trawlers – of which he himself commanded *Cape Siretoko*. Based at Aberdeen, the 10th carried out patrols along the coast of north-east Scotland, the Orkneys and Shetlands through the bitter winter of 1939 until April 1940, when they crossed to Norway.

On April 28, after the 10th had spent three nights evacuating troops from Aandalsnes and the trawlers had each made two round trips a night, lifting the best part of 4,800 men, *Cape Siretoko* was bombed and badly damaged. Talbot suffered shrapnel wounds in his left hand and arm,"not bad, but rather messy," he recalled."I still have the bloodstained chart and my tin hat which had been knocked off my head and was found to have a 2-inch gash right through it."

Yet Talbot managed to beach *Cape Siretoko* before she sank, and then, to boost morale, had an ostentatious shave before supervising the destruction of confidential equipment.He and his ship's company got ashore, and eventually came home in the cruiser *Glasgow* with King Haakon of Norway. Talbot was awarded the DSO.

Having passed the command examination before the war, Talbot hoped for a destroyer, but instead, in May 1940, he was appointed in command of the 3rd

Motor Gunboat Flotilla, with 12 boats. They had been ordered for the French Navy but were taken over after the fall of France by five Royal Navy, five Royal Canadian Navy and three Polish Navy crews. Based at Fowey, the flotilla operated at night on anti-E-boat patrols, covering Channel convoys and sweeping along the coast from Ushant to Cherbourg.

In July 1940, enemy acoustic mines closed the port of Plymouth. MGB46, Talbot's own boat, had to make a high-speed run up the Hamoaze, detonating mines as she went. The flotilla's officers were a high-spirited lot and, after an incident in a Fowey hotel, there was an official inquiry which criticised Talbot's leadership. Potentially more serious was an absurd contretemps in November.

Talbot had been ordered to stay ashore at Fowey when MGB46 put to sea. A visiting staff officer − a First World War VC whom Talbot considered to be "a slightly unbalanced fire eater" − thought this reprehensible, and wrote to the Admiralty describing Talbot as "unfitted for any type of command". The letter from Talbot's own admiral, exonerating him, was destroyed in the Blitz, so his next appointment was not a destroyer command, as he had hoped, but in the cruiser *Edinburgh* as a watch-keeper.

Talbot found *Edinburgh* a very happy ship. He was made first lieutenant on merit, while she escorted a high-speed troop convoy to the Cape and took part in two Malta convoys. On April 30 1942, *Edinburgh* was escorting convoy QP11, homeward bound from Murmansk, when she was hit by two torpedoes from U-456. At first, there seemed a chance of saving her, but after she was hit by a third torpedo from a German destroyer she had to be abandoned, and was

eventually sunk by a torpedo from the destroyer
Foresight. Talbot was among those taken off by the
minesweeper *Harrier*.

With a good report from *Edinburgh*, Talbot was at
last given a destroyer command, the 1919-vintage
modified W class *Whitshed*, escorting East Coast
convoys with the 16th Flotilla, based at Harwich. On
December 12 1942, *Whitshed* led a night action
against an enemy convoy off the harbour of Dieppe
in which a German mine destructor ship was sunk.
Talbot was awarded a Bar to his DSO.

In July 1943, Talbot had another destroyer
command, the brand new *Teazer*, in the 24th Flotilla,
once again in the Mediterranean. For 18 months
Teazer operated in support of the Army at the Anzio
and South of France landings, escorting military
convoys, bombarding coastal roads and railways,
carrying out night sweeps to intercept enemy supply
shipping in the Adriatic, and landing clandestine
parties on the Greek islands. Talbot's last wartime
appointment was as Chief of Staff to the Commodore, Western Isles, training Battle of the Atlantic
escorts at Tobermory. Commodore "Monkey"
Stephens was not an easy man to serve, but Talbot
handled him with great skill.

After the war, Roy Talbot had the happy knack of
being on the spot when anything happened. He was
in the Far East, commanding the C-in-C's dispatch
vessel *Alert*, when the frigate *Amethyst* made her dash
down the Yangtse in 1949. He was naval attaché in
Moscow when Stalin died in 1953. He was Captain
(D) of the 3rd Destroyer Squadron, commanding
Saintes, when there was trouble in Cyprus in 1955,
and he took part in Operation Musketeer, the joint

Anglo-French attempt to recover the Suez Canal.

Promoted rear-admiral, Talbot was Flag Officer Arabian Sea and Persian Gulf, when Kuwait was threatened by Iraq in 1961; he showed admirable diplomacy in dealing with visiting politicians, such as Edward Heath. As a vice-admiral and C-in-C South Atlantic and South America station, he again showed his diplomatic skill when there were renewed Argentine rumblings over the Falklands, and when Harold Wilson's government wished to introduce sanctions against South Africa.

His final appointment was C-in-C Plymouth from 1965 to 1967.

Talbot had a life-long love of horses and riding. His maternal grandfather, William Allison, an acknowledged authority on thoroughbred breeding, had named Talbot's mother Blair Athol, after the 1864 Derby winner; and Roy Talbot used his game ankle as an excuse not to take any exercise other than riding. On Malta he played in the "Sandflies" team with Mountbatten and Warburton-Lee. While standing by *Imperial*, building at Hawthorn and Leslie's yard on the Tyne, he hunted three days a week, with the Tyndale, the Hayden and the Buccleuch.

He retired to farm in Somerset, where he was appointed Deputy Lieutenant in 1973, and became chairman of the Taunton Vale Foxhounds and the Taunton Vale Polo Club.

Roy Talbot, who was appointed CB in 1961 and KBE in 1964, married, in 1940, Joyce Linley, who died in 1981; they had two daughters. He married secondly, in 1983, Lady (Elizabeth) Durlacher, who died in 1995.

FLOTILLENADMIRAL
OTTO KRETSCHMER

Flotillenadmiral Otto Kretschmer (who died on August 5 1998, aged 86) was the highest scoring U-boat "ace" of the Second World War, known to the German press as the "Wolf of the Atlantic".

Kretschmer carried out 16 patrols in the first 18 months of the war, when he spent 224 days at sea and sank 44 merchant ships totalling 266,029 tons. His record of more than 1,000 tons of shipping sunk for every day spent at sea was never equalled. He was one of only five U-boat commanders to be awarded the Knight's Cross with Swords and Oak Leaves, which was presented to him by Hitler himself.

In September 1939, Kretschmer was commanding officer of the small Type 11B U-23 which he had commanded since October 1937 and in which, despite repeated torpedo malfunctions, he sank more than 20,000 tons of shipping as well as the destroyer *Daring*, in the North Sea on February 18 1940. For his service in U-23 Kretschmer was awarded the Iron Cross 1st Class and recommended for the command of a larger U-boat.

In April 1940 he took command of the new type VII-B U-99, known as the Golden Horseshoe because of the insignia painted on its conning tower. Thus began almost a year of astounding action in the Atlantic. One of his most notable coups was during the height of what the U-boat crews called *die glüchlich Zeit* (the happy time) in the last months of 1940.

On November 3, Kretschmer attacked the outward bound convoy OB237 and sank four large vessels of more than 40,000 tons, including the armed merchant cruiser *Laurentio*. On the same day, he sank a second armed merchant cruiser, *Patroclus*, when she had stopped to pick up *Laurentio*'s survivors. Kretschmer himself thought *Patroclus*'s captain *unkriegerisch* – "unwar-wary" – to stop in such circumstances.

U-boat captains were instructed that 3,000 yards was the best range for torpedoes, which should be fired in salvoes of four or six, so as to make certain of a hit. But Kretschmer evolved his own tactics. His motto was "one torpedo – one ship". He stayed on the surface while attacking a convoy, making deadly diagonal strokes through the convoy's ranks, picking off individual ships from close range with a sniper's skill.

Trimmed down at night, with only the conning tower showing above water, U-99 was almost impossible to detect by escorts which still lacked radar; with a surface speed of 17 knots, it was faster than a corvette. Kretschmer was particularly proud of the attack which sank the armed merchant cruiser *Forfar* in the Atlantic on December 2 1940 – although he used five torpedoes."I had to submerge in the face of an advancing destroyer," he said. "But I still continued to fire, having previously cleared the bridge. I got away across the enemy's bow." U-99's war log showed one torpedo hit at a range of 3,600 metres – "a huge distance at night," Kretschmer commented.

U-99 sailed from Lorient for its eighth patrol on February 22 1941. On March 16, Kretschmer penetrated the columns of the homeward-bound convoy HX112 to make one of the most accomplished surface attacks of his career, in which he sank five ships in an hour. U-99 was clearly illuminated in the flames from burning tankers. Kretschmer said later he felt "as exposed as a man sunbathing on a beach".

He was retiring, having expended all his torpedoes, when U-99 was detected by the escort early the next morning. Kretschmer had been betrayed by his bridge staff. U-99's lookouts failed to spot the destroyer *Vanoc* until she was almost on top of them. Hearing the alarm report, the startled officer of the watch gave the order to dive – in direct contravention of Kretschmer's standing orders.

Once dived, U-99 was immediately detected by radio and attacked by the destroyer *Walker*. In what Kretschmer realised was the worst attack he had ever suffered, six depth charges burst around U-99, which plunged to 700 feet below the designed crushing depth, before pulling out of the dive. Kretschmer hoped to catch a trim at about 300 feet, when he might have a chance to work out an evasion plan.But U-99 rose uncontrollably to the surface, where *Vanoc* illuminated the U-boat with searchlight and *Walker* opened fire with main and secondary armament.

Kretschmer ordered "Abandon ship". He then had the message flashed to *Walker*: "Captain to Captain: Please save my men drifting in your direction. I am sinking." U-99 sank, but *Walker* picked up Kretschmer and all but three of the ship's company of 43.

Otto Wilhelm August Kretschmer was born on May 1 1912, the son of a schoolmaster. He went to his father's primary school and then to a Staatliche Bildungsanstalt (State Education Institution).

Too young to join the Reichsmarine, he joined "Crew 30", the class who would begin in 1930. Meanwhile, he travelled and studied in England, France and Italy. He did his basic naval training at Stralsund on the Baltic coast and was rated sea cadet in October 1930, before joining the sail training ship *Niobe*. Rated petty officer in January 1932, he served in the pocket battleship *Deutschland* and the cruiser *Emden*.

He was commissioned Leutnant in October 1934 and joined the U-boat Command in May 1936, being appointed to the 2nd U-boat Flotilla. From 1935 to 1936 he was a watch officer in U-35, serving off Spain during the Spanish Civil War.

After the sinking of U-99, Kretschmer was a prisoner for the rest of the war at Bowmanville, Ontario, where he devised a system, circumventing camp censorship, of transmitting intelligence back to Germany. It was so refined that he was able to arrange for a U-boat to rendezvous at the mouth of the St Lawrence River to pick up escaped prisoners. The prisoners were recaptured before they could be picked up, but the U-boat did appear punctually at the right place.

Released in 1947, Kretschmer married Dr Luise-Charlotte Mohnsen-Hinrichs,née Bruns,in 1948.He was the first president of the newly formed German Marine-Bund (Navy Federation) and joined the Bundesmarine in 1955.

Promoted to Kapitän zur See, he served in the United States, France, Belgium, Britain, Denmark, Norway, Greece, Portugal, the Netherlands and Turkey. Frau Dr Kretschmer launched U-1, the Bundesmarine's first U-boat,in 1962.Kretschmer was promoted to flotilla admiral in 1965 and was Chief of Staff, Allied Naval Forces Nato Baltic Approaches, until his retirement in 1970.

Nicknamed "Silent Otto", Kretschmer often incurred official displeasure by his extreme reluctance to signal while at sea. In his opinion, there was far too much signalling to and from U-boats. He suspected that the Allies had penetrated some of the German Navy's secret cyphers.

He was a household name in Germany, where his deeds were hailed in national headlines, and he was obviously very useful for the Nazi propaganda machine. But unlike some other U-boat aces he would not make propaganda speeches, nor write his autobiography for propaganda purposes.

In 1993, he took part in television programmes for the 50th anniversary of the Battle of the Atlantic. Speaking from his house in Spain, he stressed that his chief care had always been the welfare of his sailors.

Kretschmer gained the most favourable reports on his ability from his earliest days in command. But perhaps the most telling appraisal of him came from an opponent. In 1941, Captain George Creasy, Director of the Anti-Submarine Division at the Admiralty, especially asked to meet Kretschmer.

"I was anxious," Creasy recalled, "to judge for myself what manner of man a successful U-boat captain might be: to see for myself, if I could, the state of his nerves, to measure his judgment, gauge his reactions to his seniors and his juniors, the expected and the unexpected. In simple words, to size him up. I saw a young and obviously self-confident naval commander who bore himself, in the difficult conditions of recent captivity, with self-respect, modesty and courtesy.

"His record stamped him as brave and quick-witted; his appearance and manners were those of an officer and a gentleman. When he left me, I sincerely hoped that there were not too many like him."

COLONEL
PADDY STEVENS

Colonel Paddy Stevens (who died on August 30 1998, aged 76) won an MC on D-Day as a lieutenant with 41 Commando of the Royal Marines. Early that day, 41 Commando, with Stevens as second-in-command of A Troop, landed under heavy fire on Sword Beach to attack their first objective, an enemy strong point in the town of Lion-sur-Mer.

"I remember a line of detached houses," Stevens recalled, "seen through smoke, two or three tanks burning, troops on the beach, and some bodies in the water. There was a lot of shelling and machine-gun fire, not aimed specifically against our craft, but a nasty pause before we got off the ship, and I had to wade a bit. We lost quite a few men on the beach. I remember standing up because I thought I was just as good a target lying down . . . ." At one point Stevens and his troop were cut off from the main body by two enemy armoured cars, one of which Stevens attacked and wrecked with a hand grenade. The other, he said, "beat it back into cover as fast as he could".

During that day, 41 Commando suffered more than 100 casualties from a total strength of 450. A Troop alone lost 30 from 60, including the CO, and it was

Stevens who led the survivors against the final objective of the day, a fortified radar station inland at Douvres-la-Delivrande. The position was one of the strongest on the coast, and it held out for some days. Stevens led one patrol which blew a gap in the minefield and entered the radar station to gain information of great value in subsequent attacks.

The place was finally taken by 41 Commando on June 17, with the assistance of a naval bombardment and flail tanks to clear mines. After this, 41 Commando took part in the break-out from Normandy and,often marching by night,pursued the enemy across northern France. In November 1944, Stevens again led A Troop in the assault landing at Walcheren, at the mouth of the Scheldt, to clear the approaches to the great port at Antwerp. Once again, he bore a charmed life. In one attack, 41 Commando came under heavy fire. "I saw a shell burst ahead," Stevens said, "and I saw, I actually saw, a piece of shrapnel flying towards me. It hit a phosphorus grenade on my chest, ignited it... I snatched it off and threw it away."

Stevens recalled:"We had a ripple of casualties from D-Day on. I was a subaltern on D-Day, a captain on D+1, a major after Walcheren — that's all in five months. There was always a heavy toll among the officers. They were expected to lead from the front and they did." Stevens's luck finally ran out when he was wounded in the leg while leading a patrol along the bank of the Maas in February 1945. It was decided he was too brave for his own good and, despite his protests, he was sent home to recover.

Terence Morton Patrick Stevens, known as Paddy, was born on November 25 1921, the youngest of four sons in a military family. He intended to follow his father and brother into the Army but, when direct entry through Sandhurst was suspended at the outbreak of the war, he joined the Royal Marines as a probationary second lieutenant in January 1940. After training and service in the battleship *King George V* he joined 41 Commando early in 1944.

After the war, Stevens was on the staff of the RM Commando Training Unit, served for two years in the Mediterranean with 42 Commando, and was on the staff of RMA Sandhurst. Following staff and regimental appointments as a major, Stevens was promoted lieutenant-colonel, and took command of 45 Commando RM in July 1963, serving at Aden.

The following January there was a mutiny amongst troops of the Tanganyikan Army at Colito Barracks, north of Dar-es-Salaam, and President Nyerere appealed for help. In response, 45 Commando embarked in the carrier *Centaur* and flew ashore in helicopters, quelling the mutiny in a few hours and restoring order in the whole area in a few days. Later in the year, 45 Commando faced a much more serious situation in the mountainous Radfan region of the South Arabian Federation, operating against dissident tribesmen who had arms and assistance from adjacent Yemen.

The key to the campaign was a mountain codenamed Cap Badge. When its capture was first proposed, "doubts were expressed", Stevens recalled, "as to whether we could move our entire commando through that country in single file at night. I remembered how my brigade had moved out of Normandy in '44, so I said, 'OK, we'll walk it.' It was the first yomp, maybe. Once we had Cap Badge we controlled the entire country."

For his leadership of 45 Commando in the Radfan, Stevens was appointed OBE. After a course at the Imperial Defence College in 1968 and a final appointment in the Operations and Training Division of the Nato International Military Staff in Brussels, Stevens retired in 1971. He then joined the Civil Service at principal grade. Promoted to assistant secretary in 1977, he became head of S4 (Air) in the Air Force Department. As head of the Naval Law Division he was adviser to the Admiralty Board and the Chief of Naval Personnel.

Paddy Stevens seldom reminisced about his active service. To him, the past was another country, rarely visited. He was a family man, an expert builder of sandcastles and rabbit hutches, who gave his son three pieces of advice: "Don't join the military, always check the bill in a restaurant, and never buy the cheapest wine, order the second cheapest bottle."

He expressed many of his deepest thoughts in his poems. In one, he addressed his own mortality with typical irony and humour, imagining the final disposal of his mortal remains:

Those are meals that were my thoughts,
no cast of mind, just your reports,
no monument, just vapour trails,
books and clothes to jumble sales.

He married, first, Brigit Timothy. They had a son and a daughter. The marriage was dissolved. With his second wife Judy he had three daughters.

VICE-ADMIRAL
SIR "JOC" HAYES

Vice-Admiral Sir "Joc" Hayes (who died on September 7 1998, aged 85) was in the battlecruiser *Repulse* when she was sunk with the battleship *Prince of Wales* by Japanese aircraft in the South China Sea on December 10 1941.

Admiral Sir Tom Phillips, C-in-C Eastern Fleet, Captain John Leach and 327 officers and men of *Prince of Wales* were lost, along with 513 of *Repulse's* people. When told of this disaster, Winston Churchill said, "In all the war I never received a more direct shock." Yet he himself had contributed to it by dragooning a reluctant Admiralty into sending two ships to the Far East, with the object, so he told Stalin, of "keeping Japan quiet". In Hayes's own account, he tried "to convey how *Repulse* will for ever remain the centre of gravity of my naval life."

Escorted by four destroyers, the two ships had sailed from Singapore on the evening of December 8 after a report of a Japanese invasion force in the north. When nothing was seen, Phillips turned back, only to be diverted by another report that the enemy was landing at Kuantan, on the Malayan coast. Again, nothing was seen, and the ships were returning to Singapore when they were sighted by Japanese aircraft. The air attacks began at about 11 o'clock. Phillips, of whose "lethal mistakes" Hayes was very critical, did not break radio silence, evidently believing that his staff in Singapore would know, without being told, that his ships would need air cover off Kuantan.

Lacking this, both ships were repeatedly hit by

bombs and torpedoes. *Repulse* had survived one bomb hit and several near misses when three torpedoes struck her port side and she capsized, while travelling at more than 20 knots. "My movements," Hayes recalled, "were then dictated by gravity, like one of those balls on a bagatelle table which bounces off pins – the funnel, red-hot from steaming, then against the port flag-lockers, by which time, normally some 50 feet above the waterline, they were almost awash, and so overboard helplessly and down for what seemed a long time. When I bobbed up, the great iron structure of the main top, normally some hundred feet above the waterline, skidded just above my head as the ship plunged on and down with the screws still turning."

John Osler Chattock Hayes, known as "Joc", was born on Bermuda on May 9 1913, the son of an Army doctor. He went to Dartmouth as a cadet in 1927. He was a midshipman in the battleship *Royal Oak* in the Mediterranean and the cruiser *Cumberland* on the China station, and a sub-lieutenant in the light cruiser *Danae* in the West Indies. Hayes specialised as a navigating officer in 1936 and was "N" of the sloop *Fowey* in the Persian Gulf and the cadet training cruiser *Vindictive*. At the outbreak of war he was "N" of the cruiser *Cairo*, hurriedly commissioned from reserve and largely manned by the Humber Division of the RNVR.

Hayes's failure to sight a buoy one night when *Cairo* was escorting a convoy revealed that his sight was poor. A specialist who examined him said he should never have been allowed into the Navy, let alone as a bridge officer. Hayes was therefore relieved to be sent to *Repulse* as assistant navigator and signal officer in December 1940.

After *Repulse* was lost, Hayes was picked up and taken to Singapore. He was appointed naval liaison officer to the 2nd Battalion, Argyll and Sutherland Highlanders,who were fighting a rearguard action on the Malayan mainland. He had orders to "collect anything and everything you can lay hands on which floats in order to get what's left of the Army across the Strait when the moment comes." He assembled what he called "a motley armada" which duly took the Army off. Hayes had the most profound admiration and respect for the "Jocks", who appointed him an honorary Argyll and Sutherland. He and Colonel Ian MacAlister Stewart of the Argylls were the last two to walk across the Johore Causeway, being played over by a lone piper.

Hayes was then naval liaison officer to General Sir Lewis "Piggy" Heath, commanding 3 Corps. He escaped from Singapore just before it fell,going in the destroyer *Jupiter* to Batavia, and then on to Colombo. As a survivor of 3 Corps, Hayes produced a report in which he described the collapse of discipline at the end, referring particularly to some Australian troops: "The streets were full of debauched, drunken soldiers, deserters from their units, NCOs among them but not officers, breaking into any hotel they could find, shouting 'They won't be long now.'"

When Hayes's report was released into the public domain in the mid-1990s, it provoked a furious reaction from Australian politicians. But Hayes stuck to his story. His next appointment was as Staff Officer (Operations) to Rear-Admiral Louis "Turtle" Hamilton,flying his flag in the cruiser *London*. In July 1942, *London* was part of the escort of the Russian convoy PQ17 which was believed to be threatened by the battleship *Tirpitz* and ordered by the First Sea Lord to scatter, resulting in catastrophic losses amongst the merchant ships. In 1970, Hayes gave first hand evidence which greatly assisted Captain Jack Broome, PQ17's close escort commander, in his successful libel suit against David Irving, author of *The Destruction of Convoy PQ17*.

Hayes served on the staff of Admiral Mansfield in the cruiser *Orion* in 1944 and the following year was appointed OBE for his part in the relief of Greece.

In 1991, he published his memoirs, *Face the Music: a Sailor's Story*. As the title suggests, the book abounds in references to his love of music;as a midshipman,he played Wagner on a wind-up gramophone to a bemused AB in *Royal Oak*'s 15-inch gun spotting top; as a commander at HMS St Angelo on Malta, he compared the early morning sunlight and church bells in Grand Harbour, Valletta, with the orchestral opening to the third act of *Tosca*.

There are some revealing insights: how to take over a bad ship (a frigate on the South African station); how, as Commander's Appointer in the Admiralty, to temper another's disappointment at not getting the desired job; and how, as Naval Secretary, to support one's First Lord (Lord Carrington) wholeheartedly while not being overborne by the First Sea Lord (Sir Caspar John). In 1966, as Flag Officer Second-in-Command Western Fleet, flying his flag in the cruiser *Tiger*, Hayes visited Bermuda and saw again his childhood home. His last appointment, before he retired in 1966, was as Flag Officer Scotland, Northern Ireland.

He was appointed KCB in 1967. In retirement,

Hayes was chairman of the Cromarty Firth Port Authority, president of the Scottish Council of King George's Fund for Sailors, a member of the Queen's Bodyguard for Scotland (Royal Company of Archers) and, from 1977 to 1988, Lord Lieutenant of Ross and Cromarty, Skye and Lochalsh. When Hayes and his spaniel were one day sitting in the Lord Lieutenant's car, waiting on the jetty at Invergordon to greet a visiting dignitary, Hayes saw a chief petty officer he remembered as a boy seaman at St Vincent. The chief came over to the car: "Excuse me, sir. Weren't you at St Vincent?" "Yes!" said Hayes, delighted and flattered. "Thought so, sir. Recognised the dog."

Joc Hayes married, in 1939, Rosalind Mary Finlay; they had two sons and a daughter.

―――――――――

REAR-ADMIRAL
ROY FOSTER-BROWN

Rear-Admiral Roy Foster-Brown (who died on January 8 1999, aged 94) commanded the frigate squadron which located the submarine *Affray* after a prolonged search in the English Channel in 1951.

Affray sailed from Gosport on the afternoon of April 16 1951 with a training class of 23 executive and engineer officers on board for submarine experience, and four Royal Marines of the Special Boat Squadron who were to land on a beach in 18-foot collapsible canvas boats and be picked up again by the submarine. *Affray* dived that evening, some 30 miles south of the Isle of Wight, and was due to signal its position between 9 and 10am daily. When there was no signal on the 17th, shore stations tried to call it. After an hour with no reply the general signal SUBSMASH ("a submarine is overdue") was passed.

A massive search got under way which eventually involved other submarines, some 20 British, American, French and Dutch warships, a salvage team of tugs and lifting vessels, every lifeboat on the south coast, maritime patrols by naval and RAF aircraft and, for the first time, naval helicopters. *Affray* was expected to surface about 20 miles south-east of Start Point and the initial search concentrated there. But as the hours passed the search widened to include the whole Channel.

Finally, on the evening of 19th, after hopes had been raised and dashed several times, the immediate search was called off, as there was no longer any great urgency to save life. But the search by the 6th Frigate Squadron under Foster-Brown went on through the summer. "We had made 250 Asdic echo-sounding detections," Foster-Brown said, "we had evaluated 31 wrecks, 74 rocks and 34 tidal rips. We had steamed a total of 23,800 nautical miles in an area of 6,000 square miles. And we had not the slightest trace or hint of where the *Affray* might be."

At last, Foster-Brown thought back to his own days as a submariner. "I calculated that, after diving, Blackburn (*Affray*'s captain) continued for eight hours at a speed of four knots. He then rose to periscope depth at dawn on April 17 to fix his position by sighting on the Casquets lighthouse in the Channel Islands." Foster-Brown marked an X on his chart and told his navigating officer: "Tomorrow we shall search the Hurd Deep and we shall find the *Affray*." Next morning the search began of the Hurd Deep, an underwater ravine running east to west off the Channel Islands, using Type 162 specialist sounding gear. The Deep had been searched before, without success. But this time after only an hour there was the solid unmistakable contact of a submarine's hull, so strong that, as Foster-Brown said, "It nearly blew me out of my chair!"

The deep diving vessel *Reclaim* was called to the spot and lowered her newly designed underwater camera, which picked out the shape of a submarine gun platform, and then, on the side of the conning tower, the letter "Y". Moving along, the camera began slowly to trace the letters a-f-f-r-a-y. *Affray* was found on June 14, 280 feet down, near the edge of the Hurd Deep, 67 miles south-west of St Catherine's lighthouse and 37 miles south-west of its last reported diving position. Divers later discovered that its schnorkel mast (which enabled it to run its diesel engines while submerged) had been snapped off. It must have flooded so rapidly that nothing could have saved the men on board.

Foster-Brown was surprised and annoyed that his report was never acknowledged by the Admiralty, and that he was never given the credit for finding *Affray*. Two years later, when he went to the Admiralty as Director of the Signal Division, Foster-Brown called up the *Affray* file. He was shocked and incensed to find that a captain in the Admiralty, one of his rivals for promotion to rear-admiral, had claimed the credit for finding *Affray*, though he had taken no part at all in the search. The man had even claimed that any action by Foster-Brown had been carried out on his orders.

Roy Stephenson Brown (he took on the Foster at

the request of his father-in-law, who only had daughters) was born on January 16 1904 and joined the Navy as a cadet in 1917, going to Osborne and Dartmouth. His first ship as a midshipman was the cruiser *Diomede*, on the China station. Foster-Brown served in submarines from 1924 to 1928, and then specialised as a signal officer.

After service in destroyers, he was appointed Flag Lieutenant in 1936 to James Somerville, who was Rear-Admiral (Destroyers) in the Mediterranean, flying his flag in the cruiser *Galatea*. He was Fleet Signal Officer Home Fleet at the outbreak of war in 1939 and was mentioned in despatches for his service in the Norwegian campaign. From 1940 to 1944 he was Staff Signal Officer to the C-in-C Western Approaches, and then executive officer of the cruiser *Ajax* in the Mediterranean. Promoted captain in 1946, he went to the Admiralty as Director of the Air Organisation Department and then took over the 6th Frigate Squadron in 1950. In 1954 he had the honour of escorting the Queen and Prince Philip on their Commonwealth tour in the SS *Gothic*. On his return he took command of the cruiser *Ceylon* in the East Indies Fleet. Promoted rear-admiral in 1955 (his "rival" in the Admiralty was left behind), Foster-Brown was appointed Flag Officer Gibraltar before retiring in 1959. He was appointed CB in 1958.

In 1960 Foster-Brown was the narrator in 13 episodes of *Sea War*, about the Royal Navy in the Second World War. Written by his old friend, Captain Jackie Broome, and introduced by the First Sea Lord, Admiral Sir Caspar John, the series was made in black-and-white for Southern Television. Foster-Brown was also for a short period on the panel of

"What's My Line?"

He married, in 1933, Joan Wentworth Foster. They had two sons.

ADMIRAL OF THE FLEET
LORD LEWIN

Admiral of the Fleet Lord Lewin (who died on January 23 1999, aged 78) was Chief of the Defence Staff during the Falklands war in 1982.

He was on an official visit to New Zealand when in late March the first intelligence was received that Argentina intended some offensive action against the Falkland Islands in the South Atlantic: the Argentine fleet was at sea, moving into a position where an invasion of the islands was possible. Lewin telephoned London each day to keep in touch and to ask if he should return. But he was told that John Nott, the Defence Secretary, thought it would only cause alarm if the Chief of the Defence Staff publicly cut short an official visit.

Thus by the time Lewin arrived home on April 5, the Argentinians had invaded the Falklands, on the night of April 1-2, and although the Navy had no contingency plans for such a deployment, the decision had already been taken to send a task force to the South Atlantic.

The office of the Chief of the Defence Staff (CDS) rotated in turn between the three services. It was therefore fortunate that for Operation Corporate, the codename for the recovery of the islands, an enterprise in which the Navy played such a major part, the

CDS was a naval officer.

Lewin became arguably the most influential member of Margaret Thatcher's War Cabinet and rapidly established a rapport with the Prime Minister. He had clarity of thought, political awareness, unsurpassed knowledge of the Navy's men and ships, and a realistic appreciation of what was and was not possible. Above all, he refused to allow himself to be rattled when things began to go wrong. Lewin was therefore able to provide an invaluable link between the politicians at Westminster and the C-in-C Fleet, Admiral Sir John Fieldhouse, at his headquarters in Northwood, London.

When it was suggested by Nott and others that it might not be necessary actually to invade the Falklands, and that a sea blockade might suffice, Lewin disagreed. In his opinion, a blockade could never be wholly effective. Furthermore, it would subject the blockading ships to the worst of the South Atlantic winter. Most important, it would not achieve the main object: repossession of the Falklands.

However, Lewin concurred with Operation Paraquat, the recovery of South Georgia, although he knew it was purely politically motivated. But it fell to him to break the news to the Prime Minister that two helicopters carrying the SAS had crashed on Fortuna Glacier and that the very first venture in the South Atlantic appeared to have ended in disaster. It was, he said, the worst moment of the war for him. But, only an hour later, there was almost miraculous good news. In a brilliant feat of flying, the stranded SAS were rescued by helicopter.

Lewin advised on the Rules of Engagement, which laid down the circumstances under which the ships of the task force could open fire. He also encouraged the War Cabinet to support Rear-Admiral "Sandy" Woodward, the carrier battle group commander, when he requested a change in the Rules, leading to the sinking of the cruiser *General Belgrano* by the submarine *Conqueror*.

Lewin later held that the fact that the *Belgrano* had reversed course before it was sunk was irrelevant. In any case, he said, even if the War Cabinet had wished to revoke their decision to extend the Rules of Engagement, there was little chance that the message would have reached *Conqueror* in time.

The loss of the destroyer *Sheffield* after an Exocet missile strike caused a severe wobble in morale at Westminster. Lewin had already warned the War Cabinet that there were bound to be casualties and,at Mrs Thatcher's command, he appeared on television to convey the same message to the nation in robustly reassuring terms. There was much criticism at the time, and subsequently, of the Navy's handling of the media during Corporate, and much bitterness in the Navy. One admiral even went so far as to suggest that all reporters should be banned from future operations.

Lewin took a much more sophisticated, even streetwise, view. "Television is a fact of modern life," he said."It is a fact you have to take into account in all future operations. There will be many occasions when you have no control over television,so that will be a major influence on how you handle the thing."

Lewin said that he was "quite satisfied with the media" but he had no compunction about being misleading when this would deceive the enemy. "How else are you going to do it, if not through the media?" he asked. "I do not see it as deceiving the press or the public; I see it as deceiving the enemy. Anything I can do to help me to win is fair as far as I am concerned."

Like Waterloo, Corporate was "a damned close run thing", but when it was over Lewin summed it up: "For an evil military dictatorship to get away with unprovoked aggression at this part of the 20th century would have made the world a much more dangerous place to live in. It would have undermined western deterrence vis-à-vis the Soviet Union; and it is even conceivable *perestroika* would never have happened if we had not demonstrated this intention not to allow a military dictatorship to get away with it."

He was created a life peer as Baron Lewin in 1982 and appointed a Knight of the Garter in 1983, the first officer to receive the order for purely naval services since "Black Dick" Rowe in 1797.

Terence Thornton Lewin was born at Dover on November 19 1920 and went to Judd School, Tonbridge, before joining the training cruiser *Frobisher* in January 1939. He had originally thought of joining the Metropolitan Police, who were setting up an officer-level entry at Hendon College; but for that he would have had to wait until he was 20. His father suggested the Services. "Only the Navy appealed," Lewin recalled. "I lived it from the beginning; the Navy was my sort of life."

His first ship as a midshipman was the new cruiser *Belfast*, but after her back was broken by a magnetic mine in the Firth of Forth in November 1939 he joined the battleship *Valiant*, serving in the Norwegian campaign in the spring of 1940, and with

Force H at Gibraltar, taking part in the attack on the French ships at Mers el Kebir in July.

Valiant then joined the Mediterranean Fleet and, having survived Luftwaffe attacks off Norway, was equally lucky against the Regia Aeronautica. Lewin's action station was bomb look-out on the bridge, his job being to keep his binoculars fixed on any approaching Italian aircraft "and sing out as soon as the bombs were away" so that the captain could order the helm put over one way or the other.

Lewin then joined the destroyer *Highlander* as a sub-lieutenant, escorting Atlantic convoys in 1941, and was appointed next to the destroyer *Ashanti* as gunnery and watch-keeping officer, under one of the greatest of destroyer commanders, Captain Richard Onslow.

Ashanti escorted three Russian convoys between March and May 1942, and Lewin was mentioned in despatches. She also escorted ships of the Home Fleet providing distant cover for the ill-fated convoy PQ17 in July 1942. In August, *Ashanti* took part in Pedestal, escorting the badly battered tanker *Ohio* to the entrance of Grand Harbour, Valletta. Lewin, who had been closed up at his action station in *Ashanti's* gunnery control tower for 60 hours, with only short breaks, later wrote that it was Pedestal that "set the seal for all time on my already strong admiration for the men of the Merchant Navy."

In September, *Ashanti* sailed for Operation EV – the passage of convoy PQ18 to Russia and the return homeward of convoy QP14. *Ashanti* joined PQ18 on September 9 as one of 16 destroyers in the convoy's fighting escort. After a hectic passage in which PQ18 lost 13 ships, most of them to torpedo-bomber attack, *Ashanti* transferred to QP14. On the evening of the 20th, her sister ship *Somali* was torpedoed and very badly damaged. All but 80 of *Somali*'s ship's company were transferred to a trawler while *Ashanti* took *Somali* in tow. The towing cable soon parted, and all electric power in *Somali* failed.

The tow was taken up again, while Lewin led a party in *Ashanti*'s seaboat who worked for four hours, arms immersed in freezing water, to join two makeshift cables together. Their first attempt failed and everything had to be hauled in. After another cable was found, Lewin and his party successfully restored electrical power, and rigged a telephone line. Towing continued until the weather deteriorated early on the 24th, and *Somali* began to break up. Finally, in the night, after some 80 hours and 420 miles, *Somali* broke in two and sank. Many of her crew were swept away or trapped under *Ashanti*'s bilge keel in the appalling weather, but Lewin played a vital part in recovering the 35 who survived, and he was awarded the DSC.

In *Ashanti* Lewin took part in the North Africa landings, and in more convoys to and from Russia in 1942 and 1943. As part of the 10th Destroyer Flotilla in 1944, *Ashanti* provided seaward defence to the west of the D-Day landing beaches. In a night encounter off Ushant early on June 9, the Flotilla sank one German destroyer and damaged another. Lewin was mentioned in despatches. On August 5, the 10th Flotilla and the cruiser *Bellona* intercepted a German convoy off St Nazaire and sank two minesweepers and two ships from the convoy. Lewin was mentioned in despatches for the third time.

In 1945, Lewin went to HMS Excellent, the

gunnery school at Whale Island, Portsmouth, and qualified top "G" of his course, winning the Egerton Prize and being selected for the advanced "Dagger" gunnery course at Greenwich.

Terry Lewin was by now widely recognised in the Navy as a potential high-flier, and his post-war career followed the classical trajectory up towards the highest ranks in the Service, with "promotion" jobs at sea alternating with appointments in the Admiralty. After returning to HMS ·Excellent for two years on the staff, Lewin went out to the Mediterranean in 1949 to join the destroyer *Chequers*.

Promoted commander in 1953, Lewin was appointed Planning Officer on the staff of the Second Sea Lord, where he was influential in putting into effect the conclusions of the Mansergh Committee, which led to the establishment of a General List that included all executive, engineer, electrical and supply officers.Unlike some executive "deck"officers,Lewin was convinced of the need for change, and as a result had to endure in-trays full of closely reasoned hate mail, accusing him of "betraying his salt".

His first command, in 1955, was the Battle class destroyer *Corunna*. Lewin declined the appointment of executive officer of the Royal Yacht *Britannia*, to which the Flag Officer Royal Yachts replied:"I fully understand your feelings, but you have been selected." The first time Lewin received the Queen on board,she told him:"So you are the chap who did not want to come to my yacht."

Lewin said: "The extraordinary standards kept by *Britannia*'s ship's company were a revelation.The crew taught me a standard of service I have tried to apply for the rest of my life." He was appointed LVO.

Promoted captain in 1958, he was Assistant Director of Tactical and Weapons Policy. His next sea appointment, in 1961, was in command of the frigates *Urchin* and *Tenby* as Captain (F) 17th Frigate Squadron (the Dartmouth Training Squadron). In 1963, Lewin returned to Whitehall as Director of Tactical and Weapons Policy, and then, in 1966, went to sea again in command of the carrier *Hermes* for one of the happiest commissions in the ship's history. She helped to calm an explosive political situation in Aden in 1966, and the following year her helicopters mounted a dawn raid on communist agitators in Hong Kong, lowering police and troops on to two 27-storey buildings.

Promoted rear-admiral, Lewin was Assistant Chief of Naval Staff (Policy) from 1968 until 1969, when he took up his final command afloat as Flag Officer Second-in-Command, Far East Fleet. As a notable authority on Captain Cook he particularly enjoyed flying his flag in the cruiser *London*, at Gisborne, New Zealand, for the celebrations marking the 200th anniversary of Cook's landing from *Endeavour* at Poverty Bay.

Lewin went on to hold in succession the most senior posts in the Navy: Vice-Chief of the Naval Staff; C-in-C Fleet; Allied C-in-C Channel and C-in-C Eastern Atlantic Area; C-in-C Naval Home Command; Chief of the Naval Staff and First Sea Lord. Promoted Admiral of the Fleet, he was Chief of the Defence Staff from 1979 until 1982. He instigated a change in responsibilities whereby the CDS became the principal military adviser to the Government and not just the chairman of an inter-service committee.

He was appointed KCB in 1973, and GCB in 1976. He was Flag ADC to the Queen from 1975 to 1977, and First and Principal ADC from 1977 to 1979.Despite his brilliant career, Lewin deprecatingly described his time as First Sea Lord as "the dullest I ever had in the Navy".

Lewin was a natural athlete, who had been selected to represent the Navy at rugby and athletics, and he always kept himself fit; he romped home to win the Veterans' Hundred Yard Dash at *Hermes*'s sports day on Singapore in 1967. He had a deep and scholarly knowledge of naval history. His lectures and the numerous forewords he wrote for books were always informed by some apposite reference to a past naval occasion. Yet, though he often drew on the Navy's romantic past, Lewin was well aware of the brutal operational necessity which lay beneath. Of Mers el Kebir in 1940, when more than a thousand French sailors were killed by British gunfire, he said, years later, "Senior officers agonised about the decision to open fire, but for the junior officers and ratings it was just a job that had to be done as effectively as possible before going onto the next one."

Over the years, Lewin became, unobtrusively and without any wish to push himself forward, an authoritative spokesman for the Navy in general, constantly consulted by the media. He contributed to television programmes on the Falklands conflict. He wrote persuasively to the newspapers on such issues as the need to replace Polaris with Trident and also that the CDS should retain five-star rank. The news that the Navy was to leave the Royal Naval College, Greenwich, caused him great concern, and he was a sharp critic of the Government's policy.

Lewin was very generous with his time, which he gave to a wide variety of societies and organisations. He was chairman of the Trustees of the National Maritime Museum from 1987 to 1995 and president of the Society for Nautical Research, and of the Shipwrecked Fishermen and Mariners' Royal Benevolent Society. As president of the George Cross Island Association, he personally raised much of the money needed to erect the Malta Siege Bell monument overlooking Grand Harbour, and he presided over its dedication by the Queen in 1992. He was also Life Colonel Commandant, Royal Marines, an Elder Brother of Trinity House, a Freeman of the Skinners' and the Shipwrights' Companies, and joint patron, with Sir Ludovic Kennedy, of the Russian Convoy Club.

He married, in 1944, Jane Branch-Evans; they had two sons and a daughter.

COMMANDER
"JIMMY" GARDNER

Commander "Jimmy" Gardner (who died on March 26 1999, aged 84) was one of the Fleet Air Arm fighter pilots in the Battle of Britain.

In June 1940, Gardner went to No 7 Operational Training Unit at RAF Hawarden, in North Wales, for an intensive two-week course on flying Spitfires and Hurricanes. Early the next month, he and two other naval pilots, Sub-Lieutenant Dickie Cork and Midshipman Peter Patterson – neither of whom were to survive the war – joined 242 Squadron, flying

Hurricane 1s under the celebrated Douglas Bader.

Gardner had an early success on July 10 when 242 were patrolling off Lowestoft. "I came out of cloud over a small convoy of freighters going up to the East Coast," he recalled, "and there was a Heinkel 111 bombing them. I was able to latch on to him as he quickly dived back for the Dutch coast, having spotted me. I must admit I had to go full throttle to catch him up. I fired when in range and he went down halfway between the English and Dutch coasts."

Gardner shared a Dornier 17 on August 21, and shot down another on September 7. His best day was September 18, when he shot down two Dornier 17s over the Thames Estuary and was credited with a "probable". As the battle proceeded, 242 settled down to the routine of spending their nights at Coltishall and days at Duxford. There was a serious shortage of pilots, due to accidents or combat, but plenty of planes. "If your aircraft was shot up and you were OK," Gardner remembered, "the mechanics just pulled out another Hurricane and off you went again. I had my Bugatti and my Matchless motorcycle with me at Coltishall and took them out whenever I could, enjoying the peace and quiet."

Although the naval pilots were fully integrated operationally into the RAF, they wore naval uniform and guarded their Navy identities. Gardner had the flag hoist of Nelson's "England Expects" signal at Trafalgar painted on the side of his Hurricane. In general, they got on very well with Bader. "He wasn't the most diplomatic of people," Gardner said. "He had very strong opinions and stuck to these no matter who he was talking to, a senior officer or otherwise.

What he said had to go and that was that."

On November 5 1940, Gardner's Hurricane was damaged in an engagement with several Me109s, and he just managed to land at Southend. In December, he joined 252 Squadron, Coastal Command, at Chivenor, north Devon, and flew with them until April 1941. He then returned to the Navy, joining 807 Naval Air Squadron, flying Fairey Fulmars from the carrier *Ark Royal* in the Mediterranean.

In May, *Ark Royal* escorted the Tiger convoy, carrying tanks and Hurricanes through the Mediterranean to Alexandria. Gardner made four sorties on May 8, sharing an Italian Savoia S79 and shooting down two Junker 87 Stukas. His Fulmar was badly damaged, but once again he managed to struggle back and crash-land on *Ark Royal*. He was awarded the DSC for his service in *Tiger*.

Gardner's final tally as a fighter pilot was six destroyed, four shared and one "probable". He was one of 56 Fleet Air Arm pilots in the Battle of Britain, 23 of whom flew with the RAF; nine were killed.

Richard Exton Gardner, always known as Jimmy (because his father had the same Christian names) was born on July 24 1914 and went to Bryanston before joining the family firm of Yardley, the cosmetic manufacturers. He learned to fly before the war, joining the Navy and starting flying training as a leading airman at Gravesend in May 1939.

He was commissioned as a sub-lieutenant, RNVR, in September 1939, got his wings at RAF Nether-avon in April 1940, and joined 760 Naval Air Squadron at HMS Raven, Eastleigh. After *Ark Royal* was sunk in November 1941, 807 joined the carrier *Argus* for convoy duties in the western

Mediterranean.

In April 1942, Gardner was appointed as an instructor to 700 Squadron, part of the Fleet Fighter School, at HMS Heron, Yeovilton. By July, he was CO of 899 Squadron, flying Fulmars from HMS Grebe, at Dekheila, near Alexandria, and operating from Fayid for Canal Zone Defence. Part of the squadron moved to Syria to operate with 260 Wing, RAF, re-equipping with ex-RAF Hurricanes in October. They then flew in the Western Desert until disbanding in February 1943.

Gardner's long experience as a fighter pilot was now much in demand. In May 1943, he was appointed CO of 736 Squadron, flying Seafires from Yeovilton at the School of Air Combat, teaching the latest air combat techniques to experienced naval fighter pilots. In September, the squadron moved to HMS Vulture, St Merryn, Cornwall, to become the Fighter Combat School element of the School of Naval Air Warfare. Gardner remained Chief Fighter Instructor for the School of Naval Warfare until he left the Navy in March 1946, and was appointed OBE for his service there in 1945.

After the war, he rejoined Yardley, and became chairman until it was taken over by BAT in 1969.

As one of the surviving Battle of Britain pilots, Jimmy Gardner was often asked for his signature on pictures of aerial combat and other memorabilia. He always obliged good-humouredly, as his tribute to his friends who did not survive.

He married, in 1945, Jeanne Hose; they had three sons.

CAPTAIN
HUMPHRY BOYS-SMITH

Captain Humphry Boys-Smith (who died on June 24 1999, aged 94) was one of the most successful Merchant Navy officers serving in the RNR during the Second World War.

His first wartime command, late in 1939, was the trawler *Tourmaline*, escorting convoys between Aberdeen and Newcastle. On February 24 1940, *Tourmaline* was going down the Firth of Forth when an oncoming steamer, *Royal Archer*, blew up on a mine. *Tourmaline* picked up the entire crew and took them to Leith.

In April, Boys-Smith was appointed in command of the Flower class corvette *Anemone*, building at Blyth. While waiting for her to become operational, he was given command of the small Dutch coaster *Twente*, for the Dunkirk evacuation. He and his crew of five made six trips across the Channel and took off more than 1,100 soldiers.

On May 29, Boys-Smith steered *Twente* alongside the paddle steamer *Gracie Fields*, which had been bombed with 750 troops on board and was still under way while out of control. He jammed *Twente*'s bows against *Gracie Fields* and kept her there while soldiers, some of them badly injured, scrambled across. He was awarded the DSO.

Boys-Smith then commissioned *Anemone* for Western Approaches Command, based first in Liverpool and then in Londonderry. Early in January 1941, *Anemone*'s escort group was on its way to meet convoy HX99, homeward bound from Halifax, when Boys-Smith had a disagreement with the escort group commander over the group's position. Convinced that he was right, he struck out on his own. At dawn on January 7, *Anemone's* lookouts saw smoke haze astern. It was the Italian submarine *Nani*, overhauling *Anemone* in the belief that she was a convoy straggler.

Allowing the enemy to come within 3,000 yards, he then swung round to open fire. The submarine, which was faster and more heavily armed than *Anemone*, then rashly dived, and *Anemone* sank it with a series of accurate depth-charge attacks. When *Anemone* duly met the convoy, the convoy commodore signalled:"Are you the only escort?" Boys-Smith replied:"Yes."

He was awarded a Bar to his DSO, and his sinking of *Nani* was celebrated by a large two-page drawing by C E Turner in the *Illustrated London News*.

Boys-Smith next took command of the River class frigate *Spey*, based in Londonderry. On July 11, she was north-west of Madeira, escorting convoy OS33, outward bound to Freetown, Sierra Leone, when it was attacked by U-136. In a combined Allied effort, *Spey*, the sloop *Pelican* and the Free French destroyer *Leopard* sank the U-boat. Boys-Smith was mentioned in despatches.

Spey took part in the Allied Torch landings in North Africa.On November 7 1942,she stood by the American troopship *Thomas Stone*, which was torpedoed and left helpless some 150 miles from Algiers. The US battalion commander decided to embark his troops in their landing craft,to make their own way to their destination. But the landing craft, not designed for ocean passages, broke down or were swamped and sank. *Spey* took two of them in tow, but they also sank. Eventually *Spey* had 800 troops on board when she disembarked at Algiers.

Boys–Smith was awarded the DSC and a US Citation for Meritorious Service.

Serving with the 1st Support Group, *Spey* took part in several convoy actions early in 1943, including the climactic 10-day battle around the outward-bound convoy ONS5 in May. There were as many U-boats as ships in the convoy, and three and a half times as many U-boats as there were escorts.

Twelve merchant ships were lost, but six U-boats were sunk and two more lost by collision. Five U-boats reported severe damage, and 12 more reported lesser action damage. Making skilful use of radar, the escorts made some 40 attacks. On 20 occasions, U-boats signalled that they were being driven off or forced to dive.

Humphry Gilbert Boys–Smith was born on December 20 1904 and went to Pangbourne. After joining the RNR in 1921, he served in the Merchant Navy from 1922 to 1935, when he joined the Colonial Marine Service as a pilot in Haifa, Palestine.

In 1944, Boys–Smith was appointed to take a group of frigates out to the Pacific. But instead he was then sent to the Second Sea Lord's office in the Admiralty, with the rank of captain, to deal with Western Approaches officers' appointments.

He left the Navy at the end of the war to rejoin the Colonial Marine Service. From 1946 to 1950 he was Marine Superintendent of the Western Pacific High Commission, organising transport in the British South Sea Islands. He then served until 1968 as recruitment officer in the central staff department of Courtaulds in London.

Boys-Smith retired from the RNR in 1952 and was awarded the Reserve Decoration. He was a Younger Brother of Trinity House and a member of the Honourable Company of Master Mariners.

He married, in 1935, Marjorie Vicars-Miles, whom he had known since childhood. She died in 1981.

CAPTAIN
JOHN COCKBURN

Captain John Cockburn (who died on August 3 1999, aged 92) won the DSC for his leadership of the shore-based Fleet Air Arm fighters at Salerno in September 1943.

Force V, comprising the escort carriers *Attacker*, *Battler*, *Hunter* and *Stalker* (in which Cockburn was serving) plus the repair carrier *Unicorn*, had a total of 106 Seafires to provide air cover and support over the landing beaches from September 9. This they did, despite horrendous accident losses caused by the lack of wind, inexperienced pilots and the Seafire's fragile undercarriage.

It was expected that Montecorvino airfield, inshore of the main landing beaches, would be captured at once. But this was not achieved, so when Cockburn's 26 Seafires were ordered ashore on the 12th they had to use an emergency airstrip, with one narrow runway hacked out of tomato fields, at Paestum, further south.

When Cockburn landed, he saw a playing card sticking out of the sand and picked it up. It was the joker. He put it in his pocket, taking it as good omen.

Conditions at Paestum were primitive. "Every time an aircraft took off the air was full of dust and flying stones," Cockburn said. "We had no tools, not even a screwdriver, and we had to use flints to remove the cowlings and service our aircraft, refuelling them from some petrol drums we found in a corner of a field and transported in a lorry borrowed from the Americans."

Nevertheless, the Seafires were able to fly patrols of as many as 16 aircraft, controlled by the fighter direction ship *Palomares* offshore. Enemy reaction was slight, being mostly high-speed "tip and run" raids. On the second day, Cockburn took over a farmhouse near the airstrip and opened the First Fleet Air Arm mess in Europe (FFAAMIE). "We decided to have a house warming," he said. "A pig and several chickens were on the farm and these were allocated for dinner, and an Italian was sent off on a mule for 50 litres of local red wine, known as 'Screech'."

By the 14th the RAF and the USAAF were arriving in force. Though very reluctant to close the FFAAMIE, on the 15th Cockburn led the Seafires (of which, remarkably, 25 were still operational) across the Mediterranean by stages to Bizerta.

John Clayton Cockburn was born on January 21 1907 and went to Rugby before joining the training ship *Thunderer* as a naval cadet in 1926. After service in the battleships *Barham* and *Resolution*, and the minesweeper *Pangbourne*, he joined No 19 Pilots' Course at RAF Leuchars in 1931.

He spent much of the early 1930s on the China station, flying Fairey Flycatcher biplanes from the carrier *Hermes* and from the cruisers *Cumberland*, *Suffolk* and *Kent*. In the late 1930s Cockburn served with 800 Naval Air Squadron,flying Hawker Nimrod and Osprey biplanes from the carrier *Courageous* and then with 802 Squadron,flying Nimrods and Ospreys from *Glorious*.

He had his first command,718 Squadron,providing Walrus amphibians and Seafox seaplanes in support of the cruisers on the America and West Indies station. In December 1939, he took command of 804 Squadron, flying Gloster Sea Gladiator biplanes, first from Hatston in the Orkneys to counter enemy air activity over Scapa Flow, and then from *Glorious*, taking part in the Norwegian campaign in the spring of 1940.

The squadron acquitted themselves well in Norway, scoring several successes against the enemy, but in general the Fleet Air Arm's aircraft were hopelessly outclassed by the Luftwaffe. Cockburn did not endear himself to authority by writing in his report that combat had shown:"(1) that the Gladiator had insufficient performance to chase and hold enemy aircraft; (2) that the time between sighting the enemy by our own pilots and the time the enemy drops his bomb is very short, therefore Fleet Air Arm fighters should have at least eight front guns; (3) to save the fleet turning into wind frequently the FAA fighter should have a reasonable endurance, eg five hours."

Waxing caustic, Cockburn concluded "that (1) and (2) can be fulfilled by giving us Spitfires; (1), (2) and (3) by giving us practically any US Navy fighter."

In September 1940, during the Battle of Britain, 804 was based at Wick, in Caithness, under the RAF's 13 Group, charged with defending the dockyards at Scapa Flow. Cockburn's next command in June 1941 was the newly-formed 881 Squadron, flying Grumman Martlets and intended for *Ark Royal*; but when she was sunk in November 1941 the squadron went instead to *Illustrious*, took part in Operation Ironclad, the invasion of Madagascar in May 1942, and shot down six Vichy French aircraft for the loss of one of their own.

Cockburn then joined the carrier *Argus* as Lieutenant-Commander (Flying). She took part in the Harpoon convoy to Malta in June 1942 and the Torch landings in North Africa in November. His final wartime appointment was as the commander of HMS Rajaliya, the naval air station at Puttalam in Ceylon.

When peace returned, Cockburn was Commander (Flying) of HMS Gannet, the naval air station at Eglinton in Northern Ireland; then, in 1947, he joined the carrier *Implacable* as Commander (Air) when she was Home Fleet flagship. In 1949, she embarked 702 Squadron, flying de Havilland Sea Vampires for jet fighter evaluation.

In the succeeding decade, his appointments included command of HMS Peregrine, the naval air station at Ford in Sussex, naval attaché in Rio de Janeiro and, finally, Director of Air Equipment at the Admiralty.

John Cockburn was an aviator whose flying ranged from biplanes to fast jets. At Salerno, he showed a robust sense of humour and an ability to make the best of a very difficult situation. "My pilots," he said, "were an excellent bunch of thugs, as FAA fighter pilots should be." Under his leadership, they "made light of the rough living, treating the whole affair as a picnic, and thoroughly enjoying themselves."

At home in Bembridge, Isle of Wight, he was an honorary life member of the Sailing Club, and a member of the Royal Yacht Squadron. He built and sailed his own boats, catamarans and sand yachts almost to the end of his life. A keen beagler, he was vice-president of the Isle of Wight Beagles. He never married.

LIEUTENANT-COMMANDER JOHN CASSON

Lieutenant-Commander John Casson (who died on December 24 1999, aged 90) was a Fleet Air Arm fighter pilot; a codemaster for MI9 in PoW camps; a theatre director; and the author of *Lewis and Sybil* (1972), an affectionate memoir of his parents.

He was born on October 28 1909, the son of Sir Lewis Casson and Dame Sybil Thorndike. From childhood he craved not the footlights, as his parents had hoped, but the open sea. After King's College School, Wimbledon, he went to *Worcester*, the boys' training ship in the Thames, before joining the Navy as a special entry cadet in the training ship *Erebus* in 1926. His first ship as a midshipman was the old battleship *Emperor of India*.

In 1931, when he was serving in the destroyer *Velox*, Casson volunteered for flying, though his Captain (D) told him that would ruin his career. He joined No 22 Naval Pilots' Course at RAF Leuchars in January 1932. Two years later, he was serving on the China station, flying Hawker Osprey fighter biplanes from the carrier *Eagle* with 803 Naval Air

Squadron. Then he went out to the Mediterranean to fly Ospreys and Hawker Nimrod biplanes from *Glorious* as senior pilot of 802 Squadron.

From 1937 to 1938 he flew the cruiser *Glasgow's* Walrus amphibian in the Home Fleet. A spell as a divisional officer in the cadet training cruiser *Vindictive* in 1939 was followed by promotion to lieutenant-commander in April 1940. Casson was then appointed in command of 803 Squadron, flying Blackburn Skua fighter-dive-bombers from *Ark Royal* in May. He flew through the Norwegian campaign and then, on June 13, took part in an attack by *Ark Royal's* two Skua squadrons on the German battlecruisers *Scharnhorst* and *Gneisenau* in Trondheim harbour.

A rash and ill-conceived enterprise, this was nothing more than a vain attempt to take revenge on the two German ships which had sunk *Glorious* and her two escorting destroyers, with great loss of life, off northern Norway five days earlier. There was almost perpetual daylight at that time of year, and no cloud cover. Trondheim was strongly defended by guns, with two fighter airfields nearby. The Skuas were bound to be spotted as they crossed offshore islands, 80 miles short of their targets. What happened exceeded everyone's worst fears.

Of 15 Skuas, eight were shot down and their crews killed or captured. One 500lb bomb hit *Scharnhorst's* upper deck and rolled over the side without exploding. Casson and his observer, Peter Fanshawe, saw their bomb just miss *Scharnhorst's* quarterdeck before they were jumped by an Me109. Casson threw the Skua all over the sky in such violent attempts to evade that Fanshawe eventually said: "Could you steady up for a moment while I have a shot at him?" Casson replied: "I know how I can fly, but I don't know how you can shoot."

Their opponent put a bullet into Fanshawe's shoulder and another into the fuel tank.Casson heard a "hell of a rattle" and smelt petrol. Fearing that the Skua was about to catch fire, he landed it in a fjord. They could not get their dinghy out and so spent some hours in the water before a Norwegian boy in a rowing boat picked them up and took them to a farmhouse where they signed the family album with their names and ranks. (Exactly 40 years later, Casson and his wife were shown the album by the Norwegian, who by then was a middle-aged farmer.)

The Germans arrived next day to take them to hospital and then to imprisonment,first in Dulag Luft near Frankfurt and then in Stalag Luft III, famous for the Great Escape, which both Casson and Fanshawe helped to plan. As a PoW, Casson learned German and Russian, studied philosophy and theology, and directed theatricals. He had a remarkable aptitude for codes and ciphers, working for MI9, the department concerned with Escape and Evasion. He developed what he claimed was "jolly nearly a high grade cypher", using personal codewords in his own and other PoWs' letters to their families and to fictitious characters invented by Casson.When a chaplain was about to be repatriated, Casson asked him if he could take anything with him. "Only my Bible and my sermons," the chaplain replied. Overnight, Casson wrote a sermon taking Luke ch 2 v 52 as a text:"Jesus increased in wisdom and stature, and in favour with God and man." It was a genuine sermon, fit for any pulpit – but it contained several coded messages.

Casson arrived home on VE Day May 1945 and was appointed OBE for his services as a PoW. But although he loved the Navy, he decided that "he hadn't a hope in hell of promotion". After a short appointment at HMS Wagtail, a naval air station near Ayr, he resigned in 1946, and took a low-paid job as assistant stage manager at the Glasgow Citizens Theatre. He eventually rose to be producer-manager, directing his own parents and helping, among others, Stanley Baxter and Fulton Mackay in their early careers. He then accepted an offer to become senior producer for J C Williamson Theatres in Australia, for which he and his family moved to Melbourne in 1951.

Over the next 17 years Casson became a considerable figure in the Australian theatre. He gave late night Bible readings in an Australian version of *The Epilogue* on television, and played a Salvation Army preacher in *On The Beach*, the film of Nevil Shute's novel. In 1968, Casson became a communication consultant in Melbourne. He set down his experiences in a lively book, *Using Words: Verbal Communication in Industry* (1968). Back in Britain in 1970, he lectured businessmen on "how to get on with people".

Casson had the ideal temperament for a Fleet Air Arm squadron commander. There were some long faces in *Ark Royal's* wardroom that night waiting to take off for the Trondheim sortie but Casson, who was to lead the strike, seemed calmly indifferent to the prospects and, as a gifted conjuror, passed the time doing tricks.

In his later years, he gave library readings for charity which were really theatrical performances, using his favourite extracts, from Shakespeare's sonnets to Ogden Nash. At the memorial service for his cousin, the architect Sir Hugh Casson, in St Paul's Cathedral in 1999 he read W E Henley's *Margaritae Sororis* in a resounding voice, making his listeners feel they were being hailed from some distant quarterdeck. He kept himself fit to the end, fetching his newspaper by bicycle early every morning.

John Casson married, in 1935, Patricia Chester Master, who died in 1992. They had a son and two daughters.

REAR-ADMIRAL DENNIS CAMBELL

Rear-Admiral Dennis Cambell (who died on April 6 2000, aged 92) was the inventor of the angled flight deck, one of the most radical changes in post-war aircraft carrier design.

The high landing speeds and greatly increased weights of post-war aircraft made obsolescent – and dangerous – the traditional Second World War method of working a flight deck, with arrester wires and crash barriers and the forward half in use as a deck park. The solution, devised by Cambell and refined by the late Lewis Boddington of the Royal Aircraft Establishment, Farnborough, was so staggeringly simple that everybody else kicked themselves for not thinking of it.

It was to slew the direction of the approach and landing a little out to port, so that if an aircraft missed the wires it could simply take off and go round again.

The idea came to Cambell in August 1951, when he was Deputy Chief Naval Representative (Air) at the Ministry of Supply. He broached the subject at a meeting he was chairing on future aircraft design.But the suggestion was received by the Admiralty, as Cambell said,"with an indifference amounting almost to derision."

However, at the Farnborough Air Show that year Cambell met some US Navy officers who showed an immediate interest. Thus, although the first experiments, in the carrier *Triumph* in 1952, were made by painting new lines on the flight deck, the first true angled deck was fitted for trials on an American carrier, the USS *Antietam*. By July 1953, *Antietam* carried out over 4,000 launches and landings, with no accident attributable to the angled deck.In May 1953 she came for trials in the Channel, and British pilots were able to try out a British invention – on board an American ship. As eventually fitted in British carriers, first with the intermediate five degrees and then with the full ten, the angled deck was a success in every way, needing fewer arrester wires and crash barriers, making deck handling much easier and faster, and greatly reducing deaths and injuries to aircrew and deck handlers.

Dennis Royle Farquharson Cambell was born on November 13 1907 and went to Westminster before joining the training ship *Thunderer* as a special entry cadet in 1925. He served as a midshipman in the battleship *Repulse* and later in the destroyers *Wolfhound* and *Sesame*. In 1928, when *Repulse* was in Portsmouth for a short refit, he borrowed £35 from his father to learn how to fly at the Hants Aero Club. He volunteered for flying at a time when it was most unfashionable for a naval officer to do so and qualified as a pilot at RAF Leuchars in 1931.

His two brothers also became Fleet Air pilots;Brian was lost in the Atlantic during the hunt for the *Bismarck* in May 1941, and Neville was shot down and captured off Tripoli the same month. Cambell flew Fairey Flycatcher fighter biplanes with 401 and 405 Flights from the carriers *Furious* and *Glorious*. In March 1939 he got his first squadron command, 803, flying Blackburn Skuas from *Ark Royal*. On September 14 1939, three of 803's Skuas led by Cambell responded to an SOS from the merchant ship *Fanad Head* which was being shelled by a U-boat in the North Sea.

They found the U-boat on the surface and made a low-level bombing attack. But Cambell's wingmen's bombs, which were wrongly fused, blew off the tails of their Skuas. Both pilots were picked up by U-30, and became PoWs. Cambell flew back to *Ark* alone, after one of several incidents in a long flying career when, as he said,"the Grim Reaper missed me". He was awarded the DSC in 1940 for his service with 803, but then suffered from a form of disabling arthritis which was finally cured by an emergency appendectomy in 1941.

Cambell was a test pilot at Boscombe Down until March 1942 when he was appointed Commander (Air) in the old carrier *Argus* which was ferrying replacement aircraft to Malta. *Argus*, converted from an Italian liner, was known as a "gentleman's conveyance", much loved by those who served in her. Cambell was disappointed to be pulled suddenly out of her in July 1942 and sent to the Blackburn Company, which had problems with their Firebrand fighter. The Blackburn Firebrand, a big unwieldy brute of an aircraft, had failed its trials at Boscombe Down and already killed two of Blackburn's regular test pilots. Cambell successfully made its first deck landing trials on board *Illustrious* in February 1943 but despite his best efforts the Firebrand, known as "the world's worst aircraft", saw no action in the Second World War.

Although Cambell had proved himself an outstanding pilot, he was also a gifted administrator. In 1943, he went to Washington DC as Senior Naval Representative to the British Air Commission. From 1945 to 1947 he was at the Admiralty. He was glad to get back to sea in 1947 as Commander (Air) of the carrier *Glory* in the Far East, and then have his first sea command, the corvette *Tintagel Castle*, working for the Anti-Submarine School at Portland. He then returned to a desk in 1949 for a year, before going to the Ministry of Supply.

In 1955 Cambell took command of the new 50,000-ton carrier *Ark Royal*, the fourth ship of her name in the Navy, for her first commission. His 18 months in *Ark*, he felt, were the high point of his time in the Navy. "Although I reached a higher rank later on," he said, "nothing could ever equal the extraordinary feeling of power and responsibility which lay with me while I was in command of this behemoth."

After leaving *Ark Royal* in July 1956, Cambell went back to the Admiralty as Director of Naval Air Warfare. His final appointment was as Flag Officer Flying Training from 1957 to 1960; he was appointed CB and made an officer of the American Legion of Merit.

In retirement, Cambell was European sales director for Hiller and then for Hughes Helicopters, pioneers in promoting private helicopter ownership. In the late 1960s, he started a travel agency, specialising in Turkish holidays. His privately printed memoirs *If Only I'd Seen the Script...* were published in 1994.

He married, in 1933, Dorothy Downes. They had two daughters.

COMMANDER
LOFTUS PEYTON-JONES

Commander Loftus Peyton-Jones (who died on December 14 2000, aged 82) was awarded the DSO for his gallant conduct in the final stages of the Battle of the Barents Sea, in defence of the Arctic convoy JW51B against attack by heavy German warships.

The convoy, consisting of 14 merchant ships, sailed from Loch Ewe on December 22 1942. The destroyer *Achates*, of which Peyton-Jones was first lieutenant, and five other destroyers of the 17th Flotilla under Captain Robert Sherbrooke, who won the VC, joined it on Christmas Day as close fighting escort. The convoy was sighted and reported by a shadowing U-boat on December 30.

A powerful German force, consisting of the heavy cruiser *Admiral Hipper*, the pocket battleship *Lutzow* and six destroyers sailed to intercept. Sherbrooke had a plan to deal with just such a surface attack and, at the first sign of danger, he led his destroyers out on the threatened side, while the convoy turned stern on and retreated under cover of a smoke screen laid by *Achates*.

Four times *Hipper* attacked and was driven off, but during one attack she hit *Achates* with an 8-inch shell, killing everybody on her bridge. "The familiar scene was unrecognisable," Peyton-Jones recalled, "just a blackened shambles of twisted metal with the remains of a few identifiable objects sticking grotesquely out of the wreckage. Among the fantastic jumble of what had been the compass platform were lying the mercifully unidentifiable remains of my shipmates who had been standing there."

With his captain killed, Peyton-Jones took command and ordered *Achates* to continue her self-sacrificing zigzag smoke-laying run to shelter the retreating convoy – thus amply fulfilling her nick-name, *Fidus Achates* (faithful *Achates*). The Germans had their own plan. While *Hipper* attacked from the north, *Lutzow* lay in wait to the south. It worked perfectly. *Lutzow* met the convoy at a range of only two miles, while the destroyers were fully engaged beating off *Hipper*. For *Lutzow*'s six 11-inch guns, it should have been mere target practice. Instead, her captain fumbled his approach, was distracted by a snow storm, waited for it to clear, then made no attack and withdrew, having let slip the golden moment which comes to a naval officer once in a lifetime.

All 14 merchant ships reached the Kola Inlet safely. Meanwhile, *Achates* had been hit by *Hipper* again. Her sides were riddled by shrapnel and a huge hole was blown in her hull abreast of a boiler room. She lost all power, came to a stop dead in the water, swung over on her beam ends so that the sea surged into her funnels, capsized and sank. Peyton-Jones and 80 survivors (a surprisingly large number, considering the sea temperature and the ferocity of the action) were picked up by the trawler *Northern Gem*.

The Barents Sea was the climax of Peyton-Jones's time in *Achates*, which he had joined earlier that year. He was awarded the DSC for her part in the defence of convoy PQ16, which was attacked by aircraft and U-boats in May; he was mentioned in despatches after she escorted another Arctic convoy, PQ18, which suffered heavy losses to air attack in September. *Achates* also escorted the Torch convoys for the invasion of North Africa in November, during which she was credited with sinking a Vichy French submarine, and picked up survivors from the troopship *Warwick Castle*, torpedoed and sunk by U-413 off Portugal.

The son of a naval officer, Loftus Edward Peyton-Jones was born on October 7 1918 into an old Guernsey family, which included Commander Loftus William Jones who won the VC at the Battle of Jutland. He joined the Navy as a cadet at Dartmouth in 1932, serving in the training cruiser *Frobisher* and as a midshipman in the battleships *Resolution* and *Royal Sovereign*. As sub-lieutenant, he was in the cruiser *Penelope* during the Norwegian campaign in spring 1940, when she was badly damaged running aground on a rock pinnacle.

He was then appointed first lieutenant of the Hunt class destroyer *Brocklesby*, escorting coastal convoys to and from South Wales. After *Achates*, Peyton-Jones joined the submarine service, as one of a number of lieutenants with operational experience in small ships who were to be trained directly as submarine COs. This was part of a scheme introduced at a time of very severe submarine losses which had resulted in ever younger COs, who were thought "too prone to take chances". The potential COs had to make war patrols in operational submarines.

Peyton-Jones's first, and last, patrol was in *Sahib*, which was depth-charged and forced to the surface by the Italian corvette *Gabbiano* north of Sicily on April 24 1943; he and the ship's company, all but one of whom survived, became prisoners of war. Peyton-Jones was imprisoned in a camp at Padula, near Salerno. He later escaped from a train taking him to Bologna but was recaptured.

After the Italian armistice in September 1943, he escaped from Bologna and set off on an adventurous walk of more than 300 miles, through the winter of 1943-44. He travelled with a variety of other PoWs, of several services and nationalities, avoiding German patrols. Much assisted by the kindness of Italian families en route, he finally reached Terracina on the coast south of Anzio in April 1944. He put to sea in a rickety boat and was rescued by an American DUKW. For his escape from enemy hands, he was appointed MBE in 1944.

Peyton-Jones decided against returning to submarines. Instead, he had his first command, the Hunt class *Easton*, operating in the Aegean and the Adriatic. Amongst other incidents, *Easton* bombarded buildings occupied by Greek communists on the water front at Piraeus, and took the surrender of the German garrison on the island of Samos. Peyton-Jones was again mentioned in despatches.

When peace returned Peyton-Jones became a Staff Officer (Plans) on the staff of the Flag Officer Western Europe, at Fontainebleau, in the early days of Nato. In 1952 he had his second command, the frigate *Loch Veyatie*, in the anti–submarine training flotilla based in Londonderry. Promoted commander, Peyton-Jones was the Naval Member of the Joint Planning Staff at the Ministry of Defence. In 1955 he went back to sea as executive officer of the cruiser *Glasgow*, flagship of Earl Mountbatten, C–in–C Mediterranean. For two years he was Staff Officer (Operations) on the staff of the C–in–C South Atlantic at Simonstown, South Africa. His final appointment in 1961 was as the Naval Member of the Directing Staff of the RAF Staff College.

In retirement, Peyton-Jones became naval adviser to the short-lived Federal Government of the West Indies, and CO (designate) of the West Indies Navy. When Hurricane Hattie struck Belize in October 1961, he flew in with the Royal Navy and the other relief agencies. In the harbour, he boarded a burning motorboat carrying three 50-gallon drums of petrol and had it towed to safety. He was awarded the Queen's Commendation for Brave Conduct. In 1962 he founded the Trinidad and Tobago Coastguard, which he recruited, trained and commanded in anti-drug smuggling operations in the Caribbean until 1965.

Peyton-Jones's final service, from 1966 until 1985, was as overseas director of the Duke of Edinburgh's Award Scheme. To this he devoted his usual energy and dedication, travelling to more than 40 countries. On leaving he was appointed CVO. He later wrote the scheme's official history, *Challenge and Opportunity*. In 1995 he had privately printed his *Wartime Wanderings 1939-1945*, with its poignant first-hand account of *Achates*'s last moments, and a vivid travelogue of his odyssey through wartime Italy.

A life member of the Royal Naval Sailing Association, Peyton-Jones was well-known in yachting circles. At Dartmouth, he was delighted to be given charge of the college's "windfall" yachts, obtained as reparations from Germany. He and his wife cruised in the Baltic, around Britain, Ireland, Spain and France and, in summer 2000, in the Aegean in his 35-foot yacht *Caliope*. He married, in 1953, Francie Lee. They had three sons and a daughter.

CAPTAIN
PAUL BOOTHERSTONE

Captain Paul Bootherstone (who died on March 1 2001, aged 62) was awarded the DSC during the Falklands conflict of 1982 when he was in command of the Type 21 frigate *Arrow*.

On May 1, *Arrow*, her sister ship *Alacrity* and the destroyer *Glamorgan* bombarded Port Stanley airfield. *Arrow* claimed to be the first ship to open fire; she was certainly the first to be damaged by air attack, with one of her sailors slightly wounded. When the destroyer *Sheffield* was hit starboard side amidships by an Exocet missile from an Argentine Super Etendard aircraft fires broke out, passageways and compartments were choked by smoke and there was no firemen's water for fire-fighting.

The frigate *Yarmouth* went alongside *Sheffield*'s starboard side while Bootherstone put *Arrow* on the port side to lend assistance, spraying *Sheffield*'s upper deck with water. After some hours, all power in *Sheffield* failed and as the fires grew closer to the Sea

Dart missile and 4.5-inch gun ammunition, with further air attacks likely, Captain Salt of *Sheffield* decided to abandon ship. Bootherstone moved *Arrow* up alongside the destroyer's fo'c'sle to enable 225 of her men to jump across.

Nine days later, *Arrow* stood by while *Alacrity* made a transit of Falkland Sound to determine whether it was mined. Both ships were then attacked by the Argentine submarine *San Luis* and, although neither noticed this at the time, *Arrow*'s towed torpedo decoy was badly damaged. She arrived at San Carlos Water on May 24, the day after *Antelope* was sunk, and for several days was subjected to regular intense air attacks and suffered numerous near-misses.

On May 28, Bootherstone anchored *Arrow* close to shore in Grantham Sound, almost exactly where *Ardent* had been sunk a week earlier. She carried out an accurate bombardment, firing 157 shells, star-shell and explosive air bursts in support of 2 Para's attack on Goose Green. By the time Port Stanley surrendered, the South Atlantic weather had inflicted alarming cracks in her superstructure and hull. She was alongside the repair ship *Stena Seaspread* for 14 days, then set off for home. On the way, she had a joyful SODS Opera (a performance by the Ship's Operatic and Dramatic Society, which included a memorable rendering of the "Arrow Boating Song") before reaching Plymouth on July 7.

Paul Jeffrey Bootherstone was born on May 7 1938, and joined the Navy as a cadet at Dartmouth in 1956. As a midshipman, he carried out patrols off Cyprus in the minesweeper *Maxton*. He won his wings in 1961 and flew in Fairey Gannet airborne early warning aircraft from the carriers *Centaur* and

Hermes. As a pilot of above average ability he was a flying instructor, and, in 1968, was sent to fly with the US Navy in California on an exchange appointment. The next year he had his first command, the minesweeper *Brinton*.

By now it was clear that Bootherstone was a very able all-rounder. After appointments at the RN College and at HMS Heron, Yeovilton, he joined the frigate *Ambuscade* as executive officer in 1975. He was promoted commander from the ship in 1977 and joined the Department of Naval Air Warfare in the MoD. The Navy was about to fly the Sea Harrier, but had had no fixed wing experience for some years, so Bootherstone was one of that tactful group of staff officers who obtained the necessary RAF co-operation.

After *Arrow*, Bootherstone was promoted captain in 1983 and served on the staff of the Naval Secretary, for whom he was responsible for Fleet Air Arm officers' appointments. In 1985, he had his third sea command, the destroyer *Battleaxe*, then served on the staff of Flag Officer Naval Air, and from 1987 to 1989 was captain of HMS Seahawk, the naval air station at Culdrose, Cornwall.

Bootherstone attended the Canadian National Defence College, and then was naval adviser to the High Commissioner in Ottawa until his retirement in 1992. He then became chief executive of the New Masonic Samaritan Fund.

In the Falklands, Paul Bootherstone managed his sailors with great skill and tact. The work, like the air attacks, was dangerous and seemingly never-ending. There were constant machinery and hull defects. The weather was appalling, mail deliveries were uncertain and the food unpredictable. Yet he seemed imperturbable, and jollied everybody along, convincing them that all would be well in the end.

He was a keen skier and a dedicated railway buff who made a rail journey with him an education in rail history and machinery. He married, in 1961, Janet Ferris. They had two sons and two daughters.

COMMANDER
GUY CLARABUT

Commander Guy Clarabut (who died on March 9 2002, aged 82) had an uncertain start as one of the Royal Navy's youngest submarine captains when he was sent to take temporary command of *Trooper*, off the Italian naval base of Taranto, in 1943.

He first hit an elderly Italian battleship with four torpedoes; when she failed to sink, he realised that she was a target ship and that he was inside the enemy's training areas. After firing torpedoes which missed a 2,000-ton merchant ship, he surfaced and set her on fire with his guns; but he missed the satisfaction of seeing her sink because enemy aircraft forced him into a rapid dive.

Then, on July 29, Clarabut found a 1,800-ton Italian submarine entering Taranto on the surface with an escort, and duly sank it with a single torpedo. He was awarded a DSO, the news of which reached him at the same time as that of the birth of his son.

When *Trooper's* captain, Johnny Wraith, returned to fitness, Clarabut was given a choice of coming home in it or flying. He lost the toss of a coin and flew home; shortly afterwards *Trooper* went down off Leros with all hands.

Clarabut took command of *Rorqual* in the Channel, where a French corvette escorting him ran on to a mine; as senior officer, Clarabut was court-martialled. Despite the anger of the Free French, he was acquitted. He was then given *Stygian* at Trincomalee, Ceylon. This enabled him, between patrols, to fly up to Nagpor, in the North-West Frontier province, to see his father for the first time in eight years.

In 1945 Clarabut cornered a Japanese convoy behind a boom, but was unable to fire torpedoes. So he ran along the boom in 24 feet of water and, despite the attentions of enemy aircraft, did not give up until the convoy was ablaze and he had expended all his ammunition. Clarabut's return to Singapore was no less spectacular when, in company with the submarine *Spark*, he launched an attack with midget submarines against Japanese warships, sinking the cruiser *Takao*. Shortly afterwards the Japanese fleet withdrew from Singapore, and Clarabut was awarded a DSC.

Guy Stewart Chetwode Clarabut was born on July 19 1919. His father, Major-General R B Clarabut, was often so busy on frontier work that, until he was seven, young Guy was largely brought up by his bearer. He was once taken by the bearer to see a gun factory where tribesmen were making the weapons to fire at his father. On another occasion, when his father returned empty-handed from hunting, Guy was able to show him a basking crocodile which had kept him company while he built a castle on the sandy banks of the Indus.

Clarabut got his first taste of the sea at home, when his grandfather dispatched him and a young friend in a 12-foot dinghy to sail the 30 miles from Herne Bay to Rochester in order to collect a new suit of sails. But his ambition to go to Dartmouth at 13 was thwarted by three bouts of rheumatic fever, which meant a year off school. He was also stopped from playing vigorous games – though his doctor allowed him to play racquets, under the impression that it was a parlour game; he became the Cheltenham College champion.

In 1938 Clarabut joined the Navy through the special entry scheme, although he had a weak left eye as well as heart problems. When told to change eyes in the eyesight test, he removed his hand and then put it back to the same eye. He soon found himself on the China station, and took 12 weeks to return home as a watch-keeping officer aboard a 10-knot merchant ship. At Malta, he and some other young officers persuaded nurses to smuggle them onboard a hospital ship bound for Marseilles, from where they continued their journey.

After more training he was sent to the destroyer *Montrose*, which was damaged in a collision during an air raid. He was then moved on to a commandeered French ferry, and given command of a naval party on a Dutch coaster; over a fortnight, Clarabut made six crossings to rescue troops from Dunkirk. Once, he landed on the jetty, only to encounter German tanks which shelled his ship as she backed out of harbour; but he had time to rescue a small dog, which he gave to his mother.

Back at Harwich Clarabut fell into a long sleep on

the wardroom sofa, and was woken by the King and Winston Churchill, who had come to find out about the evacuation.Clarabut was promised a bright future in the Navy after the war, but he became bored. In 1955 he left to join the family business, the London and Rochester Trading Company, which eventually he turned into Crescent Shipping; he also became a director of Hays Wharf. His interests included the Medway Port Authority, the Pilotage Commission, Trinity House, the Rochester Bridge Trust, and the Admiralty Ferry Association.

He was also captain of the Medway and Rochester Golf Club, commodore of the Medway Yacht Club, and Deputy Lieutenant of Kent. In his later years he took up ocean racing, and completed several Fastnet races.

Guy Clarabut married, in 1942, Stella Strachan-Smith, who survived him together with their son and daughter.

CAPTAIN
SIR DAVID TIBBITS

Captain Sir David Tibbits (who died on May 17 2002, aged 91) was responsible for modernising the 400-year-old navigational authority Trinity House.

As Master's Deputy and chairman of the board of Trinity House, the organisation founded by King Henry VIII as "The Guild of the Holy and Undivided Trinity and St Clement at Deptford Strond", Tibbits ensured that it fully participated in the revolution taking place in international navigation during the

1970s. He established automation in lighthouses, standardised the use of helicopters to enable lighthousemen to be relieved swiftly, and phased out the use of oil for lighting beacons.

He introduced fast 40-foot launches in the pilot service, replacing the slow, heavily-manned pilot cutters. In addition to his duties relating to navigational aids and pilotage around England, Wales and the Channel Islands, Tibbits became an internationally recognised expert in safety at sea. He was an energetic member of an Anglo-French working committee for safe routing in the English Channel, and a leading member of the International Maritime Organisation.

As president of the International Association of Lighthouse Authorities, with its headquarters in Paris and 72 member nations, Tibbits rationalised the world's buoyage to reduce 40 systems to just two. His expert witness as an assessor in marine cases in the Admiralty and Queen's Bench courts was also appreciated.

Working from an office on Tower Hill, where he was surrounded by portraits of such earlier Masters as Samuel Pepys and Lord Palmerston, as well as the present one, Prince Philip, Tibbits admitted that such archaic styles as "Elder Brother" could be a handicap in discussing technical matters with governments. However, he was extremely proud that Roy Mason, President of the Board of Trade in Harold Wilson's government, told him that Trinity House was a century ahead of its time in labour relations; each year a member of the Board visited every employee on the coasts of England and Wales.

One dark night Tibbits fell into the sea while

boarding a launch, but he never ceased to issue orders (punctuated with nautical language) for his own rescue or let go of his briefcase, full of valuable papers. While drying the notes of an important Anglo-French meeting at breakfast next morning he made a stream of new orders for the prevention of similar accidents.

The son of a doctor, David Stanley Tibbits was born at Warwick on April 11 1911, educated at Dartmouth in the St Vincent term and went to sea aged 16. After serving in the battleship *Queen Elizabeth*, flagship of the Mediterranean Fleet, Tibbits became one of the youngest officers to specialise in navigation. As the junior member of his course he expected the dullest appointment until a colleague fell sick, and he was given a pierhead jump to the minesweeping sloop *Scarborough* on the American and West Indies station.

Luck continued to play a part in Tibbits's career; two days after the sloop arrived at Bermuda he met his future wife. As war loomed, he served in a minesweeping flotilla during the Abyssinian crisis, in the minesweeper *Halcyon* during the Spanish Civil War, and was navigator of the 1st Submarine Flotilla at Malta.

Tibbits was in the heavy cruiser *York* with which he saw nearly every campaign of 1939 to 1941 until she was wrecked in Suda Bay, Crete. He tried to save her when she was badly damaged by Italian explosive "suicide" motorboats, and beached her, but she then became a sitting duck for German air attacks. Eventually Tibbits was evacuated in the light cruiser *Orion*, in which he was subjected to heavy bombing. He returned home via the Cape as a passenger in the liner *Otranto* to join the cruiser *Devonshire*.

On November 22 1941, *Devonshire* found *Atlantis*, a disguised German raider which had sunk 22 merchant ships of some 150,000 tons. Tibbits identified the enemy from a picture in the American magazine *Life* and navigated *Devonshire* as she destroyed the raider. This involved launching her reconnaissance aircraft for early identification, manoeuvring outside the enemy's gun range, signalling for confirmation of false identity and setting her on fire with just four salvoes from her 8-inch guns.

Atlantis had been supplying U-boats which were still in the area, so her survivors were left in their lifeboats. Next Tibbits planned Operation Ironclad, the invasion of Madagascar. This required a difficult entry at night by a large fleet into Courier Bay, which Tibbits achieved undetected and unopposed; he was awarded the DSC.

In 1944, Tibbits worked in the stables in Southwick House, outside Portsmouth, on the plans for the D-Day landings. This was followed by appointment to the battleship *Anson*, destined for the British Pacific Fleet and the relief of Hong Kong.

With the return of peace, he was involved with the development of an action information organisation for ships and of radar. He commanded the sloop *Snipe*, which brought him to Bermuda again, and the fast minelayer *Manxman* in which he took part in the Suez operations in 1956. After commanding the navigation school HMS Dryad, Tibbits stood by the aircraft carrier *Hermes* building at Barrow-in-Furness, steamed her south under the Red Ensign and, after acceptance into the Royal Navy, entered Portsmouth wearing the White Ensign for the first time. On her first voyage to the Far East Kenneth Rose was pleased to report in *The Daily Telegraph* that for all the grim requirements of modern warfare at sea, the officers dined in black tie and the captain took tea which was brought to him on the bridge in crested china.

It was unfortunate that after a successful commission, in which he completed the new carrier's sea and flying trials, Tibbits's command had an aftermath in which £4,000 was stolen from the pay office safe during his retirement party in the wardroom. He resigned in 1961 after deciding that he was too old to be promoted admiral.

By then he had been elected a full-time Elder Brother of Trinity House, which he had joined as a Younger Brother four years earlier. His presence in the organisation seemed "a rush of fresh air" from the start. When opening a pilot station at Folkestone he was scathing about the ill-trained crew among the 800 ships that used the Channel daily, and declared that it would take much money and high standards of seamanship before effective policing could be achieved in 25 years' time.

On retiring again in 1976, Tibbits settled on Bermuda, where he was a marine consultant to the Bermudian government; a member of the port authority; and chairman of the marine pilotage commission. As chairman of the marine oil pollution contingency committee and of the search and rescue co-ordination committee, he conducted several inquiries into groundings on the Bermuda coast. He was also a strong supporter of the Anglican Cathedral.

Tibbits, who was knighted in 1976, married Mary Butterfield, a Bermudian, in 1938. She survived him with their two daughters.

COMMANDER
PETER RICHARDSON

Commander Peter Richardson (who died on June 29 2002, aged 78) was awarded a DSC in 1945 for his part in sinking two U-boats on the same day in the Outer Hebrides.

He was serving as a 20-year-old anti-submarine warfare officer on the frigate *Rupert*, which was part of the 21st Escort Group assigned by Admiral Sir Max Horton to search out U-boats lurking in the Minches between the Hebrides and the west coast of Scotland. The group escorted several convoys through the narrow waters and, in between times, hunted coves and inlets for U-boats. They were rewarded on March 27, when *Rupert* helped to sink both U-965 and U-722, and, for good measure, sank U-1021 three days later. Horton, in laconic style, noted that the cruise of the 21st Escort Group had been "a creditable affair".

To prove this was no fluke, *Rupert* and her sister ships sank U-1001 in the Western Approaches the next month.

Peter Charles Esdaile Richardson was born at Bournemouth on May 27 1924 and educated at King Edward VII School, Southampton. His grandfather was a marine artist, whose works were popular with members of the Royal Family.

Richardson joined the Navy at 18 and, after undergoing accelerated basic training, was assigned to North Atlantic convoy duties as a midshipman in the corvette *Abelia*. His talent was soon apparent, and he was loaned to the Royal Canadian Navy, which was rapidly expanding to become the fourth largest navy in the world.

In August 1942 the destroyer *Assiniboine* took part in the defence of convoy SC94, a five-day battle across 1,000 miles of the Atlantic. During the action 11 merchantmen were sunk; but of the 18 attacking U-boats, four were damaged and two sunk, one, U-210, after being rammed by "the Bones", as *Assiniboine* was affectionately known.

Richardson then served briefly in the corvette *Gifford,* before returning to the Royal Navy where he was sent to *Rupert,* a lend-lease frigate which was part of the 111th Escort Group. She safely escorted American assault ships to Omaha beach on D-Day, and was then sent on anti-submarine patrols in the Channel. When Arctic convoys to Russia were recommenced in the autumn of 1944, *Rupert* was employed to escort convoys JW61 and RA61 using new tactics; these involved employing aircraft carriers to sweep the seas of U-boats in advance of the merchant ships.

An estimated 18 U-boats were waiting at the entrance of the Kola Inlet. The escort dispersed them although none of them were sunk, due to very bad conditions for Asdic throughout the operation. It was, one commander observed, like "trying to catch several irritated and offensively-minded snakes with harmless rabbits to oppose them". On this occasion, though, the rabbits won: some 33 merchant ships safely made the return passage.

After the war, Richardson had the satisfaction of being boarding officer on several score of enemy submarines, and of towing them into the Atlantic where they were scuttled in Operation Deadlight. Some of the more modern, faster German U-boats were retained for experiments in anti-submarine tactics, in which Richardson played a full part.

Amazingly, he had received no formal training in this type of warfare, and it was not until 1949 that he went to the Navy's anti-submarine warfare school. He was then sent to Portland, where the Navy prepared ships for operations, and Richardson became the commanding officers' "teacher". This was his forte and, in between other appointments, he taught tactics and command procedures and conducted trials with the most modern anti-submarine equipment.

Then, after a period commanding anti-submarine frigates in the Dartmouth training squadron, he was sent to serve as flotilla torpedo and anti-submarine specialist on the staff of the Navy's Flag Officer Submarines. There, with the future First Sea Lord, John Fieldhouse, he helped to introduce a new long-range sonar (as Asdic had become known) and new weapons systems into *Dreadnought*, the Navy's first nuclear-powered submarine.

Richardson's great love was sailing. In 1946 he had been sent to Kiel and made responsible for a fleet of 180 "prizes", mostly abandoned yachts. He picked which ones were to be taken as reparations for war damage, and sailed them home to Britain, all without engines and safely under sail. These became known as "windfalls", and were so well chosen that for nearly 30 years they were used for adventure training, and provided the opportunity for serving men and women to participate in major races. Later in life Richardson bought one from the Navy for himself, *Sea Otter*, which his two sons set about restoring in his garden.

In 1947 Richardson was elected a life member of

the Royal Naval Sailing Association (RNSA), and in 1969 a member of the Royal Yacht Squadron. He was a member of numerous national and international sailing committees and, from 1975 to 1985, took a leading part in organising the Whitbread Round the World Race.

For 22 years he was moorings officer of the RNSA in Portsmouth harbour. When he started, the association had half a dozen grace and favour moorings, but by the end of his tenure there were more than 200 yacht berths for members, and the Crown Estate was correspondingly diminished.

Richardson lived at Portchester, Hampshire, but acquired a holiday home, Lantern House, near the Royal Yacht Squadron where he entertained well, especially during Cowes Week. He was a colourful character with a fund of humorous stories, all of them scurrilous but good-natured.

Peter Richardson was twice married, first, in 1949, to Betty Talbot-Hill, who died in 1994, and secondly to Joan Leary (née Phillips) in 1997.

LIEUTENANT-COMMANDER KEN PATTISSON

Lieutenant-Commander Ken Pattisson (who died on July 13 2002, aged 85) was the Swordfish pilot whose torpedo was most strongly believed to have fatally crippled the German battleship *Bismarck*.

In the first attack, launched from the carrier *Ark Royal* on May 26 1940, Pattisson was mistakenly led down on the British cruiser *Sheffield*, which was shadowing *Bismarck*. But he recognised her silhouette and withheld his fire, unlike his 14 colleagues whose torpedoes fortunately detonated in the heavy seas before reaching her; when *Sheffield* saw the next attack of Swordfish arriving she calmly signalled that the enemy was 15 miles north.

After rearming with torpedoes,now equipped with impact detonators and set to run shallower, 810 Squadron was launched again in worsening weather. Climbing to 9,000 feet Pattisson lost contact in a snow squall with everyone but his leader "Feather" Godfrey-Faussett who led him into an attacking dive. Shrapnel started to tear away the flimsy canvas covering his aircraft's wooden airframe. Breaking through the cloud at 900 feet, Pattisson found himself alone as he saw *Bismarck* on his starboard side.

Although conscious that his lumbering "stringbag" made an easy target for the ship's gunners as he flew straight and level towards her, Pattisson waited until he was 900 yards off and 90 feet above the waves before firing. He then started to jink wildly from side to side to put the Germans off their aim.

Later, he modestly admitted that it was "highly probable" that his torpedo hit *Bismarck*'s stern and jammed her rudders, though others who saw a large column of water rise up on her starboard side right aft, were more certain.

Bismarck steered in circles throughout the night before the Home Fleet caught up with her. At dawn next day, 810 Squadron was launched again, but was told to hold off while *King George V* and *Rodney* pounded her. Pattisson then watched from the air as *Bismarck* capsized, leaving the heads of the survivors, he recalled,"bobbing like turnips in a field". He was awarded a DSC for his part in the operation.

A piece of shrapnel which had lodged in his aircraft became a prized souvenir; but while returning to Britain as a passenger in *Springbank* in convoy HG73, he lost all his possessions when she was sunk by U-boats. Jumping from her on to the deck of the corvette *Jasmine*, Pattisson broke three ribs; his only injury, bar one high landing, in 20 years' service.

Kenneth Stuart Pattisson was born in North London on December 12 1916, and educated at Newport Grammar School on the Isle of Wight before responding to an advertisement for the Fleet Air Arm. As part of Force H, his squadron bombed Italy, which was out of range for RAF bombers, and escorted Mediterranean convoys. After *Ark Royal*, Pattisson flew in several training and trials squadrons.

As commanding officer of 815 Squadron, based in Scotland, he once drove to where a Barracuda, which had suffered engine failure, had landed in a small field. After repair, he taxied to the end of the field, tied the tail of the aircraft to a tree, and told the local farmer to cut the ropes when the engine reached full throttle; he just cleared the hedge at the opposite side of the field.

Pattisson served in the carrier *Colossus* with the British Pacific Fleet in 1945. He also commanded his old squadron, now flying Fireflies in the carrier *Theseus*, during the Korean War, and he was mentioned in despatches. Later, several desk-bound jobs did not suit him, and he retired from the Navy in 1958.

Pattisson lived most of his life on the Hampshire and Dorset coasts, and his great passion was sailing. He taught his children to sail, one of whom, Rodney, became an Olympic gold medal winner. After the Royal Navy, he took over his father's business in London, running exhibitions.He was Honorary Life-boat Secretary in Poole, 1976-86, and an active member of the Royal Naval Sailing Association.

Ken Pattisson married Margaret Collett in 1939. She predeceased him, and they had four children.

REAR-ADMIRAL
TONY STORRS

Rear-Admiral Tony Storrs (who died on August 9 2002, aged 95) started his sailing career in windjammers, and went on to clear mines off the Normandy coast before the Americans landed at Utah and Omaha beaches on D-Day.

As senior officer of the Canadian 31st Mine-sweeping Flotilla, Storrs was aware of the doubts expressed about the Royal Canadian Navy's compe-tence earlier in the war. But he trained his crews so relentlessly between March and May 1944 that the British were eventually forced to admit that they were "efficient, keen and competent".

Although minesweepers normally withdraw when they come under attack, Storrs told his ships to hold their formation even under bombardment. The operation required superb seamanship as Storrs led them close to the German guns under cover of darkness in a strong cross-tide and in poor weather. Only when German shells started falling around him did he order "in sweeps", although his own ship, the Bangor class *Caraquet*, was caught on a wreck and had to be cut clear.

Storrs's zeal, patience and cheerfulness, together with the skill and judgment he displayed in the execution of this complex task, contributed significantly to the success of Operation Neptune, the naval element of the invasion, according to the citation for the first of the two DSCs he was awarded early in 1945; the Americans also recognised his achievement with the Legion of Merit.

The son of a doctor, Antony Hubert Gleadow Storrs was born at Overton, Hampshire, on April 1 1907 and taken to Rhodesia, where both his parents died before he was 15. He returned home to go to Weymouth College, then trained in the merchant navy school ship *Worcester*, sponsored by P&O, leaving as chief cadet captain with two first-class extra certificates.

He signed indentures with John Stewart & Co to serve in *William Mitchell*, one of the last British-owned sailing freighters to ply her business between America and Australia. Her longest voyage lasted 150 days, and for protracted periods the crew never saw another ship. They amused themselves, when becalmed, by trying to capture albatrosses. This would involve extending a piece of wood with a sardine can attached to the end; when an Albatross dipped in its beak, a twist of the wood would enable the crew to hoist the bird aboard, measure its wingspan, then set it free.

There was little water for washing, but a talented Chinese cook managed to produce a small loaf of fresh bread for each man every day. Even so, Storrs could not resist the temptation to steal an egg which had been laid by the captain's chicken. In Australia,

Storrs found a qualified examiner to pass him as a master mariner in sail, though he afterwards received the advice:"Never command a sailing ship."

After the *William Mitchell* was sold, Storrs rejoined P&O and served in various ships until the onset of the Depression. He then joined the Chinese Maritime Customs which placed him in command of revenue cutters. When it became clear that Japan was going to invade China, Storrs and his wife Joy, whom he had married in 1940, set off from Foochow. This involved a long walk to reach a sampan, sleeping in a junk for several nights and taking a blockade runner up to Shanghai, where a ship took them to Victoria, British Columbia.

On joining the RCNR, Storrs first assumed command of the trawler *Armentieres* at Esquimalt, then was appointed to the destroyer *Gatineau*. His next command was the corvette *Dawson*, which, after the war with Japan began, took part in convoy duty with the US Navy between Dutch Harbour and Adak in the Aleutians.

In 1943 he was switched to the Atlantic Coast, where he was appointed commanding officer of *Drumheller*, which protected convoys at a critical stage of the Battle of the Atlantic in September 1943. They were subjected to repeated U-boat attacks. For this service Storrs was also awarded the Legion d'Honneur and the Croix de Guerre *avec palme*.

At the end of the war Storrs took command of the frigate *Antigonish*, then was given shore jobs, ending up at naval headquarters as Director of Naval Plans and Operations. In 1953 his career took a new direction when he was appointed commanding officer of the air station at Dartmouth, Nova Scotia, where he was soon offered the command of the carrier *Magnificent*. Storrs had started taking flying lessons in a Gipsy Moth while in Shanghai, and now began again in a Piper Cub fitted with floats. But Naval Headquarters in Ottawa declined to authorise him to be trained, like other Canadian flyers, by the US Navy.

His last naval appointment was as commandant of the National Defence College at Kingston, Ontario, when he became the first Reserve officer to reach admiral's rank in the RCN. Later, he became Director of Marine Operations for the Canadian Coastguard, and was involved in the founding of the Canadian Coastguard College at Sydney, Nova Scotia. Storrs was then asked to lead 35 officers in setting up a similar Coastguard service in Iran, though the project was scrapped shortly before the Shah fell.

He spent his retirement in Victoria, British Columbia, where he was survived by his wife and two sons.

VICE-ADMIRAL
"ROCKET" ROD TAYLOR

Vice-Admiral "Rocket" Rod Taylor, the former head of the Royal Australian Navy (who died on September 1 2002, aged 62), oversaw important changes in his country's relationship with Britain, while retaining the RN's respect for its sister service "down under".

The significance of this evolution, which can be easily exaggerated, was signalled in 1969 when Taylor was Operations and Bombardment Navigation Officer in the new Australian guided missile destroyer *Brisbane* which had commissioned at Newport, Rhode Island, as the Australians were changing from British to American equipment.

Brisbane, known as the "Steel Cat", was then, for political reasons, rushed into action in Vietnam without being fully worked up. There were problems with her gunfire control system, which had been cannibalised from a sister ship, and serious malfunctioning led to an explosion in one turret. But *Brisbane* steamed more than 40,000 miles to fire 7,891 rounds of 5-inch shells in support of American troops and the 1st Australian Task Force, who were fighting in Phuoc Tuy province.

The Americans later demonstrated their confidence in *Brisbane* by giving her command of the screen protecting the American carrier *Oriskany* in August 1969. Taylor's role in the conflict was recognised with a mention in despatches.

Twenty-two years later, when he was Assistant Chief of Defence Force (Operations) during the Gulf War, Taylor had learned the lessons of the Vietnam War, and immediately placed his department on a war footing when he had to deploy RAN ships to the Persian Gulf in support of Operation Desert Storm. General Peter Gration, Chief of the Australian Defence Force, was particularly pleased at the rapid dispatch of three ships and other elements of the fleet for the war zone.

Rodney Graham Taylor was born on June 11 1940 at Toowoomba, Queensland. His family had had no connection with the sea, but eventually his brother, his sister and a nephew entered the RAN. He went to the Royal Australian Naval College at Jervis Bay, aged 13,at a time when corporal punishment was still liberally meted out for minor lapses of concentration.

He soon showed determination to succeed and excelled at everything he did: rugby, cricket, in the classroom and on the parade ground. On passing out in December 1957 at Dartmouth,he was awarded the Queen's Medal by Prince Philip.

Taylor was always meticulous and deliberate, and so he naturally decided early to specialise in navigation. It was a sign of his immediate self-confidence in this role that, as a junior officer in the fast frigate *Quiberon,*Taylor realised that the fleet would be nearly two hours late arriving at Sydney Heads and signalled on his own initiative the Fleet Navigator, who quickly adjusted the time of arrival.

Taylor's training and exchange duties took him to England on five lengthy occasions in ranks from midshipman to commander. He was a "season officer" in the Royal Yacht *Britannia*; navigating officer of the British 7th Mine Countermeasures Squadron based at Malta; served on the staff at the Joint Warfare Establishment at Old Sarum; and completed the Advanced Navigation Course. He also attended the Canadian National Defence College in 1985-6. Taylor quickly rose in the RAN through a series of key sea and staff appointments.

But all he really wanted was to command a destroyer; everything else, he said, was a bonus. In 1979-80 he had his first command in the Daring class destroyer *Vampire*, creating a happy and well-trained ship by quickly learning to know every member of the ship's company by name. In 1994 Taylor was promoted vice-admiral and became Chief of Naval

Staff, a title which he changed to Chief of Navy.

The other changes which he witnessed were the withdrawal of British-built ships and RN-manned submarines from the Australian Navy theatre and their replacement, first by American-built destroyers and then Australian ANZAC class frigates and Collins class submarines.

On recovering from heart surgery in 1993, he returned to supervise major RAN manpower reforms concerning pay, conditions and rank structure as well as the repatriation of training from the UK to Australia. The RAN also led the way for other navies in becoming more tolerant towards homosexuals and women at sea. He continuously stressed the importance of preserving the Navy's values, however: tradition, ethos and professionalism – especially during a "defence efficiency review".

Taylor loved all sports, got on with everyone and had that rare gift in naval officers of not imposing his thinking on others. In retirement he helped his wife on their farm at Glenhaven, Wamboin, near Canberra, where she bred alpacas. He learned to wire fences, lay water pipes, renovate an old tractor, and bottle-feed newborn alpacas – sometimes several times a day for several months. Glenhaven also became a meeting place for friends from Taylor's 43 years of service, from his overseas appointments and courses, and his neighbours.

Taylor, who was appointed OA in 1992, was survived by his wife Judy Smith, whom he married in 1964, and a son.

CAPTAIN
PETER SAMBORNE

Captain Peter Samborne (who died on September 28 2002, aged 78) commanded Britain's first nuclear-powered submarine *Dreadnought* in the early 1960s.

Even Admiral Hyman Rickover of the US Navy – who was never slow to criticise the Royal Navy's progress in the rudest fashion – was impressed by the technical and intellectual competence of Samborne when he was selected to train in American nuclear-powered submarines. Samborne first attended No 1 Nuclear Course at the Royal Naval College, Greenwich, then spent nine months in the USS *Skipjack*, learning about the S5W power plant which was being installed in *Dreadnought*. Exceptionally for a seaman officer in the RN, Samborne qualified as engineer officer of the watch and was later regarded as one of the best nuclear engineers of his generation.

The Navy recognised the significance of a new generation of submarines not just by giving the first boat the name of a revolutionary ship (the 1905 battleship *Dreadnought*), but also by asking Her Majesty The Queen to launch her on Trafalgar Day, 1961.

All previous submarines had been taken on sea trials by the shipbuilder, but only Samborne and his crew were qualified to take the new *Dreadnought* to sea. Since Vickers had responsibility for the trials,they overcame this contractual problem by paying Samborne £1 for his services; he started a new tradition by hanging the framed pound note in the wardroom.

There were many firsts during Samborne's

command. In 1962, he got the surfaced *Dreadnought* "on the step", that is, rising through the water, like a planing speedboat; and in 1964 she crossed the Atlantic underwater at an average speed of 24 knots. That year, after more than three years in *Dreadnought*, he was appointed OBE.

Barnaby Frederick Palmer Samborne, known as Peter, was born on September 3 1924 at Timbury House, Somerset, and went to St Christopher's School, Bath, before joining Dartmouth, aged 13½. His first ship was the Town class light cruiser *Liverpool*. In 1942, while escorting the desperately needed convoy WS19 to Malta, *Liverpool* was hit in the engine room and disabled by a torpedo dropped during an Italian attack.

She could be towed only at slow speed by the destroyer *Antelope*, but she helped to save the convoy because the Italian air force concentrated their subsequent attacks upon the crippled cruiser, leaving the convoy to escape eastwards in the darkness. During the attack, Midshipman Samborne controlled *Liverpool*'s 4-inch anti-aircraft guns from the transmitting station; and the ship shot down at least seven aircraft. Samborne was mentioned in despatches for his bravery and resolution in keeping the high-angle guns firing accurately while under continuous attack and as the ship listed heavily.

Later he served briefly in the battleship *Malaya* in Force H in the Mediterranean and in the Hunt class destroyer *Lamerton* during the North African campaign and the landings on Sicily. Samborne joined the "trade",as the submarine service is known, in January 1944 and served as navigating officer and then first lieutenant of *Tuna*.

His next submarine was *Amphion*, the first of a new class designed for service in the British Pacific Fleet. He joined it while it was building at Barrow, gaining experience which would later stand him in good stead. Samborne was then appointed to Reserve Submarine Group Portsmouth, the submarine school at Gosport, and then to command Rothesay Attack Teacher; but for two decades he served almost continually at sea.

He passed the submarine commanding officers' qualifying course, the "perisher", and commanded the submarines *Sturdy*, *Tabard* and *Trenchant* until promoted commander. After the war, the Navy pioneered the use of submarines for intelligence gathering; each operation required the Prime Minister's personal approval, and in 1955 Samborne was entrusted to take *Tabard* to the Barents Sea.

Following *Dreadnought*, he was given a series of staff appointments ashore, including Deputy Chief of Staff of the Nato command on Malta from 1967 to 1970. But Samborne was unhappy in staff posts ashore. He retired as a captain, while many of the officers who had served under him in *Dreadnought* were to become admirals. These included Sir John Fieldhouse, who succeeded him in *Dreadnought*'s command and later was C-in-C Fleet during the Falklands War. In retirement from the Navy, Samborne marketed periscopes for the instrument makers Barr and Stroud.

Peter Samborne married, in 1945, Margaret Brewster. She died in 1988, and he was survived by their second son, who commanded the nuclear-powered submarine *Swiftsure* in 1987-89,and by their daughter; their elder son died in 2000.

COMMANDER
JOHN WEST

Commander John West (who died on October 16 2002, aged 89) was honoured for his role in three major naval battles during the Second World War.

At the Second Battle of Narvik on April 11 1940, he was serving in the Tribal class destroyer *Eskimo*, armed with 4.7-inch guns. When four larger German destroyers took refuge in Rombaksfjord, they filled it with a smokescreen. Frost and snow blurred the gun and director telescopes, blinding West on the bridge; but he navigated *Eskimo* at 15 knots through the narrow entrance of the fjord, where the enemy waited with 5-inch guns and torpedo tubes ready and trained.

A furious fight at less than 5,000 yards range lasted 15 minutes. As *Eskimo* turned broadside on to fire her torpedoes at the German destroyer *Hans Lüdemann*, four torpedoes streaked across the narrow waters towards her. Heading for the cliffs less than 400 yards away, *Eskimo* increased to full speed, then reversed sharply just a few feet short, shaking in every rivet.

Superb ship handling had avoided one fan of torpedoes but a second German destroyer fired another, which *Eskimo* now avoided by going full speed astern. However, a third torpedo attack blew off *Eskimo*'s bows, including the A gun. But she continued to hit the Germans repeatedly from her other mountings and reduced them to hulks. *Eskimo* then navigated backwards through the fjord entrance, dragging her fo'c'sle, which temporarily anchored her to the bottom twice.

Eskimo was in danger of sinking, and her captain

Commander St J A Micklethwait evacuated all non-essential crew for the long tow back to Scotland. West was mentioned in despatches.

In the Second Battle of Sirte on March 22 1942, West was navigating officer of the First World War cruiser *Carlisle*, which was charged with protecting the merchant ships of convoy MW10 from Alexandria to Malta. The convoy came under non-stop heavy air attack. At one stage shells from the Italian battleship *Littorio* missed Admiral Philip Vian's cruisers to fall amongst the merchant ships.

Carlisle was steering under continuous rudder as she twisted and turned to avoid attack; but she skilfully made smoke to hide the merchant ships and safely conducted her precious convoy to their dispersal point. Though almost out of fuel and ammunition, *Carlisle* also tried to tow *Breconshire* out of a minefield. This manoeuvring while under attack required navigating skill of the highest order, and West was awarded the DSC.

In late 1943 West was navigator of the cruiser *Jamaica*, consort to the battleship *Duke of York*, escorting convoys into and out of the Kola Inlet, when the German battleship *Scharnhorst* attacked convoy JW55B. It was permanently dark in the Arctic winter, and the sea was so violent on Christmas Night that few men had any sleep; but the battle plan called for the two ships to manoeuvre as one unit. West succeeded in keeping *Jamaica* so close that German fire control radar was confused by the large echoes which merged into one.

Light forces thwarted *Scharnhorst* until, at 1650 hours on Boxing Day, Admiral Sir Bruce Fraser surprised her at six miles range. British gunnery was good. By 1935 *Jamaica* was ordered to finish off the enemy with torpedoes. West was mentioned in despatches again for his faultless efficiency, coolness and skill under fire.

John Leslie West was born on February 3 1913 and entered the Royal Navy between the wars, specialising in navigation in 1941. When peace returned he served in two appointments which carried titles redolent of the age of sail: he was Master Attendant at Garden Island in Sydney, responsible for ships' movements, and Master of the Fleet or senior navigator while in the battleship *Vanguard*. His last uniformed appointment was as Assistant Queen's Harbourmaster at Portsmouth.

After leaving the Navy he served as a retired officer in the Directorate of Naval Warfare at the Ministry of Defence, where he was appointed MBE for his part in organising a long series of Nato exercises.

John West married, in 1940, Eve Haggis, who survived him with one daughter; another daughter predeceased him.

CAPTAIN
KEN MARTIN

Captain Ken Martin (who died on October 22 2002, aged 82) was one of two submariner brothers involved together in the Mediterranean and Pacific theatres during the Second World War.

In 1944 Ken Martin arrived in *Sleuth* at Fremantle, Western Australia, a week ahead of his older brother Joe in *Solent*. "Crap" Miers, VC, commanding the RN submarines of the British Pacific Fleet,hit on the idea that the brothers, who had married sisters, would form a natural team. This was poor psychology, as they worried about each other, and Ken resented serving under the tactical command of his brother, who was six years older.

Nevertheless, using their wives' Christian names as call signs, they accomplished some successful patrols at a time when the seas had been largely swept clear of Japanese shipping.

On a seven-week patrol in the Java Sea, Joe in *Solent* attacked a merchant ship and had to avoid both the counter-attack of an escort and one of his own torpedoes, which had developed a fault and circled back towards him. Later the brothers sank a minesweeper, a landing barge and a coaster, and rescued 90 survivors; but Joe had to be evacuated suffering from jaundice.

When they made their next joint patrol in the South China Sea, they sank several small ships by gunfire; then Ken, in *Sleuth*, missed a Japanese submarine, but, despite a heavy swell, was able to conn Joe's *Solent* into a counter-attack on another target.

On their last patrol in the Gulf of Siam they accounted for 15 junks and a patrol vessel. Surfacing on August 15 1945, they were in time to hear the broadcast announcing the end of the war. A few minutes later *Solent's* coxswain offered to sign on volunteers to complete 12 years service, and was greeted with hoots of derision.

Sleuth and *Solent* were the last two submarines to return from active service. Ken was awarded the DSC, and Joe a Bar to his DSC.

The son of a paymaster lieutenant, Kenneth Henry Martin was born at Plymouth on March 24 1920. After education at Colston's School,Bristol,he joined his older brother Joe at *Conway*, the merchant naval school. Joe went briefly into the Merchant Navy before moving across to the Royal Navy and "the trade", as the submarine service is known, when war broke out. Ken had gone directly into the Royal Navy as a special entry cadet in 1937, helped by having won the highest prize at *Conway*, the King's Medal.

In May 1940 all the sub-lieutenants on courses at Whale Island took part in the evacuation of Dunkirk. Ken Martin was given command of an ungainly 250-ton steam-driven mud hopper which steamed from Portsmouth with two motor launches. Defenceless and under fire from German artillery off Dunkirk, he embarked some 500 French troops, stiffened by a company of British Guards.

By the time they reached Ramsgate, it was realised how unsuited his craft was for the task, and she was sent back to Portsmouth for Martin to resume his training. Later that year he was appointed to the battleship *Hood*. When the signal came for him to go for submarine training his captain, who was fed up with the turnover of young officers, told him that he was making the biggest mistake of his life. Martin pleaded that he already had a brother in submarines and had set his heart on joining, and the captain reluctantly relented. Five months later *Hood* was sunk with the loss of all but three of her ship's company.

After an abbreviated training, Martin served in three submarines, the First World War H34 and then the more modern P35 and P31, before being sent as spare crew to Malta where, during 1941 and 1942, the submarines of the "Fighting Tenth" squadron attacked Axis supply lines.

When in harbour the submarines sat on the bottom of Marsamxett creek by day to avoid attack by enemy bombers, surfacing at night to continue maintenance. As duty officer one day, Ken Martin dived his submarine which, shortly after settling on the bottom, started to take in water.

He blew ballast to bring the submarine to the surface, but it stood on its head with the propellers out of the water, while the air battle raged overhead; it then sank back to the mud while Joe watched helplessly from a *dghaisa* for several hours. After much shifting of stores and pumping out of water, Ken and the handful of men on board managed to lighten the submarine sufficiently to bring it to the surface, where it transpired that it had sat on the flukes of an old anchor, piercing the pressure hull and making an 8-inch hole.

In July 1943, after the Italian submarine *Bronzo* had been depth-charged and captured by a force of minesweepers, Martin was sent to Syracuse to bring it back to Malta; he could not start *Bronzo*'s engines and so returned in her under tow. However, while at Syracuse he and the engineer officer sent with him were poking around the torpedo store in the Italian naval base when they captured the mechanism of a German magnetic torpedo, left behind by the Axis forces. Their efforts were not acknowledged, but Martin believed he was the first to seize such a device.

After the war, Ken Martin made national headlines. By conducting tropical trials in the submarine

Alliance, he completed a record-breaking 35 days continuously dived; he was then relieved in *Alliance* by Joe. Ken then commanded the submarine *Tally Ho* and was second-in-command of the destroyer *Duchess*. He was Commander (Submarines) in the depot ship Adamant; captain of the destroyer *Broadsword*; and Captain Seventh Submarine Squadron and of the depot ship Forth. His final appointment was as Queen's Harbourmaster and Captain of the Port at Portsmouth, where he organised the reception for Sir Alec Rose after his round-the-world voyage.

In 1970 the motor vessels *Allegro* and *Pacific Glory* collided and caught fire off the Isle of Wight, leaking large quantities of oil. Although this was technically outside his jurisdiction, Martin characteristically took charge, and initiated an emergency plan which averted disaster.

He had briefly been liaison officer on the Greek submarine *Pipinos* in 1943, and, from 1948 to 1950, he served as volunteer in the British naval mission to Greece, directing an amphibious operation against a communist stronghold at Kalamata Bay. Later, at a dinner in the Greek Navy Tactical School to celebrate the end of the civil war, Queen Frederika invited Martin to dance with her.

It was generally agreed that the Admiralty was acting untypically when it sent Martin, who by now spoke Greek well, back to Athens as naval attaché in 1963. He helped to organise a royal visit by King Paul and Queen Frederika to London, and, after the King's death, marched close by the gun carriage carrying his body. Martin was awarded the Greek Order of the Phoenix, and, later, when he visited Piraeus in his ship, *Forth*, the royal family insisted on coming on board, despite it being only a routine port visit.

In retirement Martin threw himself into family life, and enjoyed sailing, including making a transatlantic crossing in a small yacht with a scratch crew.

Ken Martin married, in 1941, Joyce Isobel Symes, who survived him with their four sons, two of whom were naval officers. His brother Joe, who married Joyce's sister Margaret, died in 1965.

MAJOR-GENERAL DEREK POUNDS

Major-General Derek Pounds (who died on November 7 2002, aged 80) led several daring commando raids behind enemy lines during the Korean War.

His involvement in these actions came after a row between the senior American commanders of the United Nations force. General Douglas MacArthur had questioned whether the proposed raids justified the risks inherent in such operations, and had then rudely asked why Admiral Turner Joy was "so keen to use Brits".

Only after several terse exchanges, in which Joy insisted on the excellent quality of the Royal Marines (many of whom had flown to the Far East in civil airliners dressed in Admiralty-issued civilian suits), did MacArthur relent. He then limited their participation to just 70 Royal Marines. Less than a week later, in August 1950, Pounds and a team of 12 were practising night amphibious raids from the high-speed destroyer transport USS *Diachenko* and the transport submarine USS *Perch*.

The following month "Pounds Force", as it was known, and two platoons of American marines were landed from the British frigate *Whitesand Bay* in a diversionary raid 80 miles south at Kunsan. As the marines approached the beach the sea was extremely phosphorescent, and their paddles created a brilliant shower of light with every stroke. They had been told there would be no resistance; but the enemy were waiting, and, after a bitter struggle, Pounds Force withdrew in organised chaos with heavy casualties. But they achieved their objective of creating a diversion as the American marines stormed ashore at Inchon, thereby securing a strategic triumph for MacArthur.

On the night of October 6-7, Pounds destroyed a railway tunnel just 80 miles south of the Soviet border, the first of a series of raids against the railway system which ran along a 120-mile stretch of coastline. Back on board the American transport destroyer *Horace A Bass*, Pounds's men drank a miniature bottle of brandy each – strictly for medicinal purposes since they were in a dry US Navy ship.

Later, as part of 41 Independent Commando, the troop helped to capture Kimpo airfield and took part in operations to recapture Seoul. Pounds was awarded the US Bronze Star; it was felt that, if he had been under British command, he would have received a DSO.

Edgar George Derek Pounds was born at Devizes, Wiltshire, on Friday October 13 1922. He was educated at Reading School. At 17, Pounds presented himself at his local recruiting office, where the only options seemed to be the Navy or the Royal Marines. As he pondered these alternatives, a large man in a blue uniform, whom he later discovered to be a colour-sergeant, put a hand on his shoulder and said: "You're a well-built lad. You'd better be a marine."

In later years, Pounds often cited this encounter as a perfect example of personnel selection and career counselling. After training with 384 King's Squad at Chatham, he was awarded the King's Badge, as the best recruit of his intake. By the end of his 36-year career he was unique in being the only general to wear this badge (sported on the left shoulder).

He qualified in naval gunnery and served in Atlantic and Russian waters in the cruiser *Kent* where he was captain of a twin 4-inch gun mounting. On being commissioned in 1942, he won the sword for outstanding ability.

In late 1944 Pounds began his long association with the commandos at the Achnacarry training centre in Scotland, and joined 45 Commando for the closing stages of the war. He next served in Hong Kong, where he helped with civil rehabilitation pro-grammes, and then in Palestine during the handover of the Mandate. Pounds saw action in Cyprus against Grivas's Eoka terrorists, for which he was mentioned in despatches, and also during the Suez landings in 1956.

After qualifying at the RAF Staff College, Brack-nell, he served on the staff of the Commandant General, Royal Marines, and then was Amphibious Operations Officer in *Bulwark*, Britain's first com-mando helicopter carrier. In the mid-1960s Pounds commanded 40 Commando in Borneo during the confrontation with Indonesia. Following a period as GSO1 on the Commandant General's staff, he went to the Ministry of Defence.

On retiring in 1974 Pounds bought himself a bookshop at Exmouth,Devon; but within the year he was recalled, and appointed to a vacant position as major-general. His final appointment was in command of Commando Forces, responsible for the operational command of reinforcement operations on both Nato flanks (Norway and Turkey) and the development of Arctic warfare.

After his second retirement in 1976, Pounds became chief executive of the British Friesian Cattle Society (now the Holstein-Friesian Society). He reorganised its administration, expanded computerisation and worked to safeguard the interests of British dairy farmers by expanding export markets, particularly in South Korea, where his war record helped. On giving this up in 1987, he occupied himself as a cattle steward and council member of the Devon Agricultural Association.

Earlier he had represented the Royal Marines at rugby, rifle and pistol shooting, and always kept himself fit, although troubled by asthma in later life. He hunted regularly when stationed in the West Country.

Pounds was a natural leader with firm opinions which he was not afraid to express forcefully on occasion, irrespective of whether this was likely to endear him to his superiors. He noted that, although he received a CB in 1975, Cheng Chau village in Hong Kong had awarded him their gold medal for his work with them in the 1950s.

Derek Pounds married, in 1944, Third Officer

Barbara Evans, WRNS. She survived him, with their son and daughter.

CAPTAIN
STAN DARLING

Captain Stan Darling (who died on November 18 2002, aged 95) was a much decorated U-boat hunter, and Australia's most successful ocean-racing navigator.

After commanding several anti-submarine vessels, varying from trawlers to frigates, on convoy escort in the Atlantic, Darling was given command of the new frigate *Loch Killin*. She was equipped with the "squid", which used a mortar to throw a depth charge ahead of a ship, so that she did not have to pass over her submerged target.

In June 1944 Darling joined Captain Johnnie Walker's Second Support Group which was deployed in the South Western Approaches and English Channel to keep the seas clear for the Normandy landings. Walker taught his officers to develop "the spirit of vicious offensive" and, after Walker's death in July, Darling embodied this. On a single patrol he sank two U-boats and assisted in the sinking of two more.

He was awarded a first DSC for his courage, resolution and skill in destroying U-333 in the Channel on July 31 1944, and a Bar for forcing U-736 to the surface and sinking her on August 6.

Darling had detected U-736 at close range; he turned towards her and, slowing just long enough to establish Asdic contact and set his weapons, fired the squid, which set off two torpedoes coming from the U-boat. The massive explosion a few yards from *Loch Killin* blew U-736 to the surface and, as a huge fountain of water settled around both vessels, *Loch Killin* ran over the German's foredecks. The German survivors of the attack were able to clamber from the U-boat's conning tower on to *Loch Killin*'s quarter-deck without wetting their feet; Darling remembered with satisfaction the German commander's expression of surprise as his boat sank beneath him.

Then, on April 15 1945, Darling sank U-1063 off Start Point, the last German sub to be sunk in the Channel; it earned him a second Bar to his DSC.

Stanley Waldron Darling was born at Bellerive, Tasmania, on August 17 1907. His father, a surveyor, was a keen sailor who took his family cruising on his 31-foot yacht; his mother was one of Tasmania's first female Justices of the Peace. Darling was educated at Hutchins School and studied Engineering at the University of Tasmania.

In 1931 he became a radio announcer with the Australian Broadcasting Commission at Hobart, transferring to its head office in Sydney in 1936. Three years later the ABC sent him to America to study acoustics. By the outbreak of the Second World War, Darling was a lieutenant-commander in the RANVR. He had become interested in sound after joining the Australian Broadcasting Commission, and his work had led him naturally towards the use of sound in detecting underwater targets (Asdic), and to his training at the Australian anti-submarine school at Rushcutters Bay.

Australians made up a fifth of the anti-submarine

specialist officers serving in British, Canadian, Norwegian and Free French ships during the Battle of the Atlantic, and Darling was one of those loaned to the Royal Navy in August 1940.

After *Loch Killin*, he went to South East Asian waters in command of the frigate *Loch Lomond*. When peace returned, he commanded the shore base HMAS Rushcutter, retiring as the RAN's senior reserve officer nine years later.

Darling returned to the ABC, where he became a highly regarded acoustics engineer, setting up studios and concert halls across Australia; he was also consulted about the design of the Sydney Opera House. With his broadcasting and naval background, he became a pioneer in the use of radio communication in offshore racing, which is now seen as essential to safety. The first radio Darling used as a peacetime sailor was an old army surplus set, which he repaired in *Peer Gynt* during the Auckland–Sydney race in 1948; he had to take it apart and solder it together again while holding all the parts to prevent them being lost overboard.

As a long-standing member of the Royal Sydney Yacht Squadron and the Cruising Yacht Club of Australia, Darling navigated five winners in the Sydney–Hobart race, which is regarded as the toughest competition in the international blue-water racing calendar. He crewed first for the Halvorsen brothers, and then for Sir Robert Crichton-Brown. In the 1954 race he skippered *Solveig* when the Halvorsen brothers fell ill, and went on to become the first yachtsman to complete 25 Sydney–Hobart races.

He also navigated Australia's earliest Admiral's Cup

challenges,in *Freya* in 1965,and in Crichton-Brown's *Balandra* which won in 1967. Five years later, Darling was coaxed out of retirement to sail Jack Rooklyn's boats, *Apollo* and then *Ballyhoo*, navigating them in races and on delivery trips from Australia to the west coast of America and to Britain.

He displayed all his skills in *Apollo* during the 1973 Fastnet race. The fog was so thick that the bows could not be seen from the cockpit. Other boats became lost, and sailed straight past the Fastnet Rock to Ireland; but Darling sat calmly with the earphones of an old wartime direction-finding radio, calling: "Fifteen minutes to go, let's get ready... 10 minutes to go... start dropping the 'chute... there it is." One crew member recalled that, as Fastnet Rock appeared out of the fog,they dropped the spinnaker and turned *Apollo* but, before they had cleared away the sail, the Rock had vanished.

Darling's seamanship and ocean-racing guile also enabled *Ballyhoo* to win the China Seas race from Hong Kong to Manila; the round-the-state race in Hawaii; and the California Cup. *Ballyhoo* returned to Australia to take line honours in the 1976 Sydney-Hobart race, then went to England for Cowes Week the following year. By now Darling lived on *Ballyhoo*. When she was sold after winning the 1977 Fastnet Race, he accompanied the new owner to the Mediterranean, the West Indies and America. He continued to sail even after breaking eight ribs in the disastrous Fastnet race of 1979.

Darling's love of classical music was sometimes a source of conflict with younger crew. Once he struck a deal whereby there would be two consecutive hours of jazz, and two hours of rock and pop, followed by two hours of classical music. On another occasion, tiring of a Rolling Stones tape that was being played continuously into the night, the 80-year-old Darling came on deck naked in the middle of a tropical rainstorm,shuffled a few dance steps to the music and sang,"I don't know if we can dig this music for too much longer."

Stan Darling had the ability to converse with anyone, and was modest and quietly spoken, rarely mentioning his wartime exploits. He was always too busy to get married.

MARINE
BILL SPARKS

Marine Bill Sparks (who died on November 30 2002, aged 80) was the last of the two surviving "Cockleshell Heroes" responsible for paddling a canoe 85 miles through enemy defences to cripple German merchant ships at Bordeaux in December 1941.

Ten Royal Marines set out from a submarine in kayaks, known as cockleshells, to attack a fleet of German armed merchantmen preparing to raid British shipping; eight were shot or drowned while Sparks and Major "Blondie" Hasler, the expedition's leader, were pursued through France and Spain by vengeful Germans for three months before they reached safety.

The operation was hazardous from the start, and was only chosen because the alternative, a bombing raid, would have caused heavy civilian casualties. Hasler's platoon spent five days in *Tuna*, escaping a U-boat attack en route. They reached their launch point in the Bay of Biscay, 10 miles from the River Gironde, but had to remain bottomed for 24 hours because of poor weather. On the evening of December 7, the sea was calmer and Hasler and Sparks launched their cockleshell, *Cachalot*, first.

Sergeant Wallace and Marine Ewart were soon captured, interrogated and shot; Corporal Sheard and Marine Moffatt were drowned. Lieutenant Mackinnon and Marine Conway went missing. Hasler and Sparks pressed on with Corporal Laver and Marine Mills. Although the Germans were now alerted, the two craft avoided sentry positions and three patrol boats in the estuary.

Sparks and Hasler were seen, but not compromised, by French civilians as they used the flood tide by night and lay in hiding by day. Sparks remembered afterwards sharing an illicit bottle of rum with Hasler, and savouring every brew of tea and the frequent use of Benzedrine tablets to stave off sleepiness. By the third night, they were feeling cold, wet and tired as they lay up on the small Ile de Cazeau, which was home to a German anti-aircraft battery, but the marines' fieldcraft was so good that enemy patrols failed to detect them. At nightfall they realised that they were sharing the island with Mackinnon and Conway, whose craft was damaged by a submerged hazard with the result that they were betrayed and executed.

On the last night of their paddle, Sparks and Hasler hid in tall reeds within easy reach of Bordeaux, where they could sleep, eat and prepare within yards of the bustling harbour. As the pair proceeded to place their limpet mines on the sides of ships, they thought that they had been seen by a sentry, and were crushed between two ships moving together. They managed to escape silently on the ebb tide, and soon found Laver and Mills who had also successfully placed their mines. When the explosions took place, four ships were severely damaged and a fifth sunk.

William Edward Sparks was born in the East End of London on September 5 1922, and left school at 14. After three years as a shoe repairer, he infuriated his father on the outbreak of war by allowing himself to be persuaded to join the Royal Marines, instead of becoming a stoker in the family tradition. Sparks first served in the battleship *Renown* on convoys to Malta and in the hunt for the *Bismarck*.

When he heard of his brother Bonny's death in the cruiser *Naiad*, he drowned his sorrows so well that his father had to persuade him to make tardy return from leave, when he was confined to barracks. There he read a notice calling for volunteers for hazardous service, and promptly volunteered as a way of avenging Bonny. He was delighted a few weeks later when Hasler selected him with 40 other volunteers. He responded to the informality and the hard work, as well as the pleasures of blowing things up. Hasler chose him as his crewman.

After completing their demolition the two remaining pairs of canoeists sank their boats and began a trek to Ruffec, 100 miles away. They spent the next two months in the hands of various agents, most notably Mary Lindell, who operated in the Lyon area. Great dangers were involved, though in one safe house Sparks felt more threatened by the overtures of the daughter of the family than by the Germans. Eventually he and Hasler were led over the Pyrenees to Spain; Layer and Mills were captured and shot.

Hasler flew home, but Sparks was placed under arrest and taken in a troopship to England, as no one in Gibraltar could corroborate his story. On arrival he was placed on a train by military police, but escaped at Euston Station and went home to see his father, who had been told that he was missing in action. Two days later Sparks reported to the Admiralty where he was again threatened with arrest, but a naval Intelli-gence officer encouraged him to slip out the back door and report to Combined Operations Head-quarters, where he was greeted with astonishment.

King George VI presented Sparks with the Distinguished Service Medal and Hasler with the DSO. Sparks served in Burma, Africa and Italy before becoming a bus driver in 1946. He spent some time in Malaya during the Emergency as a police lieutenant. When the film *The Cockleshell Heroes*, with Anthony Newley playing him, came out in 1955 Sparks made a promotional tour in America, then became a bus inspector. The one issue which upset Sparks was that his dead comrades were not properly honoured. Eventually, through the MP Sir Bernard Braine and *The Daily Telegraph*, a fund to pay for a memorial was set up; the necessary money was gathered in a month.

Two years later Sparks's invalidity pension was cut by £1,000 a year and, despite media coverage and family disagreement, he decided that he had to auction his medals. "I have tried not to feel bitter about this," he told the *Telegraph*. "But when I went to the DHSS and explained my case, I was told absolutely nothing could be done. How can I feel anything else but bitter and disappointed?"

The sale raised £31,000 at Sotheby's from an anonymous bidder. But the pain was alleviated when the new owner placed the eight medals in Sotheby's vault with instructions that Sparks was to be permitted to wear them whenever he wished.

Sparks was grateful to the French people who had helped him escape, and returned several times to Bordeaux. He met the Dubois family, who had sheltered him for some weeks,and Mary Lindell,who had survived being interned at Auschwitz;he also saw the bullet holes in the wall against which Wallace and Ewart had been shot at the Chateau Dehez.

When he was 61, Sparks re-enacted his epic journey by paddling from the mouth of the Gironde to Bordeaux to raise money for Cancer Research, with Gerry Lockyer of the Imperial War Museum as his companion. Afterwards Sparks said that, although the trip was not so dangerous as in 1942, they had known about the tides then: this time the paddling was much harder. The escape route which he and Hasler used is now a footpath dedicated to the Cockleshell Heroes.

Sparks had three sons, one of whom became a colour sergeant in the Royal Marines,and a daughter. They survived him with his second wife Irene.

LIEUTENANT-COMMANDER
"PAT" KINGSMILL

Lieutenant-Commander "Pat" Kingsmill (who died on January 1 2003, aged 82) flew one of the six elderly Swordfish which, each armed with a single torpedo, aimed to halt the largest German fleet of the Second World War as it passed through the Channel on February 21 1941.

Although the battlecruisers *Scharnhorst* and *Gneisenau*, the heavy cruiser *Prinz Eugen* and their escorts had been expected to break out from Brest to make for Norway, British inter-service liaison had failed.Most of 825 Naval Air Squadron,including the 20-year-old Kingsmill, had no experi-ence of battle. Their leader, Lieutenant-Commander Eugene Esmonde, had returned the day before from being invested with the DSO at Buckingham Palace for his part in sinking the *Bismarck*; Kingsmill was in a barber's chair when the alarm was given that the Germans were already off Calais.

Admiral Sir Bertram Ramsay, Flag Officer Dover, pleaded with the First Sea Lord not to send men to a certain death, but he gave Esmonde the authority to decide if he had sufficient fighter cover to attempt an attack. With only 10 Spitfires rather than the five squadrons he had been promised, Esmonde led his men as they took off from RAF Manston in Kent;the station commander, Wing Commander Tom Gleave, was so appalled that he stood at the end of the snowy runway and saluted each aircraft.

The Spitfires of 72 Squadron soon became engaged in dogfights with German fighters and lost sight of the Swordfish, as 825 Squadron lumbered at 90 knots an hour towards their target.Esmonde was shot down first but, with his dying action, launched his torpedo. Kingsmill, who was following him, flew so low that he was hit by ricochets from the surface of the sea as he pressed on through the smoke and bursting shells.

He watched Esmonde's aircraft erupt in a ball of fire and then his friend Brian Rose crash into the sea, before he turned towards the *Prinz Eugen* at a range of 2,000 yards. Kingsmill had already received the first of several wounds, a hit in the back. His observer, "Mac" Samples, had blood running from his boots, and his leading telegraphist air gunner, Don Bunce, had his seat shot away, so that he had to brace his legs to avoid falling into the sea.

Swordfish W5907 had one wing on fire, it had engine damage, and the controls were becoming increasingly sluggish as Kingsmill turned full circle to avoid enemy fighters, then steadied up for his torpedo drop. *Prinz Eugen* manoeuvred violently to comb the torpedo track which just missed astern.As Kingsmill turned away, his Swordfish was hit again, detonating its distress flares. Trailing ragged fabric streamers and with gaping holes in virtually every part of its wings, fuselage and tail, he tried to prevent it stalling before ditching.

Then he calmly climbed from his cockpit, crawled the length of the fuselage to the tailplane, helped his crew to escape and slipped into the icy sea. Their dinghy was destroyed by gunfire, but 10 minutes later they were rescued by a motor torpedo boat.

Kingsmill had flown at 40 feet underneath the second flight of Swordfish as they advanced into a wall of fire, and all were shot down: 825 Squadron had lived up to its motto *nihil obstat* (nothing stops us). Afterwards Admiral Ramsay wrote that this gallant sortie constituted one of the finest exhibitions of self-sacrifice and devotion to duty that the war had yet witnessed; on the bridge of the *Scharnhorst* the navigating officer felt privileged to witness the pilots knowingly and ungrudgingly flying to their doom without hesitation.

Esmonde was posthumously awarded the Victoria Cross. The survivors of the second Swordfish, Sub-Lieutenants Rose and Edgar Lee, were awarded the DSO, as were Kingsmill and Samples; Bunce received the Conspicuous Gallantry Medal. The others were awarded a mention in despatches, all that was allowed by the rules.

Charles Major Kingsmill, nicknamed Pat, was born on September 19 1920 at Edmonton, Alberta, where his family were homesteaders. They returned to England during the Depression and Kingsmill was educated at Dulwich College, before volunteering for the Royal Navy and learning to fly. One day, when he should have been studying his pilot's notes, Kingsmill took time off to play golf, and was most offended when a low flying Messerschmitt strafed him, though he was more scared that the incident would reveal his truancy from the classroom.

Kingsmill's injuries in 1941 were bullet wounds, and although he was never a patient of the plastic surgeon Sir Archibald McIndoe at Queen Victoria Hospital, East Grinstead, he took an interest in the pioneering work done there on burns and restorative surgery. After the war he served more than 15 years in London Division RNR. He worked briefly in an engineering company which installed air conditioning at Clarence House, then joined the newly created National Health Service.

At the London Hospital he ran the country's largest outpatients' department and took satisfaction that no patient had to wait more than four weeks to see a consultant. Later he worked for the North-East Kent regional health authority, and at the end of his career spent a year in Saudi Arabia, helping to commission a "state-of-the-art" hospital for the National Guard.

Kingsmill was a modest man, and few who worked with him knew of his bravery. He never wrote about his experiences, but he did record an oral history with his fellow aircrew to accompany a pamphlet by Ted Powell called *The Channel Dash Heroes*.

Pat Kingsmill married first, in 1940, Connie Durrant, whose midwife was delayed by a snowstorm when she was bearing twins; so he delivered them himself. After her death Kingsmill married, in 1957, Unity Urquhart, who survived him, with two sons and a daughter of his first marriage and a son and a daughter from his second. A daughter of his second marriage predeceased him.

MAJOR
HUGH BRUCE

Major Hugh Bruce (who died on January 9 2003, aged 83) spent three years as a prisoner of war in Colditz Castle, becoming involved in many attempts to escape from Germany's most notorious PoW camp; he later served with distinction in Cyprus, and was commanding officer of the Special Boat Service.

At 21, Bruce was part of Captain Darby Courtice's

company of 85 Royal Marines which landed at Calais shortly after midnight on May 25 1940. With one other officer, Lieutenant David Hunter, they were charged with helping French marines to defend the ancient citadel at the centre of the town. There they were attacked by the full might of XIX Panzer Corps and, by early evening, found themselves surrounded and out of ammunition. They had fought with such vigour that the official German record declared: "The enemy gives the impression of being fresh, and seems to have received reinforcements after two days of heavy fighting."

When Calais fell, there was a sudden quiet; it was a warm summer's evening. The Royal Marines put down their arms and filed out through a tunnel, but Bruce remained behind on the ramparts amongst the dead. Although there was no ship in sight and the quays were deserted, he knew that, behind the high mound of fortifications, the Germans were marshalling their prisoners. He wondered about hiding, then considered trying to swim the strip of water which separated him from the eastern arm of the break water. But the route was too exposed to the eyes of Germans already on the bastions of the harbour; so he returned to his machine-gun post and dismantled the firing mechanism.

As Bruce pulled the film out of his camera to destroy the gruesome record of the battle, he saw a German soldier coming into the citadel towards him. He was alone, and about the same age as Bruce, and, although they had no common language, they exchanged greetings. Handing the German his binoculars and miniature camera, Bruce asked, somewhat hopefully, that they be sent back after the war, and hurriedly scribbled his address. Then he took off his steel helmet and webbing equipment, picked up a small haversack containing his toothbrush and razor and two tins of meat and vegetables for his next meal, and walked out of the citadel into imprisonment.

Bruce was marched across northern France to the German frontier, and then on to Laufen camp in Bavaria. In the spring of 1941 he was moved to Posen, a punishment camp set up in response to the supposed ill-treatment of German prisoners in Canada. Here, he and his comrades were kept underground in deplorable conditions, which resulted in Bruce contracting *cairo pompholyx*, brought on by poor nutrition and lack of sunlight.

Then, after a short spell at the Biberach camp on the Swiss border, he was moved to the naval camp, or Marlag, at Sandborstal, from which he made a number of escapes. The first, with Flight Lieutenant Peter Wild, resulted in only 40 minutes of freedom after they had attached themselves to a working party, then run off whilst on a wood collecting trip in the forest. Hunter was imprisoned with him and, over the winter of 1941–42, the two men became firm friends.

With a number of colleagues they conceived, designed and built by hand a masterpiece of British engineering, a 251-yard tunnel, complete with rest bay, electric lighting and air flow system, as well as a signalling device to warn of the approach of sentries. On April 7 1942 Bruce, Hunter and 10 other officers made their escape. After 12 days on the run Bruce and Hunter were captured near Flensburg, within a few hundred yards of the Danish border. They only spent a brief spell back at Sandborstal before escaping again, this time by jumping aboard a prison lorry; they were recaptured in Hamburg by the German police.

In August 1942 the pair were imprisoned in Colditz Castle, where Bruce's skills were immediately put to good use. (He was a talented lock-picker: at a reunion at Colditz 40 years later, he managed to pick the lock of his cell before a disgruntled East German guard was able to find the correct key.)

The three Royal Marine officers – Bruce, Hunter and Courtice, their company commander at Calais – had a reputation for bravery and good humour at Colditz, where they were willing volunteers for whatever was being planned; one of their escape attempts involved a comrade impersonating a senior German NCO. But all failed. Bruce and Hunter remained in Colditz until their release in April 1945.

Hugh Glenrinnes Bruce was born on January 26 1919 at Mhow, India, where his father was serving with the Royal Army Medical Corps on attachment to the Indian Army. Young Hugh was educated at Blundells, and joined the Royal Marines in 1937. He was commissioned a year later, and served briefly in the battleship *Rodney* before being selected for the Calais force.

After the war Bruce continued in the Royal Marines, serving in British Columbia, Malta and Suez. He was second-in-command of 40 Commando, and joined the Special Boat Service in 1950, becoming its commanding officer in 1952. He engaged in a number of clandestine operations, and supervised training in Italy, Cyprus and the United States. During one exercise, he was "captured" by the RAF regiment and marched in to an office for interrogation; when ordered to halt, he escaped by continuing straight through a first floor glass window. On being sent up to inspect Kyrenia Castle, from which some Eoka men had escaped, he signalled the Governor that any Colditz man could have got away from it in 20 minutes.

Bruce was mentioned in despatches three times: for his part in the defence of Calais in 1940; for the organisation of the Sandborstal tunnel; and for anti-terrorist operations in Cyprus whilst serving with 40 Commando.

After retiring from the Royal Marines in 1957 he set up Sea Services Shipping, which surveyed the proposed route of the Channel Tunnel and provided supply ships to the oil industry. Later he established Bruce Maritime, which specialised in deep-water buoys in the North Sea. In addition to his interest in wildlife, shooting and fishing, he was a keen yachtsman. While in Colditz, he had taken part in a competition organised by the Royal Ocean Racing Club for prisoners of war to design an offshore racing yacht, and had come third, winning a prize of £20 – the £100 first prize went to another Colditz prisoner, Flight Lieutenant Welch.

Bruce competed in 10 Fastnet races (coming first of class in *Uomie* in 1953) and numerous Admiral's Cup regattas. A meticulous planner in every aspect of his life, he became a much sought after navigator and tactician; in his sixties he was engaged by the Swiss Admiral's Cup team as tactician on their 1981 challenge. He also wrote extensively on race tactics and navigation.

He founded the Royal Marines' Canoe Club, coming second in the Devizes Race in 1950 and

1951. The following year, with his Royal Marine colleague David Mitchell, he broke the world record for crossing the English Channel in a two-man canoe; a record which stood for eight years. He was a keen student of languages into old age, and published a book on family history, *The Bruces of Kildrummy*, in 1992. He was chairman of the Colditz Association until 1997. His favourite party trick was fire-breathing.

Hugh Bruce married Jean Rowland Farrant, then the head model at the house of Worth, in 1951. She survived him with their son and three daughters.

COMMANDER
TEDDY YOUNG

Commander Teddy Young (who died on January 28 2003, aged 89) designed the first covers for Penguin books and had a gallant career as a submarine officer, which led him to write the classic Second World War memoir *One of Our Submarines*.

In it, Young described how he became the first RNVR officer of the war to command a submarine. The book included a vivid account of his escape from a sinking vessel, but it was most notable for its modest humour and the nostalgic picture of a life at sea that was dangerous and uncomfortable, yet exhilarating.

One of Our Submarines was brought out in 1952 by Rupert Hart-Davis, whom Young and David Garnett had joined as co-directors in 1946. It received fine reviews, and made a considerable profit. After a year it was already in its eighth impression; in 1954 it was chosen to be the 1,000th Penguin (for which Young produced a new cover), and it has remained in print ever since.

Edward Preston Young was born on November 17 1913 in Trinidad, where his father was a general trader, and educated at Highgate School. He started work sharpening pencils at the Bodley Head, then left with Allen Lane to launch Penguin as the first major paperback imprint. Lane dispatched young Teddy off to London Zoo to draw the famous penguin logo, and it duly appeared on the bottom of Young's distinctive cover design.

Young moved to the Reprint Society shortly before the outbreak of war when, as a keen yachtsman, he joined the Royal Naval Volunteer Reserve. On learning that submariners received extra training in celestial navigation, he volunteered for submarines as a future aid to his sailing. Young was in the submarine *Umpire* on its first night at sea as part of an East Coast convoy when it was rammed and sunk by an escorting armed trawler; as third hand, he was one of only a dozen survivors from the crew of 30. Later he briefly commanded *Sealion*, and was selected for the demanding "perisher" course for submarine commanding officers.

In March 1943 Young was awarded his first DSC and, after briefly commanding a former American submarine, took command of *Storm*, which first torpedoed a Japanese minesweeper off the Andaman Islands in the Far East. His next patrol, to land a secret agent on the coast of Sumatra, was compromised, and Young's submarine was ambushed when it returned to the landing place. A few well-placed shots from its 3-inch gun silenced the enemy's crossfire, though the agent was never seen again.

For his outstanding bravery, skill and good judgment, Young was recommended for a Bar to his DSC; instead he was awarded the DSO after news arrived of his fourth and fifth patrols, during which he attacked a convoy, and sank a destroyer and two supply ships. He also sank five coasters, and surprised the Japanese when entering, by daylight and on the surface, the enemy-held Port Owen – where the channel was too narrow and too shallow to dive. There were two enemy 300-ton patrol vessels at the entrance, one of which turned towards *Storm* before being stopped by her third shot. "After that, every round was a hit," Young recorded in his report.

"The enemy replied by machine guns. As soon as the crew of this vessel started to leap overboard, aim was shifted to the second gunboat until she, too, was abandoned. We then fired further rounds at the first target, and several waterline hits were observed. Finally, as we swept past at a range of 400 yards on our way out of the anchorage, the second vessel was again plastered."

During the same patrol, Young was extremely pleased to observe a spectacular fireworks display, visible and audible for many miles, when he blew up an ammunition supply ship. He also took *Storm* through the Lombok Straits into confined waters, where he sank by gunfire several inter-island schooners carrying nickel ore for the Japanese. He established the principle that their native crews should be saved, and on one occasion swapped his prisoners for fresh fish from a fleet of outrigger fishing canoes. *Storm*'s final patrol established a record for the longest by an S-class submarine, when he operated – despite the failure of his radar – for 38 days in the Flores Sea. Young was awarded a Bar to his DSC for his unusual audacity and cool judgment.

Typically, he dismissed his achievements (which were recorded in white symbols sewn on to *Storm's* Jolly Roger) as simply "a small bag" compared with those of other submarines. Young demonstrated his publishing skills even when at sea, keeping his crew informed and amused with a daily bulletin which he wrote and illustrated himself. His drawings of well-known female figures in salacious poses were much appreciated – though some felt that the pair of lesbian penguins he would produce while drinking was his finest work.

He briefly returned to Allen Lane after the war, then joined Hart-Davis, where his fluency as a straightforward typographer was put to good use. Once, when there was a typesetters' strike, he boldly drew the firm's advertisements by hand. An outside design for the cover of *One of Our Submarines*, showing the gloomy inside of a boat, was rejected; so Young himself produced a substitute with the first three words of the title at the top, and the final word spilling down to the bottom in the shape of a submarine.

He took the title of *One of Our Submarines* from a popular poem about operations in the Pacific by the American submariner Lieutenant Melvin Martin. His first draft skated over the full horror of the escape from *Umpire*, but David Garnett persuaded him to insert a full account; this resulted in Young never again suffering from the nightmares which had plagued him since the disaster.

On leaving Hart-Davis in 1955, Young advised a

leading printer on typography, then joined the new house of Rainbird McLean, a leading designer of quality books, where he became managing director. This gave him the opportunity to write *Look at Lighthouses* (1961); *The Fifth Passenger* (1962); and *Look at Submarines* (1964).

Young finally became managing director of Sphere Books, before retiring to Domme in the Dordogne, where he and his wife Mary enjoyed writing and editing the *Shell Guide to France*.

Teddy Young married, first, Diana Graves, with whom he had two daughters; they all survived him. After their divorce he married Mary Cressall (née Strang), who died in 1991.

COMMANDER
HENRY BROOKE

Commander Henry Brooke (who died on March 30 2003, aged 89) enjoyed a bird's eye view of the final age of battleships.

While they were still in their prime he served as gunnery control officer of the battleship *Duke of York* during the Operation Torch landings in North Africa in 1942, and the following year he witnessed the heartening sight of the 16-inch gun American battle-ships *Alabama* and *South Dakota* arriving at Scapa Flow to reinforce the Home Fleet. However, the growing effectiveness of air power at sea was reducing the value of battleships.

In July 1945 he was assistant fleet gunnery officer in *King George V* when she was the last British battleship to fire her guns in anger at the bombardment of Hammatsu, Japan. Some 15 years later he was the last executive officer of the last British battleship, *Vanguard*, immediately before she was scrapped. It was therefore appropriate that he became an adviser to Lewis Gilbert when he directed the film *Sink the Bismarck*, starring Kenneth More.

An old-fashioned gunnery officer, who was ever reluctant to leave the bridge, Brooke witnessed some less conventional aspects of the Navy in early 1944 as squadron gunnery officer in the 8-inch gun cruiser *Kent* on Arctic and Norwegian operations. She had a reindeer mascot, given by well-wishers in the Russian port of Archangel, until the animal fouled the decks once too often and was donated to Edinburgh Zoo.

When, in November 1944, the Royal Navy returned to the southern Norwegian waters from which it had been driven four years earlier for want of air cover, Brooke planned and executed with textbook precision a night action against a heavily protected German convoy off Egersund. Operating so close inshore, *Kent*, together with another cruiser *Bellona* and four British and Canadian destroyers, had to manoeuvre independently to avoid the shallows as they stalked a German convoy of 10 ships under the protection of shore guns.

He illuminated the enemy with star shells and co-ordinated the squadron's fire, switching smoothly from one target to the next. The Germans fought back courageously, but five escorts were sunk, two merchant ships were blown up and others were driven ashore, for the loss of two men killed and three wounded by splinters in *Kent*. Brooke was mentioned in despatches and later awarded the DSC for his service.

Henry John Allen Brooke was born on October 21 1913, Trafalgar Day, in the British infantry lines at Maymyo, Burma. His grandmother, the widow of Brigadier-General Henry Brooke who was killed in the Second Afghan War in 1880, lived at Hampton Court, and when Brooke's father was killed in action at Gallipoli in 1915, his mother was allowed to retain the same grace-and-favour residence.

Young Henry was educated at Wellington, and joined the Navy as a special entry cadet. In 1937–38 he was a junior officer in the destroyer *Firedrake*, which was patrolling the Spanish coast during the civil war when she went to the rescue of a British freighter which was under attack by a German Heinkel bomber: this was one of the first occasions when an aerial torpedo was launched against a ship.

Brooke – known in the Service as "Larry the Bat" after a cartoon character – commanded the frigate *Roebuck* in 1954-55 and twice led convoys by night through the Suez Canal. In the port of Aqaba, Jordan, he met in his tented camp the governor Audeh bin Djad, who had fought under Lawrence of Arabia.

As Senior Officer Reserve Ships during the 1960s, he brought the frigate *Rocket* out of deep maintenance in record time, and spent his final two years as Assistant Director of Marine Services. Then, as a retired officer, during the next 11 years he travelled a quarter of a million miles, running a fleet of some 600 minor vessels of the Admiralty's port auxiliary service.

Although sometimes thought to be straight-laced and resistant to change, Brooke paid off the Royal Navy's last coal-powered ship, and brought many new types into service. He also took satisfaction in circumventing the Admiralty's Ships' Names Committee and naming a class of ships after his female relations, giving the name of his wife to a water tractor (a small tug).

He was appointed MBE in 1974, but he treasured more the silver statue of a sailor which the then First Sea Lord, Sir Henry Leach, gave him on his final retirement after 47 years on the Navy's active and retired lists.

Brooke was involved in a wide range of charitable causes, including at Chichester Cathedral. He was a member of the Royal Naval Sailing Association and the Royal Yacht Squadron, and the highlight of his year was always tea on the lawns at Cowes for the numerous members of his family.

Henry Brooke married Lesley Mary Noble in 1946. She predeceased him, and he was survived by two sons and two daughters.

REAR-ADMIRAL
SIR RICHARD TROWBRIDGE

Rear-Admiral Sir Richard Trowbridge (who died on May 4 2003, aged 83) was the first officer to rise from boy sailor to captain of the Royal Yacht *Britannia*, and the last Briton to serve as Governor of Western Australia.

A personal friend of Prince Philip since they both served in the British Pacific Fleet at the end of the Second World War, he had an unusually long-serving and successful term as Flag Officer Royal Yachts, from 1970 to 1975, when *Britannia* was enjoying one of the busiest periods of her life.

Bored at first with her dull programme, which involved being mostly alongside Portsmouth, Trowbridge energetically entered into proposals for a series of long trips, taking her to Vancouver for the Queen's visit to Canada. They went on to visit the Pacific and the Indian Oceans until the Queen had to return home when Edward Heath's Conservative government lost the first general election in 1974. Trowbridge continued in his task, taking Prince Philip on to Australia.

Five years later, when the government of Western Australia was experiencing some difficulty in finding a suitable Australian for the post of governor, Sir Charles Court, the state's premier, was in London. Calling on his old friend and fellow Western Australian William Heseltine, who was then the Queen's Private Secretary, he was delighted to be assured that "Tom" Trowbridge, whom they both knew, was the answer.

A countryman at heart, Trowbridge was enjoying his retirement in Hampshire, where he was making his household self-sufficient in fruit and vegetables, but he agreed to take the post in 1980. The days of British grandees coming over to supervise the politics of their Queen's more distant lands were drawing to a close, but Trowbridge arrived with reassuring memories of his last visit in 1945. He had landed at Perth on Christmas Eve and left four days later, after a fine but vaguely recollected party.

There were some grumbles from Labour politicians, particularly at Canberra, but naval officers were still regarded as exemplars; Trowbridge fulfilled his delicate role with a quiet hand on the tiller. On retiring three years later, he had the satisfaction of leaving an unusual legacy in the town of Claremont. His son Martin, who had spent a "gap" year there with his father, started the Trowbridge Gallery, which specialised in early maps,charts and prints of the state.

Richard John Trowbridge was born on January 21 1920 into a farming family, and educated at Andover Grammar School. But agriculture was in the doldrums, and he left school at 15 to join the Royal Navy.

Commissioned in 1940, he served at sea through-out the Second World War. He was in the destroyer *Wakeful* after the end of hostilities with Japan when she transported prisoners of war to Sydney, and Lady Mountbatten was in charge of repatriation. Trowbridge was mentioned in despatches.

This was when he met Prince Philip, who was first lieutenant of another destroyer in the 27th Destroyer Flotilla. Together they were in Tokyo Bay when the Japanese signed their surrender after atomic bombs had been dropped on Hiroshima and Nagasaki.

When peace returned Trowbridge specialised in gunnery. Although desk jobs were an anathema to him, it was as a staff gunnery officer in Singapore that he met and married his wife. Their passage home was interrupted by the Suez crisis, which meant that they were forced to enjoy a second honeymoon on a troopship which diverted them via the Cape.

Trowbridge captained the destroyer *Carysfort* in the Mediterranean from 1956 to 1958, then served as second-in-command of the cruiser *Bermuda* before returning to the gunnery school at Whale Island, Portsmouth. From 1962 to 1964 he commanded the Fishery Protection Squadron, a flotilla of small ships for whom he became a lively, noisy, and much-respected boss.

In one of his very few shore appointments Trowbridge went to Bath, on the staff of the Director Guided Weapons. But he regarded this as no more than a prelude to an appointment to command the guided missile destroyer *Hampshire*, which was the flagship of the Western Fleet. He faced the always difficult problem of incorporating the numerous admiral's staff, yet managed to make *Hampshire* one of the happiest of ships.

While *Britannia* was in refit, Trowbridge chalked up an unusual feat. The Flag Officer Royal Yachts' flag always flew, but when the restless Trowbridge secured an additional appointment to lead the British delegation supporting Princess Anne on an official visit to the Emperor of Abyssinia, he had the unique privilege of hoisting his flag in the flagship *Antrim* in the Red Sea, too.

Trowbridge was a cheerful officer with a ruddy complexion who enjoyed all forms of outdoor life, including fishing, sailing and golf. For more than 33 years he was a stalwart member of his parish at the Anglo-Saxon church of St Hubert's, Idsworth.

He never boasted of his powerful and influential contacts, and readily made friends wherever he went as both a naval officer and the Queen's representative. It was unfortunate that his life was overshadowed by exposure to asbestos which was being removed from *Britannia* during a long refit which he supervised. The opening-up of various sealed places caused clouds of dust, which almost certainly led to his final illness.

Trowbridge was appointed KCVO in 1983. He married Anne Mildred Perceval in 1955. She survived him with their two sons.

ADMIRAL
SIR DESMOND DREYER

Admiral Sir Desmond Dreyer (who died on May 15 2003, aged 93) was gunnery officer of *Ajax* at the Battle of the River Plate.

Ajax was the flagship of Commodore Henry Harwood's three cruisers which, in late 1939, discovered the German pocket battleship *Graf Spee* in the South Atlantic. Although *Graf Spee*'s 11-inch guns enjoyed vast superiority, Harwood ordered his force to attack her at once by day or night. He divided his squadron into two widely separated groups, a noteworthy departure from the orthodox battle line, and the ensuing fight showed just how far tactics and damage-control had progressed since the Battle of Jutland in 1916.

Appropriately, it was the Dreyer table, an analogue computer of cogs and clockwork invented by Dreyer's father, that helped to make the difference. It computed where the *Graf Spee* should be 60 seconds after the shells left the *Ajax*'s guns as the ships constantly altered course. Dreyer's first salvoes were confused with those of *Achilles*, but he sorted out the reports from the spotting plane, and soon *Ajax* was firing for effect at three salvoes a minute.

When *Ajax* shuddered under a massive hit, Dreyer reported from his position in the control tower that two after turrets were out of action, and ordered firing to continue from the for'd turrets. *Graf Spee*'s shooting was accurate, and the British ships were hit repeatedly, but each time the German vessel concentrated her fire on one of the enemy the others closed range and hit back. Dreyer had fired most of his 6-inch shells as *Ajax* shadowed the wounded German ship into Montevideo. Once there, *Graf Spee* was deceived into thinking that Harwood had been reinforced, and she was ignominiously scuttled.

Dreyer was awarded the DSC for his part in the battle, which was the first British action since Nelson's victories at the Nile and Trafalgar in which initiative had not been cramped by signals or stereotyped fighting instructions.

Desmond Parry Dreyer was born on April 6 1910. His father, Admiral Sir Frederic Dreyer, was Jellicoe's flag captain in the battleship *Iron Duke* during the First World War and Inspector of Merchant Navy Gunnery in the Second. Dreyer maintained that the royalties from his father's gunnery inventions paid for his education at Dartmouth, where he won the King's dirk.

Young Desmond specialised in the family business of gunnery, becoming squadron gunnery officer in a cruiser squadron after three years in *Ajax*. He first defended East Coast convoys, then took part in the abortive Norway campaign. At the Allies' withdrawal from Narvik, Dreyer was in the anti-aircraft cruiser *Cairo* which helped to destroy harbour installations. When she was bombed he transferred to *Coventry*, which re-embarked a large number of troops and equipment.

Dreyer briefly taught at the gunnery school at Whale Island, but spent most of the next few years in battleships. He was on the staff of Admiral Sir "Jack" Tovey in *King George V*, was in *Duke of York* during the North Africa landings and finally served as second-in-command of Britain's last battleship, *Vanguard*.

During the Suez Crisis Dreyer was Chief of Staff to

the Commander-in-Chief Mediterranean. As a vice-admiral in the Far East from 1962 to 1965, Dreyer's acronym was briefly FOCINCFEF until he heard the common seamen's lewd mispronunciation; a word on the golf course with Admiral Sir Varyl Begg, Commander-in-Chief Far East, caused the title to be changed.

Dreyer's task was to co-ordinate Commonwealth naval forces in their successful resistance to Indonesian incursions into the fledgling Malaysia; at one stage he commanded a third of the Royal Navy as well as Australian, Malaysian and New Zealand ships and aircraft.

Dreyer was appointed CBE in 1957, GB in 1960 and KGB in 1963 before becoming Second Sea Lord two years later. While he was serving as chief of naval personnel Denis Healey, the Defence Secretary, chose him to be Chief Adviser (Personnel and Logistics) for all three armed services in one of the Ministry of Defence's periodic reforms.

Earlier, Dreyer and his colleagues on the Board of Admiralty had tendered their resignations over Healey's decision to cancel a new generation of aircraft carriers, a gesture rejected by Admiral Sir David Luce, First Sea Lord, who alone resigned.

Dreyer was noted for his sense of humour. Once he teased his destroyer captains about their fondness for making the sternboard into the narrow Sliema Creek in Malta, and on another occasion he tested the future First Sea Lord, Sir Henry Leach, by seating him between a beautiful lady guest and a Turkish admiral, neither of whom spoke English.

In retirement Dreyer flung himself into public and charitable service, as well as working for Healey again as a member of the Prices and Incomes Board and the Armed Forces' Pay Review Board. He served as a JP, High Sheriff and Deputy Lieutenant of Hampshire.

Dreyer, who was appointed KCB in 1967, first married Elisabeth Chilton,who predeceased him,and then Marjorie Whiteley (née Gordon). From his first marriage, he was survived by a son and a daughter; another son predeceased him.

COMMANDER FRANCIS PONSONBY

Commander Francis Ponsonby (who died on May 24 2003, aged 70) was a Cold War submariner before becoming,in his last years,the diligent defence correspondent of the Armed Forces' magazine, *The Officer.*

His career in submarines was twice interrupted: first when General Sir Robert Laycock, Governor of Malta, spotted his charm and asked for him as an aide de camp in 1954; then, after he had been selected in 1959 for the submarine commanding officers' qualifying course, the "perisher", Ponsonby's natural exuberance during a night out led to a fall in which he hurt his back – the injury was to dog him for the rest of his life.

Some considered that the Old Etonian Ponsonby could not prosper in submarines, but he was chosen for the staff of Flag Officer Submarines, and returned to the "perisher" in 1962.

After attending the first nuclear engineering course at Greenwich, he was one of an elite group of submariners who helped to bring the Polaris missile into service on time and within budget.As executive officer of the starboard crew of the nuclear-powered *Resolution*, Ponsonby oversaw its building and commissioning at Barrow-in-Furness, and co-ordinated some of the first test firings. Later, after the captain of *Renown* had surfaced under a coaster off the Mull of Kintyre, Ponsonby was sent to take over command and restore confidence.

Ponsonby was an epicure. All his submarines set to sea with a cellar of good port, and, when his officers attacked the Stilton, leaving the rind, he gave them lessons on how to slice cheese properly; he also wrote knowledgeably to newspapers on the difference between shepherd's pie and cottage pie. As a stickler for etiquette, he was amused when booking himself on a Constance Spry cookery course to be reminded to pack a party frock.

Ponsonby was also notable for caring for his men. During the first Navy Days at the Clyde naval base, he arranged for families to see how their menfolk lived and worked in submarines, permitting them to inspect the safety aspects. The men's families were allowed to send 20-word weekly messages to their loved ones on board, although many had difficulty filling these up, often writing about the state of the family car or the fortunes of Rangers and Celtic. Ponsonby insisted on being able to censor these. He deemed "Am missing you and am missing sex" good for morale; but if, the following week,a girlfriend said merely "Am missing you", he would feel obliged to suppress this message.

Above all, Ponsonby was good company, laughing loudly and first at his own jokes but leaving friends feeling better for a spell in his company.

A great-nephew of Queen Victoria's private secretary Sir Henry Ponsonby, Francis Noel Ponsonby was born on June 14 1932. As the son of a professor at the London School of Economics, he was precocious and erudite.

Young Francis was a page at King George VI's coronation, for which he received a Coronation medal, although he teased his family ever afterwards that this had been awarded for secret intelligence work. At 16 he wrote to a national newspaper about the special entry cadet system by which he had gone to Dartmouth. His letter escaped the authorities' attention, and not realising the writer's youth Winston Churchill, at that time Leader of the Opposition, invited him to lunch. Wisely, Ponsonby declined.

After *Renown*, he served with Admiral Sir David Scott, Chief of British Naval Staff in Washington; then, in 1973, he was given command of the frigate *Salisbury*. He undertook the last patrol off Beira during the oil blockade of the rebellious Rhodesia, though by then the British government had lost interest in enforcement.

His next appointment was as a desk officer working for the Director of Naval Operations and Training; here he became closely involved in the Third Cod War against Iceland in the 1970s. Next he became naval attaché in Norway, helping to arrange Her Majesty The Queen's visit. He was appointed a Member of the Victorian Order and a Member of the Order of King Olav.

His final appointment was as Assistant Director of Public Relations (Royal Navy). When the Falklands War broke out in 1982, he was not at his desk in

Whitehall but making a public relations film in the South Atlantic about the ice patrol ship *Endurance*. Ponsonby immediately volunteered to become chief of staff to *Endurance*'s commander Captain Nick Barker, helping him to plan such operations as the sinking of the submarine *Santa Fe*, and the landing on South Georgia of the Royal Marines who drove off the first attempted landing by the Argentines.

Modestly, Ponsonby gave all the credit for any successes to Barker, and was appointed OBE in 1984.

When Ponsonby returned home the Chief of the Defence Staff, Lord Lewin, sent him to see The Queen, who thanked him for his first-hand report saying, "No one else can tell me anything about the Falklands except my husband, and all he twitters about is the birds."

After retiring from the Service, Ponsonby joined Vickers Shipbuilding and Engineering to sell submarines overseas. Despite his considerable technical and diplomatic skills, he proved unsuccessful. However, he raised almost £250,000 for the Wave Heritage Trust to restore the Naval Club in Hill Street, London, which is the war memorial of the RNVR.

Ponsonby next became assistant secretary to the D-Notice Committee, which vets newspaper stories that might compromise national security. He then found his niche as the Westminster correspondent for *The Officer*. His long parliamentary dispatches reported debates in a perceptive, slightly languid style, and had an authority unmatched by correspondents on national newspapers. As well as covering debates in the Commons, he recorded the mood of the parties in the Commons Defence Committee and the sleights practised in government presentation of events.At the same time, there were telling comments on who attended the defence estimates debate, who found that they had more important business, and who had bothered to do some homework before opening his mouth.

Ponsonby's writing was imbued with the authority of one who attended every meeting of the committee, even travelling to one held at the Joint Services College in Shrivenham, Wiltshire, shortly before his death.When the national press periodically rushed to meetings, the chairman made a point of ensuring that a place was reserved for him if he arrived late.

Ponsonby was chairman of the ecumenical Petersfield Area Churches Together and a local choir-master. He was writing the official history of the D-Notice Committee when he collapsed at a submarine officers' reunion.

Francis Ponsonby married, in 1960, Sally Cocup, daughter of the Deputy Chaplain of the Fleet. She survived him with their two sons and two daughters.

COMMANDANT
VONLA McBRIDE

Commandant Vonla McBride (who died on August 2 2003, aged 82) was specially selected to undertake the delicate task of overseeing the integration of the Women's Royal Naval Service into the Royal Navy in the late 1970s.

Although, since its foundation in the First World

War, the WRNS had been fiercely proud of its role in supporting the RN, the approach of the Equal Pay Act (1970) and the Sex Discrimination Act (1975) spelled the end of its independence. It was clear that the Wrens must be treated equally with their male colleagues, whose jobs they were increasingly filling with success; and that they must be placed under the Naval Discipline Act, with its harsher range of sanctions for such offences as desertion.

There were some who claimed that the WRNS Regulations were perfectly adequate, although it emerged that this advice had been obtained from a young barrister at a cocktail party. However, Their Lordships of the Admiralty had been advised that the existing Wrens' regulations would have no more effect than the rules of a village cricket club. Vonla McBride was sent for, and placed in charge of further integration.

Although no aggressive "wimmin's libber", she not only helped to extend the boundaries for women inside the Navy, but was a role model for many ambitious young women in civilian life. Among her personal achievements she was the first woman to take the salute at the passing out parade of the King's Squad, Royal Marines, and the first serving female officer to receive the freedom of the City of London.

She was welcomed in Ethiopia, where she advised the Emperor Haile Selassie on the creation of a women's service. She also achieved recognition for the contribution that women had made to winning the Second World War by the dedication of a memorial window in Guildford Cathedral, attended by Admiral of the Fleet Earl Mountbatten of Burma.

Sara Vonla Adair McBride was born on January 20

1921 into a family of Presbyterian farmers and teachers in Northern Ireland, and educated at Ballymena Academy. After reading English and French at Trinity College, Dublin, she returned to teach at Ballymena, where Ian Paisley was one of her pupils. So far her university and career had been chosen for her by her father. But Vonla McBride escaped to England, first to be a housemistress at Gardenhurst School at Burnham-on-Sea, Somerset.

Then, after reading an advertisement in *The Daily Telegraph*, she joined the Wrens because she admired the senior service and thought the uniform becoming. At the mature age of 28 Vonla McBride became a new recruit at the Wrens' training establishment HMS Dauntless, near Reading. She specialised as a personnel selection officer, one of a new breed of Wrens, replacing the wartime women psychologists who had been so successful in the recruitment of male ratings.

There were few officers in the Navy with degrees, and male officers were suspicious of her, but ratings loved their selection interviews. Once Vonla McBride asked a sailor if he resented being interviewed by her and was taken aback to be told. "Not a bit of it. It's just like talking to your mum." On another occasion, an amorous recruit explained that he wanted to join the Navy because "I wud like a Wren and, if ye're no married in three years, Ma'am, let me know." Vonla McBride was so deft at dealing with these interviews that she shortly found herself in the Admiralty working for the senior psychiatrist and helping to select other Wren personnel selection officers.

Rapid promotion followed, and soon she was fully married to the Navy. As Staff Officer to the London

Division RNR she picked up City gossip; at a naval air station she enjoyed organising the wedding of one of her Wrens on Malta. She became a Free Church choirmistress, and also played bridge with senior officers.

Invited to participate in the BBC television programme, *Animal, Vegetable or Mineral* she demurred until the producer revealed himself as her former English teacher, and told her that no Ballymena girl would ever refuse such a challenge. Vonla McBride participated in uniform. The question master was Glyn Daniel and another panellist was the well-known Captain Taprell Dorling, the author who wrote under the name of "Taffrail"; Vonla McBride studied hard and beat the men at identifying the model of an 18th-century sailing ship.

She returned to Dauntless twice as training officer and as superintendent, and was Chief Officer at the Royal Naval College, Greenwich,where she schooled a new generation of Wren officers and wrote *Never at Sea* (1966), the story of her career.

Vonla McBride was a good after-dinner speaker who rehearsed her speeches thoroughly, and timed them carefully. At Trinity College, she had been an enthusiastic member of the Dublin University Players, had walk-on parts at the Abbey Theatre, and briefly became a broadcaster for Radio Eireann. Her dreams of being a film star turned into a lifelong interest in amateur dramatics; the peak of her acting career was as Juliet in a production of *Romeo and Juliet* on Malta.

When the First Sea Lord Admiral Lord Hill-Norton voted against the admission of women to the Worshipful Company of Shipwrights he lost the motion, but he sent for Vonla McBride telling her to "fill in these forms" as he wanted her to be one of the first lady shipwrights.

In retirement Vonla McBride took up several charity appointments and non-executive director-ships. Though supposed to be the token woman on the board of Lloyds Bank, when it was still rare for women to be bank managers, she insisted on visiting branches in the London region and provided a much-needed voice for the many women whose opinions and needs were ignored. However, she confessed that at one meeting when the board discussed a loan to a major national company, she did not know what all the fuss was about: she reckoned if she spoke nicely to her bank manager he would lend her the amount of money under discussion. It was then pointed out that the loan involved millions of pounds.

Vonla McBride was Honorary ADC to the Queen, and appointed CB on her retirement as Director of the WRNS in 1979.

———

NORMAN HANCOCK

Norman Hancock (who died on August 5 2003 aged 87) was an unsung hero of the Cold War whose design of the nuclear-powered hunter-killer submarine *Swiftsure* was a generation ahead of American and Soviet models; his drawings of the through-deck cruiser *Invincible* and the anti-submarine frigate *Broadsword* still form the backbone of the modern surface Navy.

On becoming Assistant Director of Warship Design

at Bath in 1969, Hancock was so determined to produce a vessel which would be faster, stealthier and deeper diving than any contemporary boat that a disbelieving Naval Staff in London had to revise their expectations several times. He rejected the American teardrop hull and used one of equal diameter throughout which combined a longer pressure hull within a shorter overall length. This was so successful that *Swiftsure* survived when, by accident, it plunged 50 per cent deeper than had been planned.

He rigorously controlled every aspect of the design, placing the machinery on sophisticated mountings, scrutinising every shipboard system and making *Swiftsure* quieter than any previous submarine. When Vickers installed a bulkhead which, by Hancock's calculations, was a fraction too thick and too heavy, he made the shipbuilder machine the bulkhead down to its proper size, not least to remind people who was in command of the construction process.

The 13 submarines of the Swiftsure and follow-on Trafalgar classes, which were built between 1978 and 1991, employed a highly enduring design: it could be stretched and modified, both to launch cruise missiles and to be changed from propeller to pump–jet propulsion. Much of Hancock's work is still so secret that details of the use of pump jets have only incidentally been revealed in such novels as Tom Clancy's *Hunt for Red October*.

His design condensed the machinery to such a degree that, in order to maintain *Swiftsure*'s longitudinal centre of gravity, he had to introduce an empty space aft of the engine room; it was known as "Hancock's hole".

Norman Hancock was born at Plymouth on March 6 1916 and attended Plymouth Grammar School before joining the dockyard in the ancient rank of shipwright apprentice in 1932. This was then the highly selective route by which bright boys of poor background could join the elite Royal Corps of Naval Constructors; after a series of highly competitive examinations young Norman studied at the Royal Naval College, Greenwich, until his education was curtailed by the Second World War.

Hancock first worked as a constructor at the Admiralty's test tanks at Haslar, and then for Sir Stanley Goodall while studying hydrodynamics, damage to ships and advising on damage control. He disagreed with Goodall about the cause of the loss of the battlecruiser *Hood* in 1941, and was proved right. His claim that this was the result of an explosion amidships of her 4-inch gun ammunition was confirmed only in 2001 when David Mearns of Blue Water Recoveries found the wreck and made a television programme about it.

After the war Hancock, in the uniform of a constructor commander (with grey stripes between the gold stripes of his naval uniform), travelled to Germany in the back of a lorry with an escort of Royal Marines to inspect damaged German ships and drawings. He was hurried off to the Far East to assist the United States Navy's studies of the Japanese fleet; there he compared the results of the fire-bombing of north German towns with the atom bombs on Hiroshima and Nagasaki. He then observed Operation Crossroads, the atom bomb tests at Bikini Atoll in the Pacific.

After a spell on Singapore in 1949, Hancock took

charge of frigate design in Bath. Beginning with the diesel-engined frigates of the Salisbury and Leopard classes, he introduced large-scale layout drawings and detailed mock-ups for the operational spaces, a concept subsequently applied to many later designs and all submarines. From 1954 to 1959, he returned to research and development, then became professor of naval architecture at Greenwich for five years.

Hancock firmly believed that ship design was both a creative art and a branch of advanced engineering, and could only be "caught rather than taught"; he subjected his students and lecturers to a relentless regime of theory, practice and close supervision. The students were allowed Wednesday and Saturday afternoons off for sport, but during their vacations they were expected to find jobs in shipbuilding. After his own experience of German and Japanese designs, Hancock also introduced month-long tours of European industry and research.

As Director of Warship Design from 1969 to 1976, he had to persuade a reluctant Admiralty and an unenthusiastic Treasury to involve the shipbuilder in the sketch designs for the carrier *Invincible* and to supervise some 3,500 man-years of effort which produced over 50,000 drawings. Late in the design, Lieutenant-Commander D R Taylor produced the idea of a ski-jump, again to a scornful Naval Staff, but Hancock and his project manager, Arthur Honnor, were easily able to accommodate this new feature and produce the world's first jump-jet carrier. As a result *Invincible* had the highest freeboard of any ship in the Navy and a modest displacement, yet was still the biggest ship to be propelled by gas turbines.

Hancock was appointed CB when he retired from

the Royal Corps of Naval Constructors in 1976. Afterwards he worked, until 70, for Marconi when the firm needed hydrodynamic and mechanical expertise on the Stingray torpedo project.

A Liveryman of the Worshipful Company of Shipwrights and a member of the council of the Royal Institute of Naval Architecture, Hancock also played the organ for his local church, and was an amateur cabinetmaker. He loved travel, but insisted on taking two spare wheels with him on his first continental motoring holiday after the war.

Norman Hancock married, in 1940, Marie Bow; she survived him with their two sons.

LIEUTENANT-COMMANDER ADRIAN SELIGMAN

Lieutenant-Commander Adrian Seligman (who died on August 6 2003, aged 93) was a master mariner, naval officer and author; before the war he undertook a two-year voyage around the world in his own sailing ship, *Cap Pilar*.

His first contact with the Royal Navy came when he checked the chronometers of *Cap Pilar* on board the cruiser *Leander* off the coast of Spain during the Spanish Civil War. By the start of the Second World War he was a qualified first mate in steam and sail and a sub-lieutenant, RNVR. He then served in mine-sweepers and commanded a destroyer; but his unique contribution to the war was in special operations.

In the desperate winter of 1941 Seligman and a handful of Reserve officers travelled by train to

Turkey to pilot five Russian ships through the Dardanelles and past the Axis blockade of the Aegean to Syria. Passing himself off as a salvage expert, Seligman's personal task was to camouflage a small oil tanker, *Olinda*, by cutting away her catwalk and rigging a jury mast.

He had his first encounter with a German spy, who tried to stop him when they were on a snowbound train. He also managed to smuggle away from the Turkish authorities a beautiful agent, who had posed as a bar girl in Ankara while watching over him.

For several nights *Olinda* hugged the coast to avoid German patrol boats while being frequently fired upon by Turkish sentries. When she ran aground, and was caught listing at low water in daylight, Seligman got her off by calmly pumping ballast as he watched for the arrival of German bombers.

Several years later, a clerk in the Admiralty pursued him for the return of an advance of pay which he had spent during his undercover activities. In reply Seligman sent a copy of his book, *No Stars to Guide* (1947), with a note saying that "while it may contain some pages not wholly relevant to the work of the Navy accounts department, it should nevertheless give a good idea of the general circumstances of my expenditure."

Between 1942 and 1944 Seligman commanded the Levant Schooner Flotilla, equipped with Greek fishing boats and caiques which had been refitted with tank engines. They made numerous raids on islands in the Aegean, landing soldiers, collecting intelligence and supplying isolated garrisons; more important, they held down large numbers of German forces.

After the Italian armistice the Germans turned on and, in some cases, murdered their erstwhile allies, and the situation on the islands was often confused. On one island Seligman was overtaken by a staff car carrying both German and Italian officers. His only article of uniform was a naval cap which he swiftly doffed to scratch the back of his head as the vehicle swept by.

All Seligman's crews were volunteers, and their motto, "Stand Boldly On", was taken from the old seafaring adage "log, lead, latitude and stand boldly on", according to his account *War in the Islands* (1996). Later he was in command of a Flower class corvette, *Erica*, which was reported missing. After four days Seligman sent a signal saying that he was alive and had read his own obituary.

Adrian Charles Cuthbert Seligman was born at Leatherhead, Surrey, on November 26 1909, the eldest son of Dr Richard Seligman, a metallurgist of international reputation. Adrian's mother, formerly Hilda McDowell, was an authoress and sculptress who, between the wars, entertained Mahatma Gandhi and the Emperor Haile Selassie at soirées in the family home at Wimbledon.

On holidays the Seligman family travelled to Europe, each child with a rucksack carefully graded according to the bearer's age; they looked like a ragged little caravan of pack animals jostling each other down the roads and across the station platforms of Europe, he recalled. In the summers the Seligmans went to the village of St Jacut-de-la-mer, on the Brittany coast, where Adrian learned to sail in fishing boats.

Rokeby prep school, Harrow, Gonville and Caius

College, Cambridge, did not kill his love of the sea. After failing his second-year examinations in Natural Sciences, being thrown over by his girlfriend and receiving a "charmingly courteous threatening letter" from his bank manager, Seligman was in the London docks when he decided to board a small freighter. He was engaged on the spot as mess boy, and sailed that night for the Spanish coast.

From then onwards, the sea had claimed him. He sailed before the mast for three years in the Finnish square-rigger *Killoran* and then in *Olivebank* which, under Captain John Matson, raced home with a cargo of wheat in a voyage of 104 days from Australia to Queensferry in 1934. After another year as mate in a tramp steamer, Seligman's grandfather left him some money to buy a house. Instead, he purchased a 250-ton French fishing barquentine *Cap Pilar* and, advised by Commander J R Stenhouse, who had been Shackleton's first officer in *Discovery*, fitted her out for a voyage round the world. When he placed an advertisement in a national newspaper for six young men for a voyage to the South Seas, "each to contribute £100 to expenses", the *News Chronicle* reported more than 300 applicants, and offered him sponsorship.

Seligman sailed in September 1936 with his new wife, the 17-year-old daughter of his prep school headmaster, and a volunteer crew, only two of whom had been to sea before; there were also a pig called Dennis (subsequently eaten), a gramophone and a piano.

The odyssey took Seligman around the Cape of Good Hope to Sydney and Auckland, New Zealand; there followed six weeks in the South Sea islands, before they returned through the Panama Canal. His 14-month-old daughter Jessica, born in New Zealand, was listed as the ship's second stewardess when they arrived home two years and 32,500 miles later.

His book, *The Voyage of the Cap Pilar* (1939), contained some highly dramatised descriptions ("the ship seemed to cower into the sea beneath her, then gather herself and leap forward as though in terror of her life, quivering from stem to stern as a big wave exploded upon her sending clouds of spray as high as the main top"). It became an instant success, and remains a sailing classic.

After the war Seligman wrote a series of children's books about the sea while living on Malta. He then spent several years on Cyprus, where he wrote about the Turks and struck up a friendship with Rauf Denktash, the future president of Turkish Cyprus, before returning home as the Greek independence movement grew.

In 1958 he founded a technical press agency in London which translated press releases and articles about British firms into any European or Asian language for sending to some 23,000 journals. In retirement he published another sailing classic, *The Slope of the Wind* (1994), about his early experiences in sail. Seligman also related many of his often strange experiences in short stories and broadcasts, and lectured until his late eighties. One grisly tale was of a shark, disembowelled by the crew whilst his ship lay becalmed in the doldrums; thrown into the sea for dead it floated slowly around the ship before coming, full circle, upon its own entrails and consuming them.

Seligman married first, in 1936, Jane Batterbury,

with whom he had four daughters. In 1950 he married Rosemary Grimble, daughter of the diplomat Sir Arthur Grimble, with whom he had two sons.

————————

LIEUTENANT-COMMANDER ROBERT BULKELEY

Lieutenant-Commander Robert Bulkelely (who died on September 20 2003, aged 83) launched the first missiles from a submarine, and fired more rounds from his main gun than any submariner in any navy before or since.

Bulkeley commissioned the newly-built submarine *Statesman* at Cammell Laird's, Birkenhead, in September 1943, and commanded it until the end of the war, based initially at Trincomalee and then at Fremantle. On his first Far East war patrol, off Port Blair on August 22 1944, Bulkeley spotted a 5,000-ton tanker which he sank with a salvo of torpedoes fired at long range. He did not know it at the time, but this was the last enemy ship of more than 1,000 tons on the station, and he did not fire his torpedoes again in anger.

Over the next eight patrols he sank 44 vessels by gunfire or by boarding and scuttling. First Lieutenant Neil Strouts and the boarding party became expert in their small boat. They were unfazed even when the appearance of a Japanese aircraft caused *Statesman* to submerge and leave them to hide in the fishing well of a junk carrying supplies for the enemy.

After returning from patrol with all his gun

ammunition expended, it appealed to Bulkeley's scientific mind to fit rails to the side of the conning tower and experiment with firing surplus rockets intended for air-to-ground attack. But although he could point *Statesman* satisfactorily, Bulkeley realised that, as the rockets were designed to be launched at 200 knots, they would never reach their designed launch speed and stabilise in flight. Next Bulkeley landed *Statesman's* reload torpedoes and filled their space with gun ammunition. After one patrol he returned, having emptied these spaces too.

Besides his claim to be the first to fire self-propelled missiles from any submarine, he took great pride in his gunnery. He had a gunnery officer, Kit Fielden, who, Bulkeley reckoned, "had a fire-control clock in his head", and was able to make rapid and accurate alterations to range and deflection as *Statesman* and its victims swerved across the surface of the sea. Bulkeley claimed a 30 per cent hit rate, which compared well with many surface ships fitted with radar and sophisticated fire control equipment.

On April 5 1945 in the Malacca Strait, he sank all seven landing craft of a Japanese convoy. The only other submarine commander to rival this achievement was Edward Young of *Storm*. Bulkeley was awarded the DSC that year for gallantry, skill and outstanding devotion to duty whilst serving on numerous successful patrols, frequently carried out in shallow depths and difficult waters and in the presence of strong opposition.

Robert George Pierson Bulkeley was born at Acomb, Yorkshire, on April 7 1920, of a long line of naval officers. Master Gunner John Bulkeley was one of the leaders of the *Wager* mutiny in 1741 and lucky to escape hanging;Richard Bulkeley was a survivor of Nelson's San Juan expedition; and his son, also Richard, was wounded as a midshipman in *Victory* at Trafalgar in 1805, after carrying a message to the dying Nelson. Robert's father was in the British Army in India,and,after his parents divorced in 1922, the boy was brought up by his grandparents at Dovercourt, Essex, until he became a cadet at the Royal Naval College Dartmouth, aged 13.

His interest in the sea was stimulated by building model yachts – perhaps inspired by his uncle Gilbert Bulkeley, who was a member of the Royal Corps of Naval Constructors – which he then sailed on the boating pond his grandfather had built when Mayor of Harwich.

At the Admiralty Interview Board in 1933 Bulkeley was asked by an admiral what the number of the taxi which brought him to the interview had been; he gave the answer without hesitation. Years later the interviewer recognised Bulkeley and asked why he should have remembered such a detail, to which Bulkeley replied that he had not, but he knew that the admiral could not have known.

At Dartmouth Bulkeley thrived on the broad education he received, and particularly enjoyed workshop training and technical drawing. He passed out top of the Exmouth term and was awarded the King's dirk.After further courses, he was awarded the King's Telescope for seamanship in 1939, though his proudest achievement was, while still a junior at Dartmouth, winning the Meade Cup for sailing in 1936.

Unlike midshipmen in the First World War, Bulkeley and his term mates were not rushed to sea on the outbreak of war, but were allowed to finish their training. By 1940, he was sub-lieutenant of the gunroom in the battleship *Rodney*, a post in which he was supposed to set an example in leadership to all the other young officers in the ship. However, in September 1940 Bulkeley joined the submarine service, where he made an uncertain start and was sent on patrol in *Pandora*, under "Tubby" Linton, VC, and under warning for reversion to general service. Linton reported favourably on Bulkeley, who then went to *Otus* as navigating officer and carried out two supply runs to Malta.

During one of these *Otus* ran into a freshwater aquifer in the central Mediterranean, and lost buoyancy so rapidly that it sank to 350 feet, 50 feet beyond its maximum diving depth; only quick action in blowing all ballast tanks and ordering full ahead saved the submarine. The extreme pressure had broken a glass observation hatch in the gun tower, and later still it was discovered that *Otus*'s ballast tanks were so rusted with holes that it was not considered seaworthy until it had had extensive repairs in Alexandria.

Bulkeley became first lieutenant of the submarine *Tribune* in 1942 before passing his submarine command examination in January 1943 and being sent to command L27. This boat ran as a "clockwork mouse" in Cardigan Bay while the RAF carried out the first trials with sonobuoys, air-dropped submarine locating devices. Although Bulkeley had risen quickly in his submarine career, someone marked his record card "a brainy but difficult type".

After the war Bulkeley completed more than 17 years of continuous service in the "trade", between training and further commands and appointments at Admiralty experimental establishments. When he was eventually reverted to general service he left the Navy.

He emigrated to South Australia in 1959, where he started a restaurant business, but soon found work as a surveyor more congenial. After a brief return to the Alcove Hotel at Swanage in Dorset, Bulkeley became a civil engineer in the main roads department of Western Australia, where he worked until the 1980s. Several roads were named after him.

Robert Bulkeley married first, in 1940, Irene Robertson; they had a son and two daughters. He married secondly, in 1965, Betty Street, who died in 1991; they had two daughters. He later made a home with Norah Sumner (née Crafer), a teenage sweetheart whom he tracked down using the Pinkerton Detective Agency.

VICE-ADMIRAL
SIR PETER BERGER

Vice-Admiral Sir Peter Berger (who died on October 19 2003, aged 78) was awarded a DSC after the Yangtse incident.

On April 20 1949, as the civil war between Chinese communists and Nationalists entered its final stages, Berger navigated the frigate *Amethyst* up the Yangtse River to protect British interests at Nanking. Off Rose Island, some 60 miles short of her destination, *Amethyst* was shelled and heavily machine-gunned from both banks by communist forces.

Two shells hit the bridge. The captain and the Chinese pilot were mortally wounded, and Berger, badly wounded in the arm, leg and chest, was knocked out cold. The explosion jammed the steering and *Amethyst* ran aground.Some of the ship's company were ordered to swim ashore, leaving on board about 40 fit men, 12 wounded, and 15 dead.

No one could move on the upper deck without drawing the attention of snipers, but Berger, still dazed and despite loss of blood,organised sailors with small arms to defend the ship against boarding and gathered up the dead and wounded. He then supervised the destruction of secret equipment including the Typex cypher machines, which he broke with a mallet and threw into the swirling river, and burned the code books in the galley stove.

The ship's doctor had been killed while tending the wounded and for six days Berger and Geoffrey Weston, the first lieutenant, who had assumed command, dosed themselves on morphine and Benzedrine. They got *Amethyst* off the sandbank, and moved her to a slightly safer berth; but Berger collapsed and was landed on the Nationalist-held shore. Chinese peasants bore him away on what seemed like an endless journey, but all they would tell him was "another five minutes".

Berger reached Chinkiang and travelled by train to Shanghai, then on to a hospital ship where he recovered quickly enough to resume his duties, under Lieutenant-Commander John Kerans. Many months later, a gaunt Berger was on the bridge when *Amethyst* made a triumphal return to Devonport. In the film of the story, *Yangtse Incident* (1957), Richard Todd played Kerans, Donald Houston played Weston, and Michael Brill was Berger. The ship's cat also enjoyed a walk-on part,though Berger confessed that he had "hated the bloody thing".

Peter Egerton Capel Berger was born on February 11 1925 and went to Harrow before entering the Royal Navy as a cadet in 1943. He saw action at the landings in Normandy and on the south coast of France while serving in the cruiser *Ajax*. Having specialised in navigation, he was Fleet Navigating Officer Home Fleet from 1956 to 1958, and navigator of the Royal Yacht *Britannia* from 1958 to 1960.

While salvaging the High Commissioner's yacht where it had gone aground on the reefs of the Solomon Islands, he was told of the birth of his first daughter. He navigated *Britannia* through both the Panama Canal and the Welland Canal in Canada and had the Queen, President Eisenhower and the Canadian Prime Minister John Diefenbaker on board for the historic opening of the St Lawrence Seaway. At Thunder Bay, Ontario, Berger claimed two records for a ship flying the White Ensign: a height record of 600 feet above sea level, and the furthest from the sea, 2,800 miles.

Returning from the Great Lakes, the Royal Yacht lost her anchor at midnight off Montreal. It was Berger's responsibility as the navigator to ensure that the inboard end of the cable was secured, but he was exonerated after it was discovered that the chain had broken mid-length rather than run out from its locker.

From 1962 to 1964 Berger commanded the frigate *Torquay* in the Dartmouth Training Squadron, where a twitch of his famously bushy eyebrows was sufficient to admonish any wayward cadet.In the rank of captain,he was then sent to The Hague, as defence, naval and military attaché,from 1964 to 1966,returning to command the frigate *Phoebe* (better known to the public as "HMS Hero",from the television series of that name).

From 1971 to 1973 Berger was the first non-submariner to command the nuclear submarine base at Clyde, where he also developed a passion for fishing. From 1973 to 1975 he was Assistant Chief of Naval Staff (Policy) when, although the fleet withdrew from East of Suez and ran down its base in Singapore, he helped to ensure that there was a considerable investment in new ships, such as the Invincible class carriers and Type 22 frigates.

The "Cod War" with Iceland over fishing limits led to a study by Berger of the "offshore tapestry", the complex weave of British resources and risks, which included the protection of oil platforms in the North Sea from terrorist threats, as a result of which the Island class offshore patrol vessels were ordered.

Berger was Chief of Staff to the Commander-in-Chief of the Fleet, 1976–78, and from 1979 to 1981 held the four-hatted appointment of Flag Officer Plymouth; Port Admiral Devonport; Commander Central Sub Area Eastern Atlantic; and Commander Plymouth Sub Area Channel. However, he was never promoted to the Board of Admiralty and retired in 1981.

Berger was then elected a Fellow of Selwyn College, Cambridge, and served as Bursar for the next decade. The most junior college servant realised that he ran a "tight ship", but Berger knew everyone by name and showed a deep concern for the welfare of all. He frequently contacted local authorities himself to persuade them to give discretionary grants to Selwyn students, and he was so efficient at managing the college's centenary building programme that there was money left over to build a library extension. The only battle he lost was his bid to abolish free breakfasts for Fellows.

Berger was appointed LVO in 1960 and KCB in 1979. He married, in 1956, June Kathleen Pigou, who survived him, together with their three daughters.

REAR-ADMIRAL
JAN AYLEN

Rear-Admiral Jan Aylen (who died on November 5 2003, aged 93) led a special commando unit into Germany at the end of the Second World War and persuaded Helmuth Walter, the German scientist, to work for Britain.

Hating the desk job he had been given in Bath, Aylen volunteered for the 30th Assault Unit, a scruffy, undisciplined team made up of journalists, German-speaking schoolmasters, explosives experts and locksmiths (some of whom had been recently released from jail) under the direction of the Intelligence officer Commander Ian Fleming, the future creator of James Bond.

The task of 30 AU was to precede the advance following the Normandy landings, seizing weapons, material and documents before they could be found or destroyed. It was organised in a naval and a marine wing, and, as the Allies advanced, rarely a day passed without discoveries of secret documents in factory safes, of flying bombs in railway trucks, of weapons in barns or of assembly lines in mine shafts. The unit's haul included the complete naval archive of technical, scientific and operational papers which documented German evasions of the Treaty of Versailles, as well as other material which provided evidence for the prosecution of war criminals. Everything was sent to London labelled "PG", meaning "Pinched from the Germans".

Aylen crossed the Rhine with General Patton's troops then pressed ahead with two sailors in a captured fire engine which became lost when they took side roads to avoid the bombed autobahn. For a while it seemed that, in order to reach the U-boat research establishments on the Baltic coast, Aylen would have to join Operation Red Admiral, an air-borne assault on the Kiel Canal intended to forestall the Russians. But he was able to drive in the comfort of a staff car through a German army fleeing the Russians.

Charged with the task of obtaining records of naval technical aid which the Nazis had given to Japan, Aylen proceeded to Flensburg, where the rump of the German government had taken refuge. In the street he saw Grand Admiral Karl Doenitz, who had succeeded Hitler as Führer, and personally cross-examined the senior officers of the German Admiralty. Between May and November 1945, Aylen appointed himself overseer of the Walterwerke, where the Germans had experimented with high-speed submarines fuelled by hydrogen peroxide.

Helmuth Walter initially refused to co-operate,

claiming that the prototypes had been destroyed and the drawings lost. But after interrogating research department heads, Aylen found the missing blueprints and persuaded technicians to reassemble a working engine, which Walter then demonstrated to Admiral Sir Andrew Cunningham, the First Sea Lord, on his visit to Germany.

Eventually Walter and his key people agreed to bring their equipment to Vickers' shipyard at Barrow, and Aylen returned to Portsmouth in *Nordwind*, a 70-ton German naval yacht once used by the German admiralty. He was appointed OBE.

Ian Gerald Aylen, always called Jan, was born on October 12 1910 at Saltash, Cornwall, into a naval family which had included a midshipman wounded at the bombardment of Kagoshima, Japan, in 1863. At Blundell's he excelled at sport, although he preferred bird watching in the Devon countryside. He represented Kent, Hampshire and Devon at rugby, and captained the Devonport Services in 1938-39.

His father, a victim of the Geddes Axe (when hundreds of officers were made redundant after the First World War), advised him to join the Navy as an engineer to ensure that he would have a profession; so Aylen went to the Royal Naval Engineering College, Keyham, and Greenwich. His first ship was the battleship *Rodney*, then recovering from the Invergordon mutiny. Aylen went on to become engineer officer of the destroyer *Kelvin*, which during the evacuation of Crete in 1941, landed rations and ammunition at Spharkia, and helped to ferry more than 16,500 troops to Alexandria in five runs. These were ended when a Heinkel bomber dived out of the dawn sun to put a bomb under its after magazine, although it did not explode.

Aylen's abiding memory of these operations was the scent of the pine forests drawn into the destroyer's air intakes from a mile offshore. When *Kelvin* was sent to Bombay for repairs, he took a party of 50 sailors on a visit to the Khyber Pass. He always remembered pony trekking into the wilds at 15,000 feet and the sight of Nanga Parbat 80 miles away across the plains.

On March 22 1942 Aylen took part in the Second Battle of Sirte, which Cunningham described as one of the most brilliant naval actions of the war. A desperately needed Malta-bound convoy of four merchant ships, escorted by the few remaining Mediterranean cruisers and a handful of destroyers under Rear-Admiral Philip Vian, was attacked by an Italian battleship, heavy cruisers and German aircraft. *Kelvin* and Vian's other destroyers kept to leeward in order to lay a smokescreen.

After four hours' manoeuvring, the destroyers came under heavy and accurate fire, and, as *Kelvin* plunged through the suffocating black smoke at full speed to deliver her torpedoes, she emerged into daylight to be confronted at close range by the Italian battleship *Littorio*. He was awarded the DSC for his gallantry and skill during this outstanding action, which succeeded in driving off and severely damaging a superior force.

After the war, Aylen served two years as Flotilla Engineer Officer in the destroyer *Cossack*, based on Hong Kong, and then at the training establishment, HMS Caledonia, responsible for training engineering apprentices. Following another two years on the Admiralty Interview Board, he became the last Captain (E) to serve afloat as Home Fleet

Engineering Officer. As captain of the new engineering college at Manadon, Plymouth, he turned an ancient tithe barn into the college chapel.

Finally, he was Admiral Superintendent at Rosyth Dockyard, the first non-seaman to hold the appointment. On retirement he was appointed CB.

He worked for the Institute of Mechanical Engineers before settling at Honiton to rear trout at an old water mill. After retirement he became an active commentator on naval affairs via letters to *The Daily Telegraph* and articles in the *Naval Review*.

Jan Aylen married Alice Maltby in 1937. She died in 1995; their son and two daughters survived him.

CAPTAIN
HENRY ST JOHN FANCOURT

Captain Henry St John Fancourt (who died on January 8 2004, aged 103) was a midshipman at the Battle of Jutland in 1916, and was later responsible for launching the hunt for the German battleship *Bismarck* in 1941.

Fancourt was commanding Sparrowhawk, the Royal Naval Air Station at Hatston, Orkney, when the Admiralty feared *Bismarck's* break out. The weather for the previous three days had been too bad for RAF reconnaissance, but, on May 22, Fancourt ordered a Maryland from 771 Naval Air Squadron to survey the Norwegian fjords. Flying in the most difficult conditions, Commander Hank Rotherham penetrated low clouds and ack-ack fire to find that *Bismarck* had sailed, and to set in hand the hunt.

Acting on his own again, Fancourt sent 828 Squadron's Albacore torpedo-bombers to Sumburgh, ready for a strike on *Bismarck*, but she did not come within range. His resourcefulness was recognised by a mention in despatches.

In November 1942 Fancourt commanded the 4th Destroyer Flotilla, which consisted of the destroyers *Broke* and *Malcolm*, in an assault on the harbour of Algiers.Operation Terminal,as it was called, was a late addition to Operation Torch, the Allied landings in North Africa. Flying the American flag as a *ruse de guerre*, Fancourt hoped to delay any French response until he had landed some 700 American Rangers. In the darkness of November 8 the ships failed to find the entrance and came under heavy fire; *Malcolm* was badly hit and withdrew. But Fancourt, in *Broke*, commanded by Lieutenant-Commander Frank Layard, RCN, pressed on and, at the fourth attempt, broke the boom across the entrance.

Though they had practised the operation in the cruiser *Belfast*, the Rangers, from the mid-West, showed a marked reluctance to leave the shelter of *Broke*, and those who did were soon rounded up. *Broke* was forced by heavy, close-range fire to withdraw and foundered the next day trying to make Gibraltar. Though defeated, and despite many casualties amongst the British seamen and American troops,the survivors, rescued by the destroyer *Zetland*, marched proudly ashore, headed by Fancourt.He and Layard were awarded the DSO, for their "bravery and skill in the hazardous operations in which Allied forces were landed in North Africa."

The son of an Army officer, Henry Lockhart St John Fancourt was born on April 1 1900. He entered the Royal Naval College Osborne in January 1913, as war fever grew, and after training was sent to the battlecruiser *Princess Royal*, in which he served at Jutland between the British Grand Fleet and the German High Seas Fleet on May 31 1916. Midshipman Fancourt's view of the battle through the gunsights of the ship's 13.5-inch "Y" turret was limited, and when he emerged during a lull in the firing he and others cheered when they saw men clinging to the bows and stern of a wreck: only later did he learn that the men were British, and the ship was the battlecruiser *Invincible*.

"We were firing as fast as we could (about 2-3 shots per minute) at ranges of eight to 10 miles and tearing along at 28 knots," he recalled. "And then we felt a shake and learned that our X turret amidships had been hit. No-one really doubted the outcome of the battle... But the Germans were good and their gunnery was hot; there just weren't enough of them. But what they did, they did very well; they fought bravely and lost considerably fewer men than we did."

Eighteen months after Jutland, Fancourt was promoted sub-lieutenant and assigned to escort and patrol duties based at Queenstown, Ireland, before joining the battleship *Royal Oak* at Scapa Flow. To the young officer, it resembled "miles and miles of nothing at all", but, in 1919, he witnessed there the scuttling of the interned German fleet, 51 ships totalling some half a million tons.

After the First World War the Admiralty decided to send young officers to Cambridge to complete their education, and Fancourt went to Gonville and Caius. When the Admiralty's interest in naval aviation was revived, Fancourt joined No 1 Naval Pilots' Course in 1924, when he was given the dual rank of flying officer, RAF, and lieutenant, RN. Amongst several other types of aircraft he enjoyed several years flying the Fairey IIID floatplane. He joined the training carrier *Argus* and took part in operations during the Chinese civil war and riots in Shanghai in 1927, and, after moving to the carrier *Courageous* in 1929, flew reconnaissance for a naval landing party in Palestine.

During the 1920s the Royal Navy had abandoned a fore-and-aft arrester system which relied upon slow landings and wire palisades to prevent aircraft from slipping over the side. In June 1931 Fancourt was the first to try the athwartships arrester wire on *Courageous*, which became standard in the navies of the world.

Promoted lieutenant-commander in 1928, he commanded 822 Naval Air Squadron, and from 1933 played a significant part in recruiting and training officers for the Fleet Air Arm, serving in the personnel department of the Admiralty, and selecting officers for flying training. While at the shore establishment HMS Daedalus, he was badly injured when German dive-bombers destroyed the control tower at Lee-on-the-Solent in January 1941.

The next year, when Churchill had persuaded Roosevelt to allow the USS *Wasp* to ferry RAF Spitfires to Malta, Fancourt flew onboard her in a Gloster Sea Gladiator, becoming the first British officer to land on an American ship. The American equipment was heavier than the British, and Fancourt thought he might have broken the tailplane but, disdaining to appear concerned in front of allies, gave his aircraft only a cursory check before he took off. In 1943, after returning to *Argus* in command,

Fancourt flew off in a Swordfish and landed with his son, Michael, then a 16-year-old air training corps cadet, probably the first deck landing by a father and son.

After *Argus*, which sailed with Mediterranean convoys, Fancourt moved to the escort carrier *Unicorn*, also used for training, in the British Eastern and British Pacific Fleets from 1943 until 1945. Despite having held some key senior staff appointments, events conspired to deny him the necessary sea time for promotion to flag rank.

Fancourt was embittered that after 35 years' service he was "bunged out" of the Navy at one month's notice in 1951. He had flown a score of different types of aircraft, from First World War vintage biplanes to modern twin-engine aircraft, and had 1,317 hours recorded in his log.

After the Navy he worked for Rear-Admiral Sir Matthew Slattery, a colleague from No 1 Naval Pilots Course, at Short Brothers and Harland in Belfast; he finally retired again in 1965 to spend more time fly-fishing.

Fancourt married Lillian Marion Osborne (née Parkin) in 1921, whom he divorced in 1960, and then Pauline Bettina Mosley (née Kimble), who died in 2001. He was survived by his son Michael, and two daughters. Another son, who predeceased him, was Captain RNR and commanded London Division RNR.

LIEUTENANT-COMMANDER PETER WILLIAMS

Lieutenant-Commander Peter Williams (who died on January 16 2004, aged 91) ran agents, stores and stolen German plans between France and Britain in scores of operations during 1943 and 1944.

As commanding officer of Motor Gun Boat 502 and senior officer of the 15th MGB Flotilla, based at Dartmouth, he led a select band which included David Birkin, husband of Judy Campbell (the singer of "A Nightingale Sang in Berkeley Square") and father of the actress Jane Birkin; Guy Hamilton, who directed four of the early James Bond films; and Mike Marshall, the Oxford blue and England rugby player tragically killed when MGB502 hit a mine five days after VE Day.

Operation Easement II on February 26 1944 was typical: while the French Resistance assembled passengers on the coast, Williams sailed at dusk from Dartmouth towards Weymouth then, once out of sight, turned for Brittany. He had German recognition signals valid up to midnight and orders to avoid discovery and action with the enemy. On reaching the coast he cut his speed to reduce noise, wash and phosphorescence, and crept through rocks and swirling tides to anchor within a few hundred yards of the beach.

Williams then sent his surfboat inshore with muffled oars, on a rising tide to avoid footprints. The landing party remained three or four minutes at the rendezvous, known as a pinpoint, with a sailor on standby to cut the grass anchor rope in an emergency. François Mitterrand, the future President of France, was landed and five agents and a downed pilot taken off. The problem of finding the mother ship in the dark was solved by Williams's invention of a device which homed on the MGB's Asdic transmissions. Williams was back in Dartmouth for breakfast.

In Operation Scarf on April 14, Suzanne Warenghem, the agent "Charise", was one passenger. When a sailor, moved to gallantry by an unexpected glimpse of her shapely figure and that of her friend Blanche Charlet, held out his hand and muttered "Ici, mademoiselle," she replied: "It's OK, Jack, I've been on one of these boats before." As Williams stood out to sea through a narrow channel, he met three German E-boats on a reciprocal course. He was sure that he could have overwhelmed them, but he coolly kept his course and, when challenged, fumbled his reply. The Germans briefly opened fire, then ceased after 15 seconds. Subsequent reports indicated that they were reprimanded for having fired on each other.

Although warned before Operation Splint on April 26, of German light destroyers at their anchorage off Ile de Batz, Williams insisted on entering the treacherous River Treguier in search of some SIS agents and secret mail. As he left he was caught in crossfire between the enemy destroyers and the British light cruiser *Black Prince*, three Canadian destroyers and a British destroyer, and also found his boat silhouetted by starshell for the German coastal batteries. Williams frantically ordered the German recognition signals which his MGB was using to be replaced by British ones. However, the real danger came from an agent who, intent on self-defence, accidentally fired his pistol, sending the bullet ricocheting inside the armoured bridge and narrowly missing Williams.

Williams was awarded the DSC for his series of textbook operations in difficult pilotage waters; the men of his flotilla were awarded a total of 14 DSCs and 27 DSMs between them. On the 50th anniversary of D-Day in 1994, Williams was made a Chevalier of the Legion d'honneur for his wartime action. A memorial to MGB502 is now on one of the beaches Williams favoured, Beg-an-Fry, known to his men as "Eggs and Fry".

Peter Alexander Williams was born on March 12 1912, the son of a merchant navy officer. He was educated at Malvern and Worcester College, Oxford, then qualified as a solicitor. He became the youngest member of Chelsea council and joined the RNV(S)R in 1936, but, not expecting to be called up soon, he paid for a private course in coastal navigation at Captain O M Watts's chandlery in Bond Street.

He also acted as unpaid constituency secretary to Sir Samuel Hoare, First Lord of the Admiralty from 1936 to 1937. This ensured Williams's early entry to the newly established training school HMS King Alfred, at Hove, in 1939. After a few days' training, he was sent to Scapa Flow and the armed trawler *Tourmaline*.

Williams's next appointment was to Motor Anti-Submarine Boat 10, which he first saw as an empty hull in May 1940. The engines were fitted in a day, and a scratch crew arrived for the evacuation of Dunkirk. On the first test of his navigation skills he ferried Rear-Admiral William Wake-Walker across the Channel. Instead of coming to Dunkirk, they arrived in the mist at German-occupied Gravelines, where Williams recognised the enemy uniforms in time. He turned around at high speed before his boat could be shot at, but he felt that his true luck lay in the fact that the admiral was sleeping below and did not realise the mistake.

He was given command of Motor Launch 118, protecting coastal convoys through the Straits of Dover. Despite the shelling from German shore batteries, Williams found this "very tedious". As Coastal Forces expanded, he moved on to command MGB325 and, while fitting a new two-pounder Rolls-Royce gun at Portland, he met Ted Davis and Angus Letty, who worked for Captain Frank Slocum, of the Special Operations Executive. Slocum was deputy director of the Operations Division (Irregular) at the Admiralty; and, on learning of Williams's outstanding qualities and natural aptitude, he asked for his transfer. Williams began his covert activity with three crossings to Lannion Bay in France and three to Holland. On the last occasion, the surfboat capsized and his boats officer, Peter Ewell, was taken prisoner while two Dutch agents were captured and executed.

In February 1943, now in command of MGB612, Williams took part in Operation Cabaret. Two Norwegian merchant ships detained in neutral Sweden were secretly loaded with special steel and ball-bearings and awaiting escort from Gothenburg. Williams had the task of smuggling crews and weapons to the ships. However, the operation was called off after the MGBs had entered the Skagerrak and, in mountainous waves, Williams turned his small vessel into the teeth of a Force 9 gale.

For 24 hours he feared that the flat-bottomed MGB would founder. He and his coxswain, Bill

Webb, were among the few not prone to seasickness, so Webb sustained him with rum which had been "broken" in the storm. Eventually they made landfall at Berwick-upon-Tweed, 80 miles south of his destination, where Williams spent two days making temporary repairs to the boat before returning to Aberdeen.

After the war Williams practised as a solicitor, and became chairman of the East Grinstead Conservative Party. He was clerk to the Conservators of Ashdown Forest and president of Sussex Law Society. He also farmed, delivering cream and milk from his Herefords before going into his office.

Peter Williams married the daughter of the aviation pioneer A V Roe. He had met Joy Roe after spotting a good pair of legs sticking out from under a car which she was repairing. She predeceased him, and he was survived by a son and a daughter.

LIEUTENANT-COMMANDER ROBBIE ROBINSON

Lieutenant-Commander Robbie Robinson (who died on February 26 2004, aged 82) was a diver charged with clearing the Normandy beaches on June 6 1944. As a member of a landing craft obstruction clearance unit, Petty Officer Robinson had the task of opening a path through the booby-trapped obstacles on the beaches below the high water mark.

This meant defusing improvised and unfamiliar deadly explosives on the shore and underwater while

being sniped at and sprayed with machine-gun fire.
The unexpectedly heavy surf made his task all the
more tiring, but after opening an initial path his team
had cleared a gap in the enemy defences 1,000 yards
by 400 yards by the end of the first day.

Eventually, he helped to clear more than 2,500
obstacles. Two other naval divers were killed during
these operations and 10 injured. Robinson himself
was knocked out when six feet underwater by an
explosion that left him paralysed for several hours. A
Royal Engineer working close by was killed outright,
but Robinson was saved by a specially designed
Kapok jacket under his diving suit. Although left with
back trouble ever after, he returned to work on the
beaches and harbour of Cherbourg a couple of days
later.

Ronald Stephen Colin Robinson was born on
August 1 1921. His father, a gunner who had won the
Military Medal in the First World War, was the Royal
Horse Artillery's saddler on Mauritius from 1926 to
1931. Young Robbie returned home to complete his
education at the Roan School, Blackheath, and the
London Nautical School before joining the Navy as
a boy signalman, or "bunting tosser", in 1936.

He was in the cruiser *Ajax*, which was the first ship
in action during the Second World War when she
captured two German merchant ships on the first and
second days. At the Battle of the River Plate two
months later, he was wounded in the knee when
Ajax's bridge and flagdeck were hit by a shell,
bringing the foremast down. In the victory parade
through Plymouth, Robinson remembered two
women in the cheering crowd commenting, "They're
only kids".

After service in *Ajax* in the Mediterranean against the Italians off Calabria and Matapan and during the evacuation of Crete, Robinson learned to dive in Alexandria. Unable to progress as a signalman – because some "bloody fool" had recommended him for a commission – he transferred to the seaman branch so he could obtain needed sea-time. He served on three transatlantic convoys, and was fortunate to be rescued when the Flower class corvette *Auricula* was sunk in May 1942. Three months later he was a member of a beach clearance party during Operation Jubilee, the disastrous raid on Dieppe.

After D-Day, Robinson was drafted as spare crew to the submarines *Truant*, *Torbay* and *Trident*. Surprisingly for a "bubblehead" (as naval divers are known), he found submarines claustrophobic, and was pleased to be lent to the Royal Indian Navy from 1945 to 1947, initially serving in a motor launch during preparations for the Arakan campaign.

During the Korean War Robinson served with 41 Independent Company, Royal Marines, as a demolition specialist. It was attached to the US Marine Corps, and formed the rearguard at the retreat from the Chosin Reservoir. On returning to Britain, Robinson was not amused to be told that this counted as shore service and he was now top of the roster to go to sea. Soon afterwards he was promoted Commissioned Gunner and appointed to the destroyer *Crossbow* in 1953.

From 1967 to 1968 he commanded the Ton class minesweeper *Laleston*, where he recognised the talent of one of his young officers, Nigel Essenhigh, who would become First Sea Lord. However, Robinson's command ended prematurely when he was thrown across the bridge in a storm in the North Sea and injured his back again. He was sent to the sick quarters of HMS Ganges, at Shotley, the shore establishment where he had begun his training before the war; the boy trainees were impressed that he had started his career like one of them.

For his last appointment in the Navy in 1971, Robinson briefly commanded the cruiser *Belfast* before handing her over to the museum authorities. Surprisingly, despite his array of campaign medals and the dangers he had met, his only honour was an MBE. Robinson was a prodigious reader of literature, philosophy and history. When asked to draft a speech for a senior officer, he larded it with Latin tags only to receive his draft back marked: "I'm a Captain Royal Navy, not a Roman centurion!"

In retirement Robinson served for many years with the Weapons Trials Team at HMS Vernon, the Navy's school of underwater warfare founded in 1876, where torpedomen, the Navy's specialists in torpedo, mine, anti-submarine warfare and ship's electrics, were trained. When Vernon was closed, Robinson, who had qualified as a torpedoman in 1943, turned out the lights and locked the doors after 113 years at the Gunwharf (now a shopping and housing complex in Portsmouth).

Always cheerful, with a fund of salty stories, when he became too ill to attend reunion dinners he always sent a cheque to put behind the bar so that his friends could drink with him. Robinson married his childhood sweetheart, Gweneth Longman, in 1944. When she died in 1990, he continued with his long-standing practice of writing her a verse a day. He was survived by their son.

CAPTAIN
SIR ALEXANDER GLEN

Captain Sir Alexander Glen (who died on March 6 2004, aged 91) was an Arctic explorer and wartime Intelligence officer before going into the shipping industry, and eventually becoming chairman of the British Tourist Authority.

Glen had an unusual introduction to the Arctic in 1932. He thought he had accepted a friend's invitation to a debutante dance, then found that it was to go to Spitsbergen as one of the eight-man crew of a 45-foot Peterhead fishing boat owned by a Cambridge law don. The expedition committed him to 4,000 miles of sailing and two months of surveying in the mountains; it left him fascinated by the Arctic. The next year, Glen led a 16-man Oxford University summer expedition, which carried out valuable topographical and geological surveys of West Spitsbergen. In the winter he spent some months with the Lapps of northern Sweden. Then, the following summer, he returned to Spitsbergen for a few weeks in the company of Evelyn Waugh.

It was not a happy experience for the novelist, who did not like taking orders from an undergraduate. Waugh tried to make Glen (to whom he sarcastically referred in his diary as "the leader") feel out of place. But when Waugh talked to their companion, Hugh Lygon, about people and places the younger man could not know, Glen showed every sign of enjoying their conversations – and irritated Waugh further by roaring with laughter at jokes he only half-understood. For 10 hours on three days, they carried supplies up a glacier made treacherous by a thaw.

Glen shot a seal to roast over a wood fire; however, when he announced that he was going to shoot another, Waugh gave him a lengthy lecture on the sacredness of human and animal life.

At one point, as the party crossed a stream, Waugh and Lygon found themselves swept into a raging torrent, which made Waugh fear for his life, before they managed to crawl ashore. "If I hadn't joined the Church of Rome, I could never have survived your appalling incompetence," the writer spat at Glen.

The experience prepared the 23-year-old Glen to lead the more ambitious Oxford University expedition of 1935. Against advice from older experts, he established a station on the ice cap of North East Land; it contained rooms and connecting tunnels gouged out of the ice, which were occupied for about a year. The expedition carried out valuable research in glaciology as well as topographical and geological mapping. It also did important work on the propagation of radio waves in high latitudes, which contributed to the development of radar. Glen's account of the expedition was published in *Under the Pole Star* (1937).

He was awarded the Patron's Medal of the Royal Geographical Society in 1940 and, with other members of his team, the Polar Medal in silver in 1942. In addition, he received the Bruce Medal of the Royal Society of Edinburgh, and the Andree Plaque of the Royal Swedish Geographical Society.

Glen returned to Spitsbergen in very different circumstances in July 1941 when, as a member of Rear-Admiral Philip Vian's staff, he was involved in the evacuation of Norwegian and Russian coalminers and trappers. The coalmines, equipment and stores were destroyed but Glen and others still believed that an occupying force was needed to prevent the Germans using the site as a base for attacking Arctic convoys.

Less than a year later, Glen took part in a series of flights by RAF Coastal Command Catalinas from the Shetlands which showed inconclusive evidence of German occupation on Spitsbergen. As a result, he went back with a joint British and Norwegian force in a Norwegian icebreaker; it was sunk in Spitsbergen harbour by German Focke-Wulfs, with the loss of 17 lives and several wounded. The ship's survivors established themselves in rough buildings until they were resupplied by Catalina. A force of two cruisers and four destroyers, under a Norwegian commander, remained there until the end of the war.

Glen was awarded the DSC, the Norwegian War Cross and appointed a Knight of St Olav.

The son of a Glasgow shipowner, Alexander Richard Glen was born on April 18 1912 and was educated at Fettes before reading Geography at Balliol College, Oxford. After returning from his Arctic expeditions, he worked in banking in New York and London, until mobilised in the RNVR in 1939. Precluded from an executive commission because of defective eyesight, he was trained as a meteorological officer; then, after some months in the cruiser *Arethusa* in the eastern Mediterranean, he transferred to Naval Intelligence.

In January 1940 Glen was posted to Belgrade as assistant naval attaché at the British legation, which was trying to influence the Yugoslavs to join the Allied cause. But when a coup d'etat transferred power from the hands of the neutral Prince Paul to the 17-year-old King Peter, German retribution was swift, and Belgrade was bombed for three days. Glen and the rest of the legation set off on an adventurous road journey to Tirana in Albania where they were treated chivalrously by the occupying Italians, who flew them to Foggia, in Italy. In an apparent act of goodwill, two months later they were sent home through unoccupied France and Spain.

Following his Spitsbergen adventure, Lieutenant-Commander Glen (as he had become) returned by motor torpedo boat to Yugoslavia, where he joined Brigadier Fitzroy Maclean's mission to the partisans. In the confusion of Balkan loyalties, Maclean persuaded the British government to support Tito's partisans, and Glen served with distinction in dangerous clandestine operations in Yugoslavia, Albania and Bulgaria. He accompanied Tito to his first meeting with Stalin. The Soviet leader leaned down from a dais to pick up the partisan leader by his armpits, saying, "Remember, I may be old but I am still very strong";Tito retained his dignity.

Glen ended the war on the British staff in Athens. In addition to a Bar to his DSC, he was awarded the Czechoslovak War Cross. After demobilisation, he continued to do some part-time work for Naval Intelligence; he was wondering how best to invest his family's trust money when a Norwegian shipowner advised him to join a syndicate which was buying the shipbroker H Clarkson & Co. The firm had eight employees at an old-fashioned office in the City of London where the clerks worked on handwritten ledgers while seated on high stools.

But under Glen's chairmanship, from 1965 to 1973, Clarkson diversified to become a pioneer of package holidays in conjunction with Court Line, a charter airline. Glen also became chairman of Clarkson's parent company, Shipping Industrial Holdings (SIH). When the holiday industry suffered a severe downturn after the 1973-74 oil crisis, SIH sold Clarkson to Court Line, which went bankrupt soon afterwards, leaving 120,000 holidaymakers stranded or out of pocket; Glen resigned.

His other business interests included members of the boards of British European Airways (1964-70), the Tote (1976-84) and the British National Export Council (1966-72). He was chairman of the British Tourist Authority from 1969 to 1977, and also of the Advisory Council of the Victoria and Albert Museum from 1978 to 1984, during which he organised a very successful public appeal. Glen was appointed CBE in 1964 and KBE in 1967.

Bald, bespectacled, jovial and portly in later life, he had immense resilience of mind and body, and invincible optimism. In 1975 he published his memoirs, *Footholds Against a Whirlwind Sand*, and in 2002 *Target Danube* about clandestine activities.

Sandy Glen married first, in 1936 (dissolved 1945), Nina Nixon; they had a son who predeceased Glen. He married secondly, in 1947, Baroness Zora de Collaert, whom he had met in Yugoslavia during the war; she died in 2003.

INDEX

(Italics denotes main entry)

Index